RE-IMAGINING THE MODERN AMERICAN WEST

THE MODERN AMERICAN WEST

Gerald D. Nash, editor

Carl Abbott
The Metropolitan Frontier:
Cities in the Modern American West

Richard W. Etulain
Re-imagining the Modern American West:
A Century of Fiction, History, and Art

RE-IMAGINING THE MODERN

AMERICAN West

A Century of Fiction, History, and Art

RICHARD W. ETULAIN

THE UNIVERSITY OF ARIZONA PRESS

TUCSON

The University of Arizona Press
Copyright © 1996
The Arizona Board of Regents
This book is printed on acid-free, archival-quality paper.
Manufactured in the United States of America

01 00 99 98 97 96   6 5 4 3 2 1

Library of Congress Cataloging-in-Publication Data
Etulain, Richard W.
Re-imagining the modern American West : a century of fiction,
history, and art / Richard W. Etulain.
p.   cm. — (The Modern American West)
Includes index.
ISBN 0-8165-1133-0 (cloth : alk. paper). — ISBN 0-8165-1683-9
(paper : alk. paper)
1. West (U.S.) — Historiography.   2. West (U.S.) — In literature.
3. West (U.S.) — In art.   I. Title.   II. Series.
F591.E86   1996
978'.0072 — dc20   96-10109
CIP

British Cataloguing-in-Publication Data
A catalogue record for this book is available from the British Library.

TO JOYCE

for a lifetime of support

CONTENTS

FIGURES

PREFACE

This book is an introductory, nontheoretical study of a complex subject. Describing the main cultural-intellectual contours of the twentieth-century American West is a challenging task. In the following pages, however, I will provide an overview of three important facets of modern western life: fiction, history, and painting. The ensuing chapters discuss key novelists, historians, and artists who lived during the century that stretched from the 1890s to the 1990s and whose works help us to understand the shifting interpretations of the modern West.

Three terms used here need explanation. I use *frontier* to refer to those works, especially during the early twentieth century, that dramatized the experiences of newcomers entering the West to confront new landscapes and new peoples. Moreover, frontier novelists, historians, and painters often emphasized a closing frontier, implying that Americans would have to adjust to new sociocultural experiences that were part of a vanishing frontier. Frontier images and themes dominate the work of numerous writers of fiction, including Owen Wister, Mary Hallock Foote, Jack London, Frank Norris, and Zane Grey; of historians like Frederick Jackson Turner and Frederic Logan Paxson; and of artists such as Frederic Remington, Charles Russell, and others who lived and painted in the Southwest. Ironically, these inventors of a frontier West, in praising the pioneer West so extensively and positively, often killed what they loved; they served as major forces in bringing about the quick sociocultural transformations that they lamented as signs of a vanishing frontier.

Beginning in the 1920s, but even earlier in the writings of Mary Austin and Willa Cather, authors and artists discovered another defining vision — the American West as *region*. Unlike frontier writers and painters, the regionalists focused on life *in* the West rather than *to* the West. Regionalists were convinced that the pioneer West had disappeared over the horizon and that the area was developing cultural identities uniquely its own. In addition to Austin and Cather, writers like H. L. Davis, Vardis Fisher, Ruth Suckow, and John Steinbeck depicted a maturing West, spawning characters who illustrated the diverse cultures of several subregional areas. Historians like Walter Prescott Webb, Herbert Eugene Bolton, and James C. Malin were equally intrigued with tracing these influences in their regional histories. Additionally, in the interwar years, the artists Thomas Hart Benton, Grant Wood, John Steuart Curry, and Peter Hurd turned to regionalism as a way of describing cultural changes they encountered in the Midwest and Southwest.

Following the powerful transformations that World War II and the 1960s imposed on the West, many novelists, historians, and artists began to depict the West as an emerging *postregion*. Challenging earlier frontier images and moving beyond regional emphases, these writers and painters stressed not so much the shaping power of place on personality and character as the momentous influences of race and ethnicity, gender, and a new environmentalism as crucial elements of a postregional West. For the first time, numerous ethnic voices emerged: Native Americans such as N. Scott Momaday, Leslie Marmon Silko, James Welch, and Louise Erdrich; Hispanic writers such as Rudolfo Anaya; and Asians like Amy Tan altered and enriched fiction about the West. Similarly, the New Western historians Patricia Nelson Limerick, Richard White, and Donald Worster rejected earlier, more positive frontier interpretations of the West in favor of less triumphalist, revisionist views of the West as region. In addition, pathbreaking artwork by Abstract Expressionists, Figurativists, Photo Realists, and a host of other experimental painters, particularly on the Pacific Coast and in the Southwest, signaled that a broad-based postregionalism characterized much of the contemporary West.

Of course, there is a danger of oversimplifying when one speaks of frontier, regional, and postregional inventions of the American West. Although frontier interpretations dominated the first decades of the new century and regional views were challenging frontier perspectives by the 1920s, the continuing popularity of fictional and cinematic Westerns, plus the amazing craving for Louis L'Amour novels (one of the bestselling American authors of all time), indicates that the West as frontier remains wonderfully alive up to the present. Nor should one conclude that the World War II era and the 1960s completely destroyed regionalism. The enduring popularity of novelists such as John Steinbeck, Wallace Stegner, and A. B. Guthrie, Jr., is proof enough of the continuing importance of western regionalism. In truth, during the past generation western culture has exhibited remarkable diversity; frontier, regional, and postregional images vie for dominance in a swiftly changing West that forces writers and artists continually to redefine cultural developments.

Readers will notice that this book owes more to the pioneering works of the western cultural historians Vernon Louis Parrington, Franklin Walker, Henry Nash Smith, and Kevin Starr than to contemporary theorists such as Claude Lévi-Strauss, Clifford Geertz, and James Clifford, among many others. I do not mean to denigrate those intrigued with the "culture concept"; I have simply not used that approach. My goal here is to provide what no other western historian has yet attempted: an overview of the cultural and intellectual history of the twentieth-century West. Specialists will obviously find familiar items here, but new offerings on other topics should enlarge and spice their menu. Served together, these main and side dishes provide a repast hitherto unavailable on the modern West.

Like any other scholar working on a long-range project, I have accumulated numerous debts. First, I am grateful to several editors for allowing me to use here portions of my previously published works. For these permissions my thanks go to David Holtby at the University of New Mexico Press, John Drayton at the University of Oklahoma Press, Bill Regier and Dan Ross at the University of Nebraska Press, Chuck Rankin at *Montana: The Magazine of Western History,* and to Norris Hundley, Jr., of the *Pacific Historical Review.* The most extensive borrowings are noted in appropriate footnotes. I am also indebted to the University of New Mexico for a sabbatical leave during which much of a first draft of this volume was completed. The support of Deans B. Hobson Wildenthal and William Gordon, and History Chair Jonathan Porter, is also much appreciated. Along the way, Pat Devejian, Traci Hukill, Florence Goulesque, Liz Abeyta, Jill Howard, David Key, and Jen Clark have helped in the preparation of the manuscript. More recently, Frank Szasz improved every section of the book through his general comments and careful copyediting.

Finally, Joanne O'Hare and Alan M. Schroder at the University of Arizona Press have been particularly helpful and encouraging.

More personal are the large debts I owe to teachers, colleagues, and friends. Many years ago when I was an undergraduate at Northwest Nazarene College, Marian Washburn and Bob Woodward encouraged my interdisciplinary interests, as did Professors "Bing" Bingham and Earl Pomeroy while I was a graduate student at the University of Oregon. Later, Bob Swanson at Idaho State University and Jerry Nash and Frank Szasz at the University of New Mexico, through their conversations, friendship, and support, spurred me on. Most of all, I owe extraordinary thanks to my wife, Joyce, for putting up with my impatience, my eighty-hour weeks, and my frequent absences. No excessively driven student could find a more accepting partner.

PROLOGUE:
IMAGINING A PIONEER
AMERICAN WEST

When the youthful but already celebrated American writer Stephen Crane swung west across the Great Plains and Texas in 1895, he was surprised to find a West less divergent from the East than he had been led to believe.[1] He soon discovered that the industrial and urban East had already invaded the West. In Nebraska, "yellow trolley-cars with clanging gongs," he wrote, were "an almost universal condition," convincing him that "travellers tumbling over each other in their haste to trumpet the radical differences between Eastern and Western life" had "created a generally wrong opinion." Crane's contemporary, journalist Richard Harding Davis, sounded a similar note three years earlier in *The West from a Car-Window*. Tourists to the West, Davis wrote, too often "show the differences that exist between the places they have visited and their own home. Of the similarities they say nothing."[2]

Other visitors, however, experienced a West that broke from tradition. When novelist Owen Wister arrived in the late 1800s, he was impressed with its novel qualities—the remoteness of Wyoming, the free-and-easy ways of people in the Southwest and Northwest, and the more general differences between East and West. In 1889 the brilliant English writer and traveler Rudyard Kipling ventured up the Pacific Coast, across Montana and Utah, and finally through Denver and Omaha. Like Wister, he enthusiastically embraced western scenery, celebrated what he considered the independent, open spirit of much of the West, and especially noted its go-ahead, tub-thumping patriotism and progressive energy. Yet in his *American Notes* (1891) he also hinted that westerners suffered from American materialism, that they were inclined to sell off their abundant natural resources, and that they catered too willingly to the hordes of builders and tourists who swarmed like angry ants over sections of the region.[3]

These conflicting reactions are keys to understanding the image of the nineteenth-century pioneer West. Crane and Davis were on target in viewing the trans-Mississippi West as a cultural colony of the East, in which eastern and European influences traveled west with the immigrants. Conversely, the unique terrain and space, the novel social and ethnic mixes, and the rapidity of settlement that Wister and Kipling noted also shaped the region's culture. Although most Americans of the nineteenth century looked upon the West beyond the Mississippi as being at odds with the rest of the United States, a glance at the histories, literature, and art that depicted the pioneer West reveals a more complex, often ambiguous, experience. The struggle of the West to find its identity—as an offshoot of the East, as a separate region, or as an amalgam of East and West—represents the major tension of western pioneer culture during the nineteenth century.

The image of the American frontier as a Wild West gradually crystallized over several centuries. Well before Europeans first visited the American West in the sixteenth century, they had dreamed about it. Some dreams drew upon age-old visions of the West as Eden, as paradise, as the destiny of nations, or as the direction of all great empires. Other European or New World visions, more closely tied to first experiences in the New World, envisioned the West as Cíbola (the Spaniards' fabled Seven Cities of Gold), as a Passage to India, as the home of larger-than-life heroes, or as the Great American Desert and Garden of the World.[4]

American experiences on the earliest frontiers of the New World added other ingredients to ideas that clustered around the region. New England Puritans, for instance, spoke of the frontier as a howling wilderness, infested with the Devil and his minions, and peopled with barbaric Indians. Yet economic circumstances soon forced them to move out onto that evil frontier. In facing this necessity, Puritans constructed Indian captivity narratives that depicted these experiences as spiritual tests. Gradually, these accounts were transformed into non-Puritan narratives with military or hunter heroes like Daniel Boone serving as the bringers of civilization to a remote region that uncivilized Indians inhabited.[5]

These varied images shaped the visions of people writing about the West in the nineteenth century. Despite their variety, these myths about the West contained a unifying core: since the West was less advanced than the East, it needed civilizing. Progress dictated that less advanced peoples and cultures must give way to those who followed the higher laws of progress and civilization. The West was truly wild—in need of giant doses of society and culture, something the East alone could provide.

This Wild West ideology powered most thinking and planning about the West in the nineteenth century. Religious and educational leaders such as Lyman Beecher and his daughter Catharine pointed to the frontier as a vital part of the country's future but also as a territory that needed to be saved through an infusion of ministers and teachers. Political and economic spokesmen reiterated this need to win the West from lesser peoples and to preserve it for worthy Americans. Not surprisingly, given this widespread consensus about the West, much of the writing about the region in the nineteenth century depicted it as a wild and unsettled section.

Following the Civil War, depictions of the Wild West were largely of two kinds. One celebrated historical figures as larger-than-life characters in history, biography, and fiction; the other spawned legendary figures, usually based on oral traditions, who figured prominently in folklore and literature. Biographers and historians often used historical figures such as Billy the Kid, Calamity Jane, Wild Bill Hickok, and Kit Carson to create the sensational heroes and heroines needed to subdue a Wild West. In these romantic accounts, Billy the Kid kills a bad man for each of his twenty-one years, Calamity Jane rides and shoots like a hellcat, Wild Bill is flashingly quick with his fists and guns, and the small, wiry Kit Carson becomes a ring-tailed roarer, a gigantic Samson. Since the West was a wild, forbidding place, only historical individuals depicted as strong-armed demigods could pave the way for western settlement.[6]

The most significant of the historical figures who became legends in their own time was William Frederick "Buffalo Bill" Cody. A former Pony Express rider, buffalo hunter, scout, and Indian fighter, Cody also fathered Buffalo Bill's Wild West, which did more than any other attraction to popularize the West as a wild frontier. An experienced pioneer, a compelling dramatist of his own exploits, and a perceptive judge of Americans' instincts, Cody opened a Wild West exhibition in 1883 that dramatized one frenetic appearance after another: stagecoach holdups, trick riding and shooting, Indian fights, and attention-grabbing appearances of Annie Oakley ("Little Sure Shot"), Buck Taylor ("King of the Cowboys"), and Chief Sitting Bull. So successful was the

Wild West show that it toured the United States for many years and even made appearances in several European cities. It also inspired several competitors. Others, seeing the popularity of Buffalo Bill's extravaganzas, copied his program, and together they began a tradition of frontier exhibitions that lasted well into the 1930s. If audiences had questions about the nature of the American West, Cody and his Wild West, along with other such blowouts, assured them that it was indeed a land of riders, ropers, and renegades — superheroes of the sagebrush. Conversely, there were no places here for farmers and city folk.

In the fertile twilight zone between fact and imagination, legendary frontier heroes took root in the late nineteenth and early twentieth centuries. In the northern West, the gigantic lumberjack Paul Bunyan and his enormous companion, Babe the Blue Ox, stalked through forests and lumber camps like a whirlwind armed with sharp axes. When Paul mistakenly dragged his spiked pole, he gouged out the Grand Canyon. Together Paul and Babe hollowed out Puget Sound — with Paul using a glacier for a scoop — as a place to store their logs. Following in Bunyan's seven-league strides were Pecos Bill, the "supercowboy of the Southwest," who rode a "mountain lion with barbed wire reins"; or Febold Feboldson, the titanic Nebraska farmer who fashioned knots in the tails of tornadoes as they flashed across the plains.[7] Here was a pantheon of manufactured, gargantuan western heroes whose mien and deeds vivified the fearless, mighty people needed to save and settle the West.

At the same time that popular histories, biographies, newspaper stories, Wild West shows, and tall tales were launching the careers of several historical and legendary Wild West heroes and heroines, the dime novel Western provided a new outlet for other sensational figures. The discovery of an inexpensive method of printing newspapers and books, especially nickel and dime novels produced on pulp paper, allowed publishing firms to churn out thousands of cheap novels for the tidal wave of new readers after the Civil War. More than half of these sensationalized novels dealt with the frontier or American West, greatly increasing the possibilities for overly dramatic and sentimentalized depictions.

From the 1860s on, dozens of authors, nearly all of whom were easterners with little knowledge of the West, utilized new heroes such as Kit Carson, Billy the Kid, Calamity Jane, and Buffalo Bill for their dime novels. No matter that the lives of these protagonists were created without fear or research, eastern readers bought dime novels by the hundreds of thousands, evidently believing much of what they read. Not content with simply tinkering with the lives of historical figures, other writers created fictional frontier figures such as Deadwood Dick, Rattlesnake Ned, and the Black Avenger. These heroes too were endowed with the physical prowess, stamina, and derring-do that characterized their historical brothers and sisters. Authors of dime novels were more than happy to provide whatever kind of characters satisfied the wish needs of their readers.[8]

But the pell-mell actions of these stereotyped characters — who could ride like the wind, kill several Indians with one hand, and win the heroine's attention — soon became tiresome. By the 1890s, sales of dime novels had fallen off dramatically. They did so just as the cowboy — the newest, most romantic figure — galloped onto the scene. Although some of the earliest literary and artistic depictions of the cowpuncher treated him as unruly and in need of a dose of refinement, when novelist Owen Wister and artist Frederic Remington became his champions in the 1890s they pictured him as a buoyant, romantic hero stripped of the excessive heroics of earlier Wild West characters but sufficiently vivacious and charming to gain large audiences. The publication of Wister's cowboy stories in leading magazines of the 1890s — often accompanied by Remington illustrations — and the eventual appearance of Wister's classic Western *The Virginian* (1902) proved decisive. They prepared the way for a long line of popular Westerns, stretching from the works of Zane Grey, Ernest Haycox, and Luke Short to the Westerns of the most popular writer of them all, Louis L'Amour. Even though these popular Westerns were more literary than the dime novels, they too pandered to the hunger for a Wild West that arose well before 1900 and that continues to the present. Although the Wild West traditions did not totally dominate the literary West, they outstripped other western literary and historiographical traditions of the nineteenth century.[9]

Not all the explorers, travelers, and writers fell victim to the strong-armed, hairy-chested school of Wild West literature, however. Indeed, beginning early in the nineteenth century, travelers and authors had attempted to depict what they considered the real West, or at least one ostensibly based on fact. These efforts, appearing throughout the century, provided an alternative vision of the far frontier.

In the opening decades of the nineteenth century, such explorers as Meriwether Lewis, William Clark, Zebulon Pike, and Stephen H. Long (Long's account was written by Edwin James) produced factual records of their expeditions, emphasizing first of all what they saw and did. Rather than providing imaginative reshapings of their experiences, these writers stressed the flora and fauna they encountered, described the terrain they crossed, and furnished straightforward descriptions of western Indian groups. Even though nearly two-thirds of the Lewis and Clark journals were excised by the prudish Philadelphia lawyer Nicholas Biddle before they were published and much of their freshness emasculated, and even though James's account of Long's expedition misled Americans for nearly a half century into thinking the central and lower plains were a Great American Desert, these accounts were much less romanticized and exaggerated than works emanating from the Wild West tradition.[10]

From the 1820s to the 1840s, three other well-known eastern literary figures — James Fenimore Cooper, Washington Irving, and Francis Parkman — published notable works about the West. Born into the country gentry of upstate New York, and with little knowledge of the western wilderness, Cooper created the most notable frontier hero of the nineteenth century, Natty Bumppo, or the Deerslayer, in his five-volume Leatherstocking Tales. Obviously drawn to his hero and the wilderness he inhabited, Cooper nonetheless betrayed an ambivalence about Natty's uncivilized and sometimes boorish behavior. As English writer and critic D. H. Lawrence explained, Cooper loved Natty and his wildness, but he seemed afraid that he might belch at dinner.

The historical accounts of Irving and Parkman, both of whom made short visits to the West, also exhibit conceptual ambiguities. During a month-long stay in present-day Oklahoma, Irving took copious notes and later read widely in historical works for his writings on the West. Still, when he prepared such works as *A Tour of the Prairies* (1835), *Astoria* (1836), and *The Adventures of Captain Bonneville* (1837) for publication, he "shaped" his notes, separating the uncivilized West from the cultured East, romanticizing the wilderness through which his explorers trudged, and making explicit social distinctions between his unpolished frontiersmen and their sophisticated eastern companions. Boston Brahmin Francis Parkman followed a similar pattern of love for the primitive and pristine wilderness but snobbish distaste for many of those who inhabited this Eden. From his earliest years, Parkman cultivated a "cult of masculinity," much as three other easterners — Theodore Roosevelt, Owen Wister, and Frederic Remington — would do at the end of the century. Yet once in the wilderness with Indians and frontiersmen — "the society of savages and men little better than savages" — Parkman produced his classic account *The*

Oregon Trail (1849), a book that is as much an illustration of the ethnocentrism of a proper Bostonian as a factual account of the frontier in the late 1840s.[11]

Richard Henry Dana and Susan Shelby Magoffin—two other sophisticated nonwesterners—also illustrate this ambivalent attitude toward the West. A New Englander and Harvard student, Dana shipped out as a common seaman and visited Mexican California in the 1830s. From this voyage and a brief stay on the West Coast came his popular book *Two Years Before the Mast* (1840), in which Dana provided telling descriptions of life on the California coast; but his narrative, filtered through his puritanical predilections, depicted Californios as lazy, illiterate, and unprogressive.

As a young, well-educated bride on her way in 1846 from Kentucky to Mexico, and as one of the first Anglo women to travel the Santa Fe Trail, Magoffin praised the politeness of New Mexicans and drew appealing word pictures of their food and dances but was repulsed by other scenes. "The women slap about with their arms and necks bare, perhaps their bosoms exposed (and they are none of the prettiest or whitest)," she wrote in *Down the Santa Fe Trail and into Mexico*; and when they crossed a creek, she added "they pull their dresses . . . up above their knees and paddle through the water like ducks. . . . I am constrained to keep my veil drawn closely over my face all the time to protect my blushes."[12] Still other visitors to the Southwest complained of the cigarillos Mexicanas smoked and the low-necked dresses they wore.

By the outbreak of the Civil War, literature and historical writing about the West had hardened into recognizable patterns. Some travelers had written factual records of what they had seen and done; others (like Irving, Parkman, and Magoffin) wrote accounts that were as much revelations of the writer's biases as historical narratives. All these books were by outsiders, the West as viewed through eastern eyes. Although these writings exhibited no single viewpoint, they often revealed an ambivalence that cherished the open landscape and freedom of the West yet hesitated to embrace frontier characters or the West's sociocultural life.

If, before the Civil War, Europeans and easterners produced the bulk of the literature about the West, by the mid-1860s writers with extensive western experience had begun to treat the West. When Mark Twain's lively sketch "The Celebrated Jumping Frog of Calaveras County" appeared in a New York journal in 1865, and when Bret Harte's local-color stories were published in California's *Overland Monthly* in the late 1860s, these writers were immediately hailed as something novel, as authentic new voices from the American West.

And they were. In emphasizing three particulars—setting, local customs, and dialect—the local colorists set important precedents. Departing from the extreme idealizations of setting and character in romantic literature of the pre-Civil War era, they moved toward the greater verisimilitude of the realists of the late nineteenth century. But these two authors—and other local-color writers such as Joaquin Miller and Alfred Henry Lewis—were also reluctant realists. Even if Harte wrote about prostitutes and gamblers, Twain about uncouth miners and other frontiersmen, and Lewis about common cowboys and cowtown citizens, they usually treated these ungenteel characters romantically. They gave them hearts of gold and pure motives beneath their rough and crude exteriors. Utilizing vulgar characters from unfamiliar settings and speaking regional dialects, western local-color writers compromised their realism by excessively idealizing their undesirables. They had no wish to affront eastern drawing room and editorial sensibilities.

The center for much western local-color writing was the San Francisco Bay area. As the leading city of the West by the 1860s, San Francisco boasted numerous newspapers and several literary magazines. When the *Overland Monthly* began publication as a western imitation of New England's *Atlantic Monthly* in 1868, the Bay Area now had its important regional journal. In addition, Twain's presence in the Mother Lode country and in San Francisco in the 1860s, his popular sketches, and his humorous account of trail and mining camp life in the Far West in *Roughing It* (1872) and Harte's notorious stories "The Luck of Roaring Camp," "The Outcasts of Poker Flat," and "Tennessee's Partner" all pointed to San Francisco and California as the vortex of western literary activity. Twain soon left for Hawaii and then Connecticut, and Harte followed to the East Coast and Europe, but San Francisco drew other writers. At the turn of the century, newcomers such as Frank Norris and Jack London became its new literary lions.

By the 1880s, authors had introduced readers to a vast, unpeopled West, with awesome stretches of plains and mountains, a host of varied Indian groups, and new character types, such as trappers, miners, and cowboys. The local-color writers pioneered in dealing with the novel settings, customs, and speech patterns of this new country, but at the same time they overlooked most westerners—those who lived on farms or in cities. Their sketches and stories also owed as much to their ties to the European and eastern literary traditions of Charles Dickens, Robert Louis Stevenson, and Nathaniel Hawthorne as to the new frontier life they had encountered. In this sense, western

American literature remained balanced between the new and the old, the West and the East, as the nineteenth century drew to a close.

Just as earlier artists of the sixteenth and seventeenth centuries had struggled to present portraits of the inhabitants and settings of the New World to European audiences, so eastern and foreign painters in the early nineteenth century attempted to capture the flora and fauna, the animals, and the Indians for their viewers. In most cases their art seemed to reflect as much what painters were predisposed to see as what appeared before their eyes. To expect otherwise, of course, is to misunderstand the shaping power of social conditioning and cultural baggage. The American West of these artists, like that of their literary brethren, was an amalgam of what they already believed with the new scenes and peoples they encountered.[13]

Since a variety of artists from diverse backgrounds came west to paint, they portrayed a richly varied region in their artistic works. From the earliest views of the frontier West in the opening decades of the nineteenth century to the gigantic paintings of Albert Bierstadt and Thomas Moran toward the end of the century, diversity and multiplicity were key ingredients of art about the West. Like those who wrote most of the literature about the region, these artists were all nonwesterners. Every notable painter of the nineteenth century who emphasized the West was either a European or an American from the East.

If artists who traveled west before 1830 had difficulty capturing western settings and wildlife, three painters in the 1830s — George Catlin, Karl Bodmer, and Alfred Jacob Miller — provided the first memorable art about the West. The least well trained of the triumvirate, the American George Catlin visited the Mandans and other Plains Indians early in the decade and later made trips to the Southern Plains and the West Coast. He is best known for his remarkably descriptive and sympathetic images of Plains natives, which epitomize his raw talents as a portrait painter. His first exhibitions in the 1830s and the publication of his *Letters and Notes on the Manners, Customs, and Conditions of the North American Indians* (2 vols., 1841) and his *North American Indian Portfolio* (1844) illustrate his profound interest in color and Indian dress, but he was unable to depict Indians in action or to catch their emotions.

Rivaling Catlin as the first notable artist of western Indians, Swiss draftsman Karl Bodmer accompanied Prince Maximilian of Wied Neuwied in a memorable tour of portions of the upper Missouri during 1833–34. Despite the bitter cold and arduous working conditions that limited the range of his palette,

Bodmer drew notable battle scenes of Indians in *Assiniboine-Cree Attack on a Piegan Camp Outside Fort McKenzie* (1833) and a scene rich in ethnographic detail in *Interior of a Mandan Earth Lodge* (1833).

Whereas Catlin and Bodmer were intrigued with Plains Indians, American artist Alfred Jacob Miller (1810–1874) provided the only noteworthy group of portraits dealing with the mountain men. Traveling west with his wealthy Scots sponsor, Sir William Drummond Stewart, in the summer of 1837, Miller drew on his training in European Romantic art to place his trappers, as well as his Indians, against romantic backdrops that sometimes overshadowed his subjects. Miller also used his oils and watercolors to sketch out the spacious expanses of western land and thereby betrayed his limited interest in the details of people and specific settings, characteristics that so intrigued Catlin and Bodmer. On the other hand, his romantic notions about frontiersmen and landscapes were a notable prefiguration of Albert Bierstadt's compelling scenes.

If Catlin, Bodmer, and Miller ventured west alone or with their patrons, other artists accompanied government-sponsored explorations or railroad survey parties. In the days before cameras or extensive, detailed maps of western terrain, these artists provided government officials — and general viewers — with descriptive, visual images of the routes explorers and surveyors traversed. Traveling with the noted explorer John C. Frémont such artists as Edward and Richard Kern contributed significant topographical and scientific details to the Frémont reports. John Mix Stanley did much the same for several explorers of the West and for a railroad survey into the Pacific Northwest.

The premier representative of the landscape craze that influenced European and American artists during the middle decades of the nineteenth century was Albert Bierstadt. Born in Germany but reared in the United States, Bierstadt returned in 1853 to his natal land for artistic training. Imbued with the proper enthusiasm for Romanticism while in Europe, he returned to the United States and first traveled west in 1859 as part of the Lander expedition to the South Pass and the Rockies. Later he also visited California and Yosemite. Not unexpectedly, Bierstadt was astounded with the "grandeur and magnitude" of western mountains. Caught up in the then-popular ideas of the sublime and picturesque, Bierstadt produced gigantic oils of the Rockies, the Yellowstone area, and Yosemite. Some of his immense paintings — like *Storm in the Rocky Mountains* (1866?) and *The Domes of the Yellowstone* (1867)–measured seven by twelve or nine by fifteen feet. Even though these dramatic landscapes captured the fancy of Europeans and Americans and brought huge prices in the 1860s and 1870s, later in the century they impressed people as far too romantic and unrealistic. By his death in 1902, Bierstadt had been forgotten, his enormous canvases no longer sought after by collectors and patrons.

Thomas Moran was also born abroad, raised in the United States, and then trained in Europe. Much influenced by the English landscape artist J.M.W. Turner, Moran's first artistic works about the West, following his trip with the Hayden expedition to the Yellowstone region in 1871–72, betrayed Turnerian influences in his use of light and color and in his sunrises and sunsets. Moran's watercolors of the Yellowstone — along with the valuable photographs of William Henry Jackson — helped establish the area as a national park in 1872. Arguing that art should present the "scenic grandeur" of the West, Moran made his paintings conform more to his vision of the frontier than to the scenes that lay before him. His notable paintings of the West illustrated his attachment to a romantic vision that sought more to promote his idealized western wilderness than to depict what he saw accurately.

Bierstadt and Moran were like local-color writers in depicting a romantic, descriptive West. They were also unwilling to portray a West undergoing notable economic shifts that transformed its cultural life in the 1890s. These artists and writers, working in an atmosphere of longing for a frontier viewed as quickly passing, tried to recapture what they considered the open landscapes and the exotic lifestyles of earlier generations — all while the West was cantering toward the twentieth century. In their reluctance to face these changes, in their desire to hold on to a previous, vanishing frontier, they helped keep alive an older West that earlier writers, artists, and tourists had invented. This image of the Old West would continue well into the twentieth century in the art of Frederic Remington and Charles Russell, the fiction of Owen Wister and Zane Grey, and the western films of William S. Hart and Tom Mix.

By the 1880s, then, writers, historians, and painters had helped to invent a pioneer West already well known to many Americans. Portraying the trans-Mississippi frontier in the first half of the nineteenth century as a vast area of mysterious landscapes and natives, they continued to stress in the post–Civil War era the unique settings and residents of the West, even if some of its subregions were now settled and its inhabitants considerably less mysterious. Some hinted that the frontier was rapidly disappearing. Indeed, the launching of Buffalo Bill's Wild West show in 1883 signaled a turning point in these visions of the West; now, in addition to celebrating a heroic earlier frontier, one might simultaneously lament its passing. This ambivalent marriage of celebration and lament became a major theme of writers and painters between the 1890s and the 1920s.

I

THE WEST AS FRONTIER

INTRODUCTION

B y the end of the nineteenth century, most Americans were convinced
that the trans-Mississippi West had become a place apart. Simultaneously, they seemed increasingly afraid that the open frontier, or
Wild West, was vanishing before inrushing hordes of settlers. Even visitors
from abroad seemed to agree. In his widely quoted evaluation of the American West in the *American Commonwealth* in 1893, English traveler and diplo-
mat James Lord Bryce declared that "the West is the most American part of
America . . . the part where those features which distinguish America from
Europe come out in the strongest relief." But nineteen years later, in a new
edition, Bryce admitted that the West represented "a phase of life which is
now swiftly disappearing and may never be again seen elsewhere. . . . [Regions
of the West] are becoming like the older parts of the Republic."[1] Like many
Americans, Bryce relished the Old West even as it seemed to be passing from
the scene.

Dozens of American novelists, historians, and artists, as well as hosts of
travelers, agreed with Lord Bryce. If they echoed many of the reactions visitors to the West formulated during the nineteenth century, they concurrently
advanced new views as rapid changes transformed that West and the varying
cultures it represented. From the 1890s to the mid-1920s, writers and artists
endeavored to depict the American West as a lively frontier undergoing dramatic change—perhaps under such a barrage that the frontier would disappear
forever.

In other ways, frontier writers and artists in the first decades of the twentieth century also shared Lord Bryce's convictions that (1) the West represented a pioneer place and society markedly distant physically and culturally from the American East and that (2) regrettably, those differences were now rapidly disappearing. Like him, they also stressed the novel landscapes and peoples of the West. Moreover, their narratives (often with an autobiographical slant) spotlighted people coming *into* the West.

These similarities in content and form aside, the motivations of frontier storytellers were as varied as they were numerous. Some middle-class white males, like Owen Wister and Frederic Remington, rushed west out of wanderlust, to escape their eastern backgrounds, to view and experience the frontier, and eventually to use its natural and human landscapes in their fiction and paintings. Others, such as Mary Hallock Foote and Frederic Logan Paxson, came west following their families or occupations. For Foote, the West was initially an alien and uncivilized setting against which she hurled feminine frustrations and discontents, whereas easterner Paxson quickly acclimated to the West and embraced its frontier history. Meanwhile, for Frederick Jackson Turner, the West was primarily a cis-Mississippi frontier, where agriculturalists and other early pioneers modeled democracy and individualism for later immigrants. Finally, for native westerner Jack London and adopted westerners Frank Norris, Zane Grey, and Charles Russell the West wore a variety of faces, nearly all smilingly alive with possibilities for their fiction and art. Except for Foote, most of these writers and painters relished the West as frontier, as something of an antimodernist escape valve from the rising pressures of immigration, urbanization, and industrialization that were assaulting the East — all the more reason for them to lament signs of a closing frontier, since they had hoped it would continue to be a safe haven from the disruptive and threatening influences invading from the East.

Chapter 1

FRONTIER NOVELS

Owen Wister was perplexed. How could a Philadelphia-born, Harvard-educated man dramatize his western experiences? How could he depict a West where, it seemed to him, the future of America would be tested? After experimenting with several anecdotal and picaresque yarns, Wister hit upon a story line that many nineteenth-century travelers and tourists had employed and that would remain a popular plot for writers of Westerns after him. He decided to capitalize on the story of a greenhorn easterner coming into a new country, confronting a Wild West barely settled let alone civilized. Although autobiographical, Wister's narrative framework clearly echoed much of what earlier explorers and other sightseers had experienced.[1]

In *The Virginian* (1902), the immensely popular novel dedicated to President Theodore Roosevelt, Wister created a memorable story that dozens of contemporary and later writers imitated, stealing many of its ideas and stereotypes along the way. More than any other contemporary novelist writing about the West, Wister supplied the archetypal fictional narrative of the frontier. This became an American West like that depicted in the contemporary historical writings of Frederick Jackson Turner and Frederic Logan Paxson, the paintings of Frederic Remington and Charles Russell, the popular Westerns of Zane Grey and Max Brand, and later in the films of John Ford and John Wayne.

Wister's *Virginian* is a pivotal text in western literature because it sums up major nineteenth-century fictional, historiographical, and artistic interpretations of a frontier West. It also reflects eastern cultural attitudes at the century's turn and provides a model story line for narrating the "civilizing" and passing of that frontier. Wister's novel additionally illustrates eastern establishment attitudes toward a primitive frontier and remains a revealing fictional document about gender, heroism, and violence.

But in other ways *The Virginian* is an even more revealing example of frontier fiction. More than an illustration of the cultural conflicts between East and West, more than a model for the popular Western, more than a reflection of gender tensions of its time—and it is all these things—Wister's novel epitomizes its creator's attempt to dramatize the sociocultural conflicts involved in a closing frontier. As central to western literary history as Turner's frontier essay is to western historiography, *The Virginian* depicts the closing decades of that experience. Published halfway between the Civil War and the mid-1920s when Wild West images were being burned into the American consciousness, *The Virginian* serves as a frontier western literary epiphany, much as the works of Willa Cather, John Steinbeck, and Joan Didion would for later regional and postregional trends.

From his first trip west in 1885 until the publication of *The Virginian* in 1902, Owen Wister loved the rural landscapes of the frontier West with the intensity of a newly smitten swain. His western journals brim with the reactions of a young man caught up in novel scenery. Traveling through the sparsely inhabited areas of Wyoming, he enjoys the "continual passing of green void, without any growing things higher than a tuft of grass." Vista after vista enthralls him: "I can't possibly say how extraordinary and beautiful the valleys we've been going through are." Even more enthusiastic and revealing, his comment that "one must come to the West to realize what one may have most probably believed all one's life long—that it is a very much bigger place than the East, and the future of America is just bubbling and seething in bare legs and pinafores here." These extraordinary places begin to work their magic on Wister. As he recorded early on, "This existence is heavenly in its monotony and sweetness. Wish I were going to do it every summer. I'm beginning to be able to feel I'm something of an animal and not a stinking brain alone."[2]

But, gradually, by the mid-1890s, Wister exhibited less positive reactions to other western settings. Except for San Antonio, Salt Lake City, and a few small western towns, Wister thought western cities "perfectly hateful." Indeed—like his contemporaries Roosevelt, Remington, and Turner—Wister seemed automatically to consider the West a rural frontier, feeling ill at ease with western urban places. He likewise wondered if the frontier West hadn't spawned excessively violent men. "I begin to conclude from five seasons of observation," Wister recorded in his journal, "that life in this negligent irresponsible wilderness tends to turn people shiftless, cruel, and incompetent."[3]

Wister's first stories and books illustrate these ambivalent reactions to a swiftly changing frontier. Wister pictures his early heroes, such as Specimen Jones and Lin McLean, as cowboys, soldiers, or townsmen, not yet fully adapted to a fresh and demanding setting. Often on the move, frequently described as picaresque protagonists, these men seem unable to marry, put down roots, or establish communities. Life in little Coulee City in Washington state illustrates the settings the men inhabit: "Blowing over this waste came sudden noisome smells from the undrained filth of the town that huddled there in the midst of unlimited nothing. It is a shapeless litter of boxes, inhabited by men whose lives are an aimless drifting."[4]

Generally, however, Wister said much less about the West's native inhabitants than about its frontier settings. Perhaps because he had little direct contact with Indians, perhaps because he embraced many of the negative stereotypes of Indians that his friends held, or perhaps because his publishers and readers expressed more interest in cowboys and soldiers, Wister treated few Indians in his stories and novels. When he did, the results were rarely significant. In one early story from 1894, the villain is described as not of much use in the West because he doesn't know how to kill Indians. The next year Wister described Indians on the Colville Reservation as drunken derelicts. "Most white men know when they have had enough whiskey," the narrator asserts, but "most Indians do not. This is a difference between the races of which government has taken notice." And in the story "Little Big Horn Medicine," the young Crow chief Cheschpah is pictured as ignorant, superstitious, and childlike. The chief seems but one of the "crafty rabbits" misunderstood by easterners "rancid with philanthropy and ignorance," whom Wister satirizes as often as he stereotypes Indians. When Wister attempts to dramatize a young Indian woman married to a white man and caught between her culture and that of her husband, he describes her as "laughing like a child" and liking to think "her race could outwit the soldiers now and then."[5]

Wister's attitudes toward other racial and ethnic groups in the West were not much different from those he exhibited toward Indians. Most often supercilious and at worst virulently racist, Wister wrote little about these groups. On one occasion he urges Chicago freighters to move to California "and drive out the Chinese." When he describes Mexicans they appear as wandering, romantic, nonchalant peoples. "There is plenty of charm of its Latin variety" in "the Spanish or Mexican atmosphere," he told his mother, but his stories set in the Southwest nearly always include Mexican protagonists like that in "La Tinaja Bonita," a man described as having "no visible means of support; . . . nothing could worry him for longer than three minutes." Other "wandering Mexicans . . . , bright in rags and swarthy in nakedness," put a narrator "somehow in mind of the Old Testament."[6]

Truth to tell, Wister was much more intrigued with the passing of the frontier, how outsiders like himself reacted to the passing, and what the disappearance signified for the region and the nation. In a key essay, "The Evolution of the Cow-Puncher," written at the urging of his friend Frederic Remington, Wister glorifies Anglo-Saxons as the progenitors of the cowboy—"deep in him lay virtues and vices coarse and elemental as theirs"—and romanticizes him as a courageous civilizer of the Wild West. In fact, these vigorous, adventurous outdoor types have done their job too well; the Old West is disappearing, and Wister laments its passing, as well as the disappearance of the superb man on horseback. For example, in the opening sentence of *Lin McLean* (1897), his only novel before *The Virginian*, Wister explicitly announced the theme of that book and much of his other fiction. The story is set in "the old days, the happy days, when Wyoming was a Territory with a future instead of a State with a past, and the unfenced cattle grazed upon her ranges by prosperous thousands." The novel ends with the marriage and domestication of the hero, who leaves off riding to take up life in his ranch house.[7]

The Virginian, which incorporated many of the themes Wister had introduced in the previous decade, clearly illustrates his pivotal role as a writer of frontier western literature. Like the format of many exploration, travel, history, and fiction narratives of the nineteenth century, *The Virginian* is structured around the arrival of newcomers to the West. Notably in the portraits of the greenhorn narrator and of the heroine Molly Wood but also in the lives of earlier entrants—the Virginian, Balaam, Shorty, and the Judge—Wister focuses on the first years of their own settlement in Wyoming rather than beginning with the earlier waves of explorers, trappers, and overlanders as did the historian Turner. The new arrivals in *The Virginian*, like the eastern authors Richard Henry Dana, Washington Irving, and Francis Parkman in their writings, betray their alien prejudices, dismissing many western ways as provincial, uncouth, even dangerous. Not until Wister's narrator understands western male camaraderie and the necessity of listening more than talking and exhibits the courage and willingness to face down troublemakers is he initiated into the hero's inner circle. Not until Molly Wood comprehends the Virginian's need to prove himself against the rustlers and the villainous Trampas—and appreciates the hero's gentler and empathetic sides—is she a satisfactory "western" woman for him. Especially the Virginian but also the Judge and his family, the other cowboys, and even the maturing narrator and Molly are agents of social and moral order, jousting against skulking Indians, rapacious rustlers, and representatives of disorder to bring stability and civilization to the frontier. Finally, a hanging, a shootout, a marriage, and the Virginian's promotion to foreman represent Wister's ordered steps away from frontier instability and toward postfrontier stasis.

These rapid and certain strides toward civilization were intense and real for Wister since he too came west as a greenhorn in 1885 and returned more than a dozen times before the publication of *The Virginian*. With these visits he convinced himself that he had seen the frontier canter to its close. In a handful of later stories, in interviews, and in his correspondence, he spoke nostalgically of the Old West, but he was unable to recover the intensity that powered his writing in the 1890s. *The Virginian,* then, is a revealing document about the stages of Wister's life, as well as his shifting attitudes about the West.

The parallels between *The Virginian* and Frederick Jackson Turner's thesis are illuminating. Much of what the Wisconsin historian asserted in his pathbreaking essay of 1893, as we shall see, is central to Wister's novel. For Wister, like Turner, the frontier is a laboratory for democracy. When the Virginian displays his worth through astute leadership and then becomes a foreman, partner, and entrepreneur, Wister illustrates what he argued in the chapter "The Game and the Nation": " 'Let the best man win, whoever he is.' Let the best man win! That is America's word. That is true democracy. And true democracy and true aristocracy are one and the same thing."[8] The hero's advancement is possible because the frontier is an especially inviting arena for men of ambition, exertion, and horse sense. The leveling effects of a democratic frontier are likewise evident in the gradual acceptance of the eastern greenhorn once he understands the demands of Wister's egalitarian frontier code. Wister's frontier also encourages extraordinary feats of individualism, especially as represented in the hero's leadership under challenge, his valiant stance against Trampas, and his decisive reactions to Balaam, maltreater of horses.

Revealingly, the limitations in Wister's fictional frontier replicate similar blind spots in Turner's historiographical frontier. Neither focuses on Indians; non–Anglo-Saxons are ignored or harpooned; and women are often stereotyped or marginalized. Nor is either frontier writer, early on, interested in discussing the postfrontier West. In its emphases, as well as in its omissions, Wister's *Virginian* is a thoroughgoing illustration of much of Turner's frontier thesis.

In the mid-1890s when Owen Wister's editor received a letter from author Mary Hallock Foote commending Wister's treatment of the West in his earliest fiction, editor and author alike celebrated the letter as an indication that a leading western writer not only knew of Wister's work but held it in high regard. Although Foote's literary career had been underway for scarcely a dozen years, she had already placed numerous stories and sketches in leading magazines such as *Scribner's Monthly, The Atlantic,* and *Century Magazine,* had seen two collections of short fiction published, and had published five novels. Reviewers praised Foote's descriptive powers in setting scenes and in describing frontier characters, her insightful comparisons of East and West, and her appealing western women. By the time Foote completed her final novel during World War I, she had been writing about the West for nearly four decades, watching it rush from the frontier of General George Armstrong Custer to a region of urban and industrial might.

Judging from Foote's early years, however, no one would have predicted she would become a well-known *western* author; her life seemed headed in quite different directions. Born in 1847 in the upper Hudson River Valley, Mary Hallock grew up in a comfortable pastoral setting in a Quaker family (she would "me" and "thee" her own family well into the twentieth century). Educated at the Female Collegiate Seminary in Poughkeepsie and later at the Cooper Union Institute School of Design, where she met her lifelong friend Helena de Kay (Gilder), Mary was already well launched as a young illustrator before she married aspiring engineer Arthur De Wint Foote in 1876 and joined him in New Almaden, California. But she was a reluctant westerner for much of her life. Years later in her autobiography she wrote of her hesitations: "No girl ever wanted less to 'go West' with any man, or paid a man a greater compliment by doing so."[9] And Mary followed Arthur—usually reluctantly—throughout the West, from California to Colorado to Idaho and then finally back to California. Only their last years in Grass Valley, where she lived into the 1930s, seemed satisfying. In all, she lived in the West for more than fifty years, longer than any of the other frontier novelists treated here, even though that residence never entirely reflected the "angle of repose" she so diligently sought. Yet in her early and persisting attachment to the East, in her alienation from the West, and in her abiding interest in women's roles in the mining camps and small towns of the West, she added memorable vistas to frontier literature.

Foote's first novel, *The Led-Horse Claim* (1883),[10] illustrated emphases common in much of her early fiction. Drawing upon knowledge of western mining gained from her husband's expertise and their lives in California and Colorado mining camps, she focused especially on a vicious struggle that ended the family's stay in Leadville. On this bedrock of personal and historical detail she erected a romantic plot of Romeo-and-Juliet interfamily love and conflict. Although young mining engineers occupy much of the center stage, Cecil Conrath, the sister of one of the competing superintendents (the unscrupulous one) falls in love with George Hilgard, her brother's opponent and a man perhaps involved in his death. Cecil's difficulties in sorting out family and romantic dilemmas foreshadow similar conflicts that buffet many of Foote's young heroines. Finally, some of this melodrama is played out in competitions between a cultured East and an uncouth West, a theme central to Foote's frontier fiction.

Shallow characterizations and an inordinate use of chance and circumstance mar Foote's first novel, but other components of the work are more satisfactory. For example, she grasped well the extent to which frontier mining operations were in the hands of eastern capitalists. The Led-Horse mine "proudly boasted in its prospectuses," but, Foote writes, "the men who held it were engaged in larger schemes, which made the fate of the Led-Horse of comparatively little consequence" (33). In pointing out how much western colonies were at the mercy of eastern investors, Foote pinpointed a sore spot for westerners during the nineteenth and early twentieth centuries. Nor, like Wister, does Foote overlook the detrimental effects of a raw West on newcomers unable to meet its demands. The uncivilized frontier prematurely ages young women and frequently impels young men toward actions they would think the better of in a less precarious setting. A half dozen years later, Foote expanded on the shaping power of the new West when she wrote that the area "socially, . . . is a genesis, a formless record of beginnings, tragic, grotesque, sorrowful, unrelated, except as illustrations of a tendency toward confusion and failure, with contrasting lights of character, and high personal achievement."[11]

Foote's experiences in writing *The Led-Horse Claim* also reveal much about her times, her editors, and Foote herself. Forty years later she realized how sentimental her heroine was, how strange Cecil seemed to a generation acquainted with the Realists, the Naturalists, and new writers like Ernest Hemingway and F. Scott Fitzgerald. "What a silly sort of heroine she would seem today," Foote mused, representing "the woman's point of view, the *protected* point of view."[12] Moreover, she had tried to end the novel realistically and to separate Cecil and George, but her editor wanted a happy ending, and she caved in to his demands. Still, readers and reviewers generally reacted well to Foote's novel and frequently saluted her as a new woman writer of the West worthy of comparison with Bret Harte.

After a few months' residence in Leadville, the Footes retreated to Mary's parents on the Hudson while Arthur looked for other work in the West. A brief trip to Mexico in 1881 spawned some of Mary's most romantic writing, and during her stay in New York she drew on their recent experiences in Colorado for a second novel, *John Bodewin's Testimony* (1886). Meanwhile, Arthur had landed a position as the chief engineer and manager of the Idaho Mining and Irrigation Company. When his letter with that news arrived, Mary went "back to bed and turned [her] face to the wall." The move to "darkest Idaho," Mary thought, "meant farewell [to] music, art, gossip of the workshop, schools that we knew about, . . . old friends better loved than ever and harder to part from — all the old backgrounds receding hopelessly and forever." Mary needed to be convinced of her husband's strongest convictions about the success of this incredible venture in Idaho, with its "thousands of acres of desert empty of history," before she gave in and joined him in 1884.[13]

The next dozen years in the Boise area were filled with disappointment, failure, and family conflict. They were also Mary's most fruitful period as a writer. During these frustrating years in Idaho she produced several novels and dozens of stories, often providing the financial stability that Arthur's work could not, supporting the family and a maid or governess (or both) and adding to her reputation as the leading woman writer of the West. Such novels as *The Chosen Valley* (1892) and *Coeur d'Alene* (1894) were products of the Boise years, but her shorter works, nearly all set in Idaho, are even more intriguing. They illustrate Foote's descriptive powers, her ambivalences about the West, and her reactions to the political and social movements of the 1890s.

The Idaho stories reiterate Foote's ability to set appealing scenes and to describe revealingly the background of her fiction. Better than the other frontier writers, perhaps because of her training as an artist and illustrator, Foote built on the notable achievements of the local-color writers in portraying place, furnishing numerous memorable portraits of the rural West. Dotting her stories are hamlets like Arco, "a poor little seed of civilization dropped by the wayside," "another name for desolation on the very edge of that weird stone sea [of lava flows]." In another story, an eastern minister "resign[s] his dream" in the face of this "primeval waste," this "vast arid silence."[14] Here and elsewhere Foote creates her own Egdon Heath in remote southwestern Idaho.

Unlike other women regionalists such as Mary Austin and Willa Cather, Foote rarely uses settings to picture a frontier West vigorously shaping character over time. Rather, she utilizes western scenes to make comparisons with a static eastern society and culture. Some stories depict an eastern woman's exile in an isolated Far West, a motif in her first story that William Dean Howells accepted for *The Atlantic*. In "A Cloud on the Mountain," Mrs. Tully, once "a woman of some social pretentions, in the small Eastern village where she was born," is now a tired, prematurely old farm wife, worn out with childbearing, hard work, and "the monotony of their life in the hills." But her daughter Ruth Mary, in her late teens, is "haunted by no flesh-pots of the past"; she is attracted to the very western scenes that depress her mother. The same detrimental effect of an uncultured West on sophisticated eastern immigrants is raised in "On a Side-Track," where one character refers to a disturbingly uncivilized town: "'If you knew Pocatello, you would know what a privilege it was to have [a] house to go to. . . . There are many little things a woman needs a man to do for her in a place like Pocatello.'"

Yet, gradually and often obliquely, Foote begins to see the positive elements of Idaho and the West. One young westerner is described thus: he "showed in his striking person that union of good blood with hard conditions so often seen in the old-young graduates of the life schools of the West."[15] Even some settings seem less arid and forbidding. Historian Rodman Paul succinctly describes Foote's growing ambivalence toward the West: "Throughout the Idaho years a critical attitude toward most of the people of this rural west, other than her husband's engineering crew, marched side by side with Mary Hallock Foote's admiring appreciation of the beauty of mountain, cañon, and desert."[16]

On other topics Foote remained unrepentantly one-sided. Like most frontier novelists, Foote said little about Indians, but in one story treating Native Americans she clearly sees the Indian heritage of the mixed-blood girl, Meta, as the mongrelization of her Scottish side. From Meta's Native heritage she inherited daring and innocence but also wildness and primitive qualities. Since "the wild hill lily [cannot change] her natal stain," writes Foote, "the woman who looks the squaw is the squaw, when it comes to the flowering time of her life." On labor and political reform groups Foote was similarly outspoken. Coxey's Army, a portion of which marched through Idaho, is described as "begging and bullying its way eastward." The Coxeyites are "defiant train-stealers," or "that ridiculous army" — the same views that flavored Foote's letters to her beloved Helena.[17] All Populists are equally dangerous, and so are union radicals. These groups challenged the status quo of the conservatism that controlled Foote's opinions about society, East and West.

Foote likewise worried that the newness, the openness, of the West might encourage a threatening individualism, a dangerous chafing against standards. Even though she reluctantly came to appreciate more of the western scene by the 1890s, she continued to exhibit strong reservations. In one revealing letter to Mrs. Gilder, Foote disclosed her most persistent feelings: "For us, a home here [in the West] for a few years is inevitable, so there is nothing for it but to make the best of it. The best is not at all bad: it is only that there are people in the East I love, who draw my thoughts and longings away from what I should be wrapped up in, here. The only way to come west happily is to embrace the country, people, life, everything as colonists do, jealously maintaining its superiority and refusing to see a blemish. I love my West when I am in the East."[18]

Once the Footes abandoned Idaho in 1895, fleeing from their decade-long frustrations and failures there, and arrived in Grass Valley, California, where they were to remain nearly forty years, family circumstances changed dramatically. Along with them came new emphases in Mary's fiction. Although nearly all her stories and novels still revolved around romantic plots, her fictional treatment of the West began to move in different directions. For instance, several of the seven novels and the handful of stories she produced after resettling in northern California dealt with urban or coastal topics — e.g., *The Prodigal* (1900) and *The Ground-Swell* (1919), for example. Foote also produced her first historical novels, *The Royal Americans* (1910) and *The Picked Company* (1912), which, respectively, dealt with the American Revolution and immigration to the Oregon Country rather than with the frontier West of her own years. Abandoning the young-man-meets-young-girl scenario that dominated her fiction of the 1890s, Foote depicts parents wrestling with the marital choices of their offspring, as the Footes were doing in these years. Her final three novels drew much from her own life (*The Valley Road*, 1915); from the life of her best friend, Helena de Kay Gilder (*Edith Bonham*, 1917); and from the life of her daughter

Agnes, whose death in May 1904 was a staggering blow to Foote (*The Ground-Swell*, 1919).

Most significant, however, were Foote's transformed visions of the West. As her own life reached something of an "angle of repose" in Grass Valley, her characters are less at odds with their western settings. The stronger and more resourceful heroes and heroines in *The Prodigal, The Picked Company,* and *The Ground-Swell* find the West a place in which to demonstrate their courage and tenacity. Here, the West emerges as a free arena allowing, even encouraging, their energetic actions. What Lee Ann Johnson, Foote's biographer, says of her penultimate novel is true of most of her fiction after 1900: "Through the guise of fiction, Foote sought in *Edith Bonham* to affirm her own commitment and that of those closest to her; the novel offers reassurance that life can be lived in the West without compromise to one's integrity and vision."[19]

Foote's final book—her memoirs written in the 1920s when she was in her seventies—reflects this new acceptance of the West. Gone are most of the negative views of the frontier and the westerners who peopled her earliest fiction and letters. Even the troubled years in Idaho seem less traumatic. Had Foote come to accept the West? Were her last writings a testament of her acceptance of life in that alien country for more than half a century? Perhaps. One of her final requests was to be buried in Grass Valley.

Jack London's career and his vision of the West were dramatically at odds with those of other frontier novelists. A lifetime resident of the West except for sporadic trips elsewhere, London knew a region far different from that of Wister and Foote. Coming from social origins far below other contemporary interpreters of the frontier, London was attuned to class differences and social conflicts that other novelists overlooked. For the most part, his West, especially his much-loved Klondike, epitomized a frontier of opportunity for the bold and strong. But toward the end of his short career he fashioned an oxymoronic West, a civilized wilderness, breaking from most of the literary Wests of his era.

Born the illegitimate son of a wandering astrologer father and a socially dislocated mother, London experienced an uncertain boyhood even though his adoptive father, John London, despite poor health, courageously tried to support his family. Left much to himself, Jack gained a reputation as a youthful oyster pirate and waterfront tough. Later he joined the Oakland contingent of Coxey's Army and hoboed across the United States, returning compliments of the "boxcar Pullmans" of the Canadian Pacific. In short order he completed high school, flew through a college cram course, and enrolled for one semester at the University of California. Then wanderlust struck again, and he joined the thousands who streamed northward trying to hit pay dirt in the Klondike. London returned in late summer of 1898 as broke as most of the other dreamers.

Without a job or income, London tried to find work and also turned to writing, hoping to capitalize on his recent trip to the Klondike. While in the Northland, he took extensive notes and soaked up local-color details of the dog teams and their drivers, the mixed dialects of the region, and the customs of that inchoate society. Working with the intensity of a motivated madman, London turned out dozens of stories and sketches (all rejected) before the *Overland Monthly* and other journals began accepting his fiction. By 1900 the lordly Boston publisher Houghton Mifflin had printed a first collection of stories. The flood had begun. Three years later, London's career hit an early high when the *Saturday Evening Post* published his novella *The Call of the Wild*. The slim volume sold 10,000 copies on the first day of its subsequent book publication. London's frenzied attempt to mine his Northland experiences struck a rich vein, one that he continued to mine the rest of his career and the first of several "frontiers" that power his fiction.[20]

Even in his earliest Klondike stories, London clearly echoed emphases in the fiction of Wister and other frontier novelists. But London's frontier remained a primitive shaping force, at once more evident and more powerful than in the landscapes and settings of his contemporaries. In his first story in the *Overland Monthly*, "To the Man on Trail," London uses his hero, the Malamute Kid, to depict the physical and psychological pressures of the Klondike, the uncertain Indian-white relationships that characterized that area, and the brotherhood among men in the Northland. Published a month later, the story "The White Silence" revealingly illustrates London's abundant talents in describing a coercive environment. His "white silence"—the blank, white, indifferent setting that surrounds the story's characters—reminds one of the settings in Hamlin Garland's midwestern stories or Frank Norris's ranch country in *The Octopus*.[21]

In these stories and later ones such as "In a Far Country," "An Odyssey of the North," and "The Law of Life," and in his first novel, *A Daughter of the Snows* (1902), London repeatedly focused on either stalwart or "incapable" characters and their reactions to a demanding environment. In the first of these tales, the opening paragraph palpably summarizes London's early views of human relationships with the environment: "It were better for the man who cannot fit himself to the new groove to return to his own country; if he delay too long, he will surely die." Two greedy, lazy, selfish men — "the effete scions of civilization" — are destroyed because they cannot withstand the relentless frontier environment.[22] Here is an early example of London's social Darwinism, the "survival of the fittest" theme so much at the center of his depictions of frontier society and culture.

The reason for London's astonishingly rapid artistic development becomes clear when one realizes that a year later, in one white-hot month of writing, he produced *The Call of the Wild* (1903), which not only catapulted him to lasting fame but also constituted his best frontier fiction. Stressing again the dramatic relationships between men, animals, and nature in a wilderness environment, London provided a memorable work of fiction emphasizing themes that echoed ideas in Wister's *The Virginian* and Norris's *The Octopus*.

The Call of the Wild is the story of Buck, a magnificent half–St. Bernard and half–Scottish shepherd yanked from his placid, civilized existence on a California ranch and thrown into new, traumatic environment that tests all his strengths and instincts. As London writes, Buck "had been suddenly jerked from the heart of civilization and flung into the heart of things primordial." He soon discovers he is in a land that knows "no law but the law of club and fang." But like London's successful humans, Buck learns to adjust. His splendid energies and understanding allow him to survive when less fit beasts and people are destroyed in the coercive environment of the Northland. Although Buck is attracted to John Thornton, a miner who loves him, the "call of the wild" is upon him, and when Buck becomes friends with a wolf and strikes, drags down, and finally kills a giant moose, the primitive has clearly taken control. When nearby natives plunder Thornton's camp and kill him, Buck is forced to join the surrounding primordial world and run with his wolf brothers in the wild. The closing sentence of London's novel, surely one of the best illustrations of the author's prose, catches the mood of the book: "When the long winter nights come on and the wolves follow their meat into the lower valleys, he [Buck] may be seen running at the head of the pack through the pale moonlight or glimmering borealis, leaping gigantic above his fellows, his great throat a-bellow as he sings a song of the younger world, which is the song of the pack."[23]

London also capitalized on his own experiences and voracious reading to focus on another frontier — that of class conflict — especially in the lives of tramps and in quarrels between owners and laborers. London met thousands of men on the road when he hoboed across the United States and Canada in the 1890s and spent a month in prison for vagrancy, and when he lived disguised as a homeless worker in the slums of London, England. These men were not irresponsible workers in flight from families and duties, he concluded, but victims of a competitive economic system that pounded them into submission. As he wrote of his own conversion to socialism, "it was hammered into me" at the same time individualism and blond-beast Nietzschism were "pretty effectively hammered out" of him.[24]

When London began to write about the dramatic emergence of hundreds of thousands of unemployed workers and tramps, he emphasized a ruinous capitalist system that, in times of economic and social stress, pummeled healthy and dependable men into submission and ruin. In his view, the closing of the frontier was a major reason for these dramatic changes in the American system. The "farthest West has been reached," London wrote in his essay "The Class Struggle," and now "an immense volume of surplus capital roams for investment and nips in the bud the patient efforts of the embryo capitalist to rise through slow increment from small beginnings. The gateway of opportunity after opportunity has been closed, and closed for all time."[25]

But when London came to write about the tramp as a sympathetic hero of a vanishing frontier, he could not produce an attractive protagonist. In essays such as "The Road" (1899) and "The Tramp" (1904), stories like "Local-Color" (1903) and "The Hobo and the Fairy" (1911), and in his only full-length work on tramps, *The Road* (1907), he wavered ambivalently between treating the hobo as an adventuresome countercultural hero and as the innocent prey of a ruthless industrial system. On one occasion he wrote, "I became a tramp — well, because of the life that was in me, of the wanderlust in my blood that would not let me rest. Sociology was merely incidental; it came afterward." Yet he also asserted that all capitalist societies contain a surplus labor force and that a closing frontier produced tramps as a "by-product of an economic necessity."

To many Americans in the early twentieth century, of course, tramps were not appealing figures. Just as many objected to the uncouth cowboy until Wister, Remington, and others romanticized him in the 1890s, so editors refused to publish fiction dealing with tramps in the decades before and after 1900. Since the hobo was not an inspiring subject for girls or for the readers of coffee-table books — two of the irrefutable tests of acceptable fiction in the late nineteenth century — even London's editor and publisher, George Brett of

Macmillan, and his libertine friend, George Sterling, thought London's tramp writings would undercut the sales of his other fiction. Disagreeing vociferously with these attitudes, London nonetheless gradually shied away from the hobo in his later fiction even though he continued to believe that tramps epitomized an important facet of a closing frontier.[26]

In his last years, London was increasingly attracted to a third frontier. After his divorce from his first wife, Bessie, and marriage to Charmian Kittredge in 1905, London became more and more fascinated with the back-to-the-land ideas that rippled through American society during the Progressive Era. But London's captivation with land and farming is more than a mere flight from cities and an embracing of rural life. He came to believe that farming—particularly a scientific agriculture that combined hard work, the latest fertilizers, crossbreeding, and crop rotation—was one answer to an America facing a frontierless future.

The Valley of the Moon (1913), the best-known of London's many later works of agrarian fiction, suggests one solution for postfrontier society. Drawing upon London's own experiences in abandoning urban Oakland and retreating to his beloved Ranch in the Sonoma Valley, the long novel meanders through two lengthy sections: first, the growing discontent of Billy and Saxon Roberts with strife-torn Oakland; and, second, their prolonged search for an ideal farm. Eventually they avoid both an unsettled area and an intensely cultivated one. London writes at length of their dissatisfaction with the bonanza farming of the nineteenth century, which brought wealth to a few and poverty to many, and which ruined the soils of many areas. Human greed, Billy thinks, brought a premature end to the frontier.

When Billy and Saxon arrive in the Valley of the Moon, London makes clear the kind of farming that will sustain and heal them. Billy argues that the land surface must be changed. Looking over his dreamed-of landscape, he rhapsodizes: "It's no good as it is. . . . But it's the best ever if it's handled right. All it needs is a little common sense and 'a lot of drainage.'" And they set to work to improve and utilize the land, just as London did with his growing acreage. They irrigate the land, run electricity to the site, make bricks from soil in marginal areas, and welcome the nearby railroad as the necessary mode of transportation. The closing scene illustrates the fructuous quality of London's agricultural vision. As the couple envision the productivity of their scientifically planned farm, Saxon shyly tells Billy that she is pregnant with their second child (the first had died stillborn in the city), and as Billy expresses joy at her announcement, they gaze "up the side of the knoll where a doe and a spotted fawn looked down upon them from a tiny space between trees."[27]

In unifying the garden and the machine in the final pages of his novel, London was creating a new kind of frontier. Gradually abandoning the wilderness frontier of man-versus-nature in his Northland writings like *The Call of the Wild* and moving away from a closing frontier that spawned alienated workers and tramps, London maneuvered toward a civilized frontier that echoed the ideas of Progressives like Theodore Roosevelt, Charles Beard, and participants in the Country Life Movement. Like London, these Progressives wanted to combine the old (land) and the new (science) to produce a pragmatic, productive, and less exploitive society.

In the era of the closing frontier, Jack London suggested a plan — not a solution but a scheme that would bring about a new culture built on the judicious use of agricultural land, the beneficial employment of natural resources, and what he considered a new brotherhood of people. Stressing less his earlier Northland and class-conflict frontiers, he promoted a new oxymoronic frontier, one that combined farmland and technology into a civilized wilderness. In this new culture Jack London was convinced that an open marriage of the machine and the garden could and should exist. Three or four generations later, postregional novelists were much less optimistic about this possible union.

Frank Norris has worn a variety of assigned hats since the turn of the century. Some think of him as a Naturalist, the wearer of a Zolaesque hardhat. Others picture him as a literary blood brother of Kipling, Wister, and Remington, donning his Anglo-Saxon sun helmet. Still others describe him as an adolescent, still garbed in a boyish cap. Most have not thought of him as wearing a large western hat, but perhaps they should: Norris was a major interpreter of both the frontier and the postfrontier West at the close of the nineteenth century. Accordingly, he shared similar perspectives with authors Wister, London, and Hamlin Garland, and also other pioneers of western fiction.

Norris came west from Chicago, his birthplace, at age fourteen in 1884. The son of a self-made Victorian gentleman who moved to Oakland and then San Francisco to avoid the cold of the Great Lakes region, Norris followed an erratic educational path of, first, private and public schools in the Bay Area and then artistic training in California and in schools in London and Paris. Next he returned west to enter the University of California as a special student with a new major in writing. Alienated from his composition instructors at Berkeley, Norris moved in 1892 to Harvard for further training in creative writing. Thereafter, brief stints followed as a journalist, an editorial assistant, and a manuscript reader in New York and San Francisco. His own novels began to appear in 1898, with *McTeague* (1899) and *The Octopus* (1901) winning positive accolades. But his health, always precarious since the mid-1890s, turned dramatically worse overnight, and he died from peritonitis in October 1902.

Frank Norris is a complicated, sometimes inconsistent fiction writer as his writings about the frontier clearly attest. He echoes Wister's Anglo-Saxonism, his heroes frequently betray London's primitivism, and he often depicts the West as a recently closed frontier, a popular theme among western writers at the turn of the century. But he also focuses more on the metropolitan West than did most of his contemporaries, and along with Hamlin Garland he was one of the first to develop a preliminary credo of western literary criticism.

Early in his career, Norris trumpeted the West as a fertile region ripe for literary exploitation. In 1897 he pointed to the "Great Opportunities for Fiction Writers in San Francisco," especially for those who wrote stories of "strong, brutal men, with red-hot blood in 'em." And he effused, "we don't want literature, we want life." New York was stuffed with writers trying to turn out polished, stylistic, effete literature, he continued; but in San Francisco, "the tales are here . . . the public is here. . . . Strike but the right note, and strike it with all your might, strike it with iron instead of velvet, and the clang of it shall go the round of the nations." [28]

Like Wister and Foote, Norris also felt compelled to make comparisons between the east and west coasts, where he had been educated and where he held his first writing positions. Soon after he was hired as a reader by the famous muckraking editor S. S. McClure, he wrote to an acquaintance: "New York is not California, nor New York City San Francisco, and I am afraid that because of the difference I shall never become reconciled to the East or ever come to really like New York. . . . There is not much color here and very little of the picturesque." [29]

At the same time that the East took a lower rung on the ladder of Norris's emotional and cultural attachments, he was already beginning to champion western scenes, experiences, and peoples. With boyish exuberance he describes the western hero and heroine in *Blix* (1899): "And so they went along in that fine, clear, Western morning, on the edge of the Continent, both of them young and strong and vigorous . . . their imaginations thronging with pictures of vigorous action and adventure. . . . The day was young, the country was young, and the civilization to which they belonged, teeming there upon the green, Western fringe of the continent, was young and heady and tumultuous with the boisterous, red blood of a new race."[30]

In the four short years between the publication of his first novel in 1898 and his premature death in 1902, Norris often wrote about the importance of using the frontier or the recent West for fiction. In January 1902, for example, in disagreeing with an earlier writer who had called for a less frenetic western literature that focused on the quieter aspects of urban businessmen and solid farmers, Norris argued that the true westerner was "the adventurer." Even though dime novelists and other sensationalists had distorted the frontier past through their *sole* emphasis on the Deadwood Dicks and the Buffalo Bills, they were correct in stressing "the man of deeds, the man of action, the adventurer, the pioneer, . . . the great figure, the true figure." And when *the* epic of the West was written, when the Great American Novel centered on the West, as it should, that notable work would not focus on "one locality but [on] the huge conglomerate West; and the true knight of the song shall be the fighter, . . . blood brother to Roland and Grettir the Strong, the one distinctive and romantic figure of American life."[31]

Norris added that writers must realize, too, that although "the frontier [was] gone at last," its story was still our "neglected epic." If Americans pondered the meaning of the westward-moving frontiers that had marched from the swamps of Friesland across Europe, the United States, and now the Pacific and had returned to Europe, they would begin to sense a new patriotism, which was "the brotherhood of man" and the knowledge "that the whole world [was] our nation and simple humanity our countrymen." (Although Norris posited a larger view here than did most frontier writers, he patently limited the circle of his "brothers" to Anglo-Saxons.) Unfortunately, Norris adds, Americans have not capitalized on the grand literary theme of the westward movement across their continent. Instead we have "neglected it and overlooked it, and abandoned the one great field for American epic literature to the yellow-backs and dime-novels." Following a note much like Turner's sermonizing in western historiography, Norris sounded the tocsin for a literature that moved past the "charlatanism" of James Fenimore Cooper and well beyond the falseness of the dime novel and the Wild West show. In allowing these prevaricators to sensationalize titanic battles with Indians and to treat the West as nothing but "road agents and desperadoes," we had overlooked the real westerner, who was not "a lawbreaker, but a lawmaker; . . . a fighter for peace, a calm, grave, strong man who hated the lawbreaker as the hound hates the wolf." This loyal, courageous, and valiant figure, Norris asserted, should be *the* protagonist of our national epic. Our American story must be his fight, his deeds—and those of thousands of others like him who had swept across the West, subduing the wilderness "at a single stroke."[32]

Norris contended that "naturalism" was the best approach to writing fiction about the West, but he meant something very specific by that term. Describing "realism" and "romanticism" as opposing techniques of writing that emphasized facts and feelings, Norris concluded that naturalism was a "transcending synthesis." Whereas realism used surface facts and commonplace details, romanticism burrowed beneath the surface to discover man's emotions, the inward skies of his consciousness. Naturalism, on the other hand, would juxtapose the most useful elements of realism and romanticism and then add two ingredients that other authors overlooked: lower-class life and a sensational approach. The final ideal equation would thus read: realism (facts) plus romanticism (the true) equal naturalism (truth).[33]

Several of these ideas about the importance of the frontier and the West and the most appropriate formulas for fiction writing inform Norris's two most important novels, *McTeague* (1899) and *The Octopus* (1901). A one-to-one correspondence between Norris's theories and his fiction is too much to expect; his ideas were too often preliminary, fuzzy, and contradictory. But these novels do clearly illustrate his western literary credo and demonstrate how rapidly he developed as a literary artist as well.

Subtitled *A Story of San Francisco* and drawing upon an actual murder case, *McTeague* illustrates Norris's conviction that San Francisco was a prime topic for western writing. To depict a diverse West, Norris transports his hero, McTeague, from California's frontier mining camps into throbbing, urban San Francisco. Learning the rudiments of dentistry but practicing without a license, McTeague gradually falls in love with Trina Sieppe, the daughter of immigrants. His infatuation leads to a proposal, which she first rejects and then accepts. Five years of placid marriage follow, but when she wins a $5,000 lottery and when an earlier rival for Trina notifies authorities of McTeague's illegal practice of dentistry, their lives suddenly spiral downward. When McTeague loses his job and as Trina hordes her money, they both atavistically revert to a primitivistic status, he from buffoon to beast, she from miserliness to avarice.[34] In a moment of passionate brutality, McTeague murders Trina, steals her money, and escapes to Death Valley. Closely followed, he kills his pursuer, only to realize he is now handcuffed to his dead body. "All about him," Norris writes, "vast, interminable, stretched the measureless leagues of Death Valley."[35]

McTeague illustrates several of Norris's prescriptions for acceptable western fiction. In his Polk Street setting, he unifies minute descriptions of urban life with the turbulent emotional lives of his major characters, thereby carrying out the central provisions of his naturalistic credo. Concurrently, his western protagonist, McTeague, is the passionate, red-blooded adventurer Norris described as the archetypal westerner. And in suggesting how much this rugged frontier beast seems out of place in the urban West, so much so that he eventually retreats to the open frontier when under stress, Norris dramatizes a West in transition, caught, if McTeague symbolizes these sociocultural pressures, between a vanishing frontier and an emerging urban West. Critic Don B. Graham succinctly summarizes this West of *McTeague*: "Norris's image of the West in this novel — city and frontier — is a grim one indeed. It is a land of pulsing and unfocused energies, a place where civilization has failed to provide an adequate environment for the dispossessed frontiersman and urban peasant."[36]

The Octopus, deservedly recognized as its creator's most significant novel, illustrates Norris's major precepts about western fiction even as it foreshadows later developments in western regionalism. The sprawling, throbbing story of farmers and ranchers in conflict with an octopuslike railroad (based on a real situation that climaxed in a shootout at Mussel Slough in May 1880), Norris's novel is likewise a narrative of western city and frontier, jousting with one another for dominance. And his major figures — Magnus Derrick, Annixter, Vanamee, and Presley — embody the qualities of character that Norris urged western writers to embody in their works. Derrick epitomizes the hardworking Anglo-Saxon pioneer; Annixter, the courageous, college-educated fighter and lover; Vanamee, the wandering sheepherder mystic; and Presley, the eastern poet come to the West to write its epic history. Norris's masterpiece overflows with power, of scope and scale unlike anything any previous novelist had written about the West.

Moreover, *The Octopus* depicts a gigantic struggle between humans and nature. Those who misread the novel *solely* as a naturalistic or muckraking tract oversimplify the work. Although ambitious and hardworking, the ranchers and farmers are selfish and greedy, ripping up the land, destroying what lies in their way, and selling their souls for more land and security. S. Behrman and Shelgrim are more than merely wily, malicious agents of the bank and the railroad; they too seem caught in the immutable laws that lie behind them. As Shelgrim tells Presley, "Blame conditions, not men!" Stupefied and dumbfounded by "this new conception," Presley wonders: "Forces, conditions, laws of supply and demand—were these then the enemies, after all?" But he's unwilling to go that far, for nature was not an enemy; "there was no malevolence in Nature," just "colossal indifference."

Of all protagonists in Norris's fiction, Presley comes closest to learning the necessary lessons. At first, as an eastern aesthete, he is too literary, too uninvolved, too hamstrung with distancing romantic notions to care much for the dilemmas of the ranchers. Presley "searched for the True Romance, and, in the end, found grain rates and unjust freight tariffs." But he gradually perceives the real and commonplace behind the truth he sought, slowly coming to empathize with those writhing in the tentacles of the octopus. Witnessing and finally participating in the ranchers' cause, Presley publishes his poem "The Toilers" in support of the downtrodden, makes rabble-rousing speeches against the railroad, and even throws a bomb at Behrman. Yet his conversation with Shelgrim and his reflections in the novel's final pages suggest he has learned the ultimate lesson Norris called for: as significant as the events of California's interior valley and coast are, they are but parts of a larger picture. Men lose their lives, Presley reflects, "*but the* WHEAT *remained . . .* and all things, surely, inevitably, resistlessly work together for good."[37] Here is Norris's contention that the American West was but one frontier of a global community, but one segment of a worldwide story.

Within a decade, then, Frank Norris offered several portraits of a West in transition. Of all the frontier novelists, he centered most on the urban West, peopling his fiction with appealing metropolitan figures. Like his contemporaries, he used eastern and western differences to spell out sociocultural conflicts and similar to them he clearly reflected his Anglo-Saxon biases through his negative reactions to Jewish, Hispanic, and Chinese characters. But Norris likewise adumbrated later regional perspectives. In *The Octopus,* and in less-pronounced respects in *McTeague* and his short stories, Norris tentatively showed how westerners were beginning, in their ranch and urban experiences, to develop semblances of a regional identity. Like London's *Valley of the Moon, The Octopus* prefigures the regionalist stress on relationships between people and the land that led to unique cultural identities. And, finally, in its overflowing, rambling quality, *The Octopus* foreshadows the form and content of such regionalist novels as H. L. Davis's *Honey in the Horn,* Wallace Stegner's *Big Rock Candy Mountain,* and John Steinbeck's *Grapes of Wrath.*

At the same time that Wister, Foote, London, and Norris were turning out major fiction about the frontier West, another cluster of writers during the first three decades of the twentieth century were producing dozens of novels known as Westerns. Capitalizing on the popularity of *The Virginian* and the rising cinematic Western, especially after the release of *The Great Train Robbery* (1903), the Western appealed to mushrooming numbers of readers and became one of the country's most popular fictional genres after World War I.

Replacing the dime novel Western, which rapidly declined in popularity after 1900, the new fictional Western quickly adopted a formula of ingredients that have remained throughout this century. The Western is most often an adventure story set during the late nineteenth century in the trans-Mississippi West. Utilizing plots and character types similar to those of Sir Walter Scott and Robert Louis Stevenson, the Western features a courageous hero, often a cowboy or at least a man on horseback, who combats evil by opposing villainous characters or institutions and who establishes (or reestablishes) order, frequently through violent, redeeming acts. For his deeds, he is rewarded with a virtuous young woman, who, despite her initial hesitations about the hero and his violence, is finally drawn to him. During the twentieth century, hundreds of authors have tinkered with the format of the Western, but the essential formula of a powerful masculine protagonist, the evil or at least amoral villain, and the attractive and romantic heroine have remained. Over time, ethnic groups less frequently serve as opponents, women take more active roles, the hero may be a good-bad man, and the definition of a good community may vary a bit, but the Western still remains recognizable for its familiar formula.

Early in the twentieth century, such writers as Zane Grey, B. M. Bower, Clarence Mulford, and Max Brand (Frederick Faust) became synonymous with the Western. Grey wrote dozens of Westerns known for their extensive and moving descriptions and emotional, often sentimental, characters. Bower, the only well-known female author of Westerns and recognized particularly for *Chip of the Flying U* (1906) and other cowboy fiction, treated women, families, and divorce more often than did other writers. Brand, the best-known of Faust's many pen names, repeatedly utilized epic heroes and plots while avoiding specific western locations or historical events. Meanwhile, Mulford's hero, *Hopalong Cassidy* (1910), was based on his creator's extensive historical research on the West. More often than not, these writers seemed satisfied to stress the major components of frontier fiction: pioneers entering a new country who fight with Indians, other newcomers, and the land, hoping to tame, settle, and civilize the new frontier. This format remained widely popular even after regional and postregional writers emerged in the interwar and post–World War II decades, as the later Westerns of Ernest Haycox, Luke Short (Frederick Glidden), and Louis L'Amour amply demonstrate.

Of the early-twentieth-century writers, Zane Grey became the most esteemed and widely recognized author of Westerns. Once his career was established, he topped bestseller lists nearly every year between 1914 and 1928, and his novels continued to sell well up to and following his death in 1939. In several ways Grey seemed an unlikely prospect for a notable career in writing popular Westerns even though his forebears included stalwart frontiersmen and Indian fighters. An undisciplined college student addicted to escapist reading, Grey became known for his murderous curveball as a pitcher for the University of Pennsylvania, not for his academic prowess. Later, as a struggling dentist in New York City, he dreamed more of writing Western romances than of pulling impacted teeth. Trying his hand at frontier novels, he was forced to publish them at his own expense (*Betty Zane,* 1903) or to see them issued through minor publishers (*The Spirit of the Border,* 1906, and *The Last Trail,* 1909).

Meanwhile he married, and under the lash of new responsibilities and through the indefatigable encouragement and financial support of his wife, Lina, Grey went west with Colonel C. J. "Buffalo" Jones to see the region first-hand and to write about it. When he finished Jones's story, he submitted the manuscript to an editor at Harpers, who told Grey: "I don't see anything in this to convince me you can write either narrative or fiction."[38] Staggered, Grey thought of giving up but decided to publish the work elsewhere. Then he used his fresh experiences in the West for a new novel, *The Heritage of the Desert* (1910), which Harpers promptly published. Swinging into a faster-paced rhythm, Grey finished his most successful Western, *Riders of the Purple Sage* (1912), which gained positive reviews and sold two million copies during his lifetime and perhaps twice that since his death. More important, it is an archetypal Western, including standard elements of that popular genre and illustrating major themes of frontier fiction.

Selecting one Western to illustrate the thousands written between 1900 and the 1920s is risky indeed, yet the plot, characterizations, and thematic emphases of Grey's *Riders of the Purple Sage* are remarkably representative of numerous Westerns. In the first place, the isolated, semicivilized Utah border country, barely a generation after the first Mormon settlements, molds the outlooks of all who dare to enter its stern domain. Indeed, so intense and coercive is its fierce mien that those who encounter the canyon and sage country are forced to revert to earlier, less civilized acts to survive.

In this demanding setting, Grey uses members of the Church of Jesus Christ of Latter-day Saints as other writers had utilized Indians, as inhumane and brutal opponents, "savages." The Mormon women exhibit palpable warmth and a sense of family, but the male leaders exude selfishness and brutality, driven, Grey suggests, by monumental, all-inclusive religious motives that batter down dissent, freedom, and love. From the novel's opening chapters to its dramatic conclusion, the Mormons lurk as a dark presence, bent on dominating and keeping control of a setting and cast of characters reminiscent of Old Testament times.[39]

The six major figures of the novel are forced to negotiate with the rugged physical terrain that surrounds them and with the unrelenting, patriarchal Mormons. One heroine, Jane Withersteen, who inherited her father's forceful independence as well as his devotion to the LDS Church, faces a struggle to the death with church leaders who want her to submit to their leadership and to become a plural wife. Ambitious and defiant, she tries to hold on to her father's sprawling ranch and cattle herds and yet remain loyal to the church's teachings even while she opposes its leadership.

The other female lead, Bess Oldring (whose real name, we learn later, is Elizabeth Erne) is the shadowy Masked Rider of the Oldring rustler gang. Taken captive as a young girl, she has ridden for several years with the outlaws in this isolated border country. She remains innocent, and when mistakenly shot down as one of the ruthless renegades, she gradually recovers — and changes — in the Edenic setting of remote Surprise Valley and under the watchful care of Bern Venters, whose redeeming love sparks her attraction to him.

Venters vividly symbolizes Grey's depiction of what the compelling physical and social environment does to immigrants to frontier Utah. Initially a small rancher and hired rider, he is forced into working for others after the Mormons drive him from his land, forcing him to ride for Jane Withersteen. After he tracks down some of her stolen cattle, stumbles into Surprise Valley, and accidentally shoots the Masked Rider, he reverts to a wild man, living off the bounty of the hidden refuge. Gradually, however, his growing love for Bess and the feelings she returns redeem him, although hardening his bitter resentment toward the Mormons and outlaws. Later, he murders Oldring and with Bess flees the frontier.

The gigantic hero of Grey's novel is Lassiter, the cowboy and gunman driven to that position by the wickedness of his world. He is Frank Norris's lawbringer and Wister's Virginian, and he prefigures Brand's gunslingers and the mighty Shane. His vicious black guns symbolize his masculinity and underlying violence. In turn, Jane tries to unman him, to get him to take off his guns, thereby saving her Mormon men and the outlaws from his revenge. Larger than life, he comes "silhouetted against the western sky," dressed in black leather, exhibiting "the leanness, the red burn of the sun, and the set changelessness that came from years of silence and solitude."[40] Here is the hero of stern visage and flashing guns, the man "who's gotta do what a man's gotta do," the righter of wrongs, and the masculine essence to attractive women like Jane, who eventually falls in love with him.

The two Mormons, Elder Tull and Bishop Dyer, introduced as black-hearted villains, remain implacable opponents throughout the novel. These "savages" forfeit all sympathy because of their greedy, self-righteous attitudes toward Jane, other women, and Gentiles (non-Mormons). Indeed, Grey suggests they are more devilish than the Gentile rustlers because of their bigoted, unchristian attitudes.

In spinning out his lively plot set in this dramatic landscape and involving these lively characters, Grey follows popular themes of frontier fiction and pioneers others that prove as durable as the Western itself. His barren Utah is as much an arena for testing strength and courage as is Wister's sprawling Wyoming ranch country. Like the Virginian, Lassiter and Venters must prove their manhood against stiff opposition. In Grey's novel the Mormons as well as the demanding environment serve as agents for testing the heroes. These men front villains who would destroy a community or who would bar it to newcomers of other beliefs. Within this isolated setting, Grey relates a story of nascent frontier, one in the making, not yet a well-organized community with its own regional identity created over time. This to-the-West theme, with its attendant test of newcomers in a cauldron of conflict, became a central emphasis in Westerns, as it was in much of the fiction of Wister, Foote, and London.

The moral drama Grey so sincerely creates in *Riders of the Purple Sage* and in most of his other Westerns parallels the white-hat-versus-black-hat dichotomy that powers many cinematic Westerns from *The Great Train Robbery* into the 1920s. So often organized around the transformation of a Broncho Billy or William S. Hart from a bad man to a good man, these films depict the frontier as a demanding stage on which courage and stamina have to battle endlessly lurking evils. In *The Battle of Elderbush Gulch* (1913) noted director D. W. Griffith portrays the heroes' opponents as rapacious, dog-eating, murderous Indians, whereas in Hart's *Hell's Hinges* (1916) the hero reverses his own moral complacency, with the aid of a virtuous woman, and helps dispose of a weak, ineffectual minister to save the good people remaining in this modern-day Sodom and Gomorrah. In their penchant for creating ethical dramas played out in dusty, arid landscapes and settlements in need of both civilizing and community, Zane Grey and William S. Hart partnered in inventing a frontier West.

Once homogenized, these ingredients established a mythic West that powers fictional Westerns from Grey through L'Amour. In Western films, the frontier is also a Wild West in need of double doses of civilization, the kinds of change that only the dynamic heroes of Wister's and Grey's novels and the willful protagonists of Hart and Mix movies can carry out. When the frontier finally closes, as it does in Hart's wonderfully emblematic *Tumbleweeds* (1925), that change occurs when the pretty daughter of incoming nesters captures the heart of Hart's roving cowboy. Romanticism and romance aside, many Western films of the first three decades followed the familiar pattern of frontier fiction, in which strong masculine heroes conquer the demanding landscapes and challenging natives of the New Country. The same story drives the histories of Frederick Jackson Turner and Frederic Logan Paxson and structures many of the paintings of Frederic Remington and Charles Russell. In contrast, the contemporary writers Mary Austin and Willa Cather were already depicting a West at variance with this Wild West, but not until the 1920s and 1930s did their regional West furnish a major challenge to the frontier as the predominant fictional and cinematic image of the American West.

Chapter 2

FRONTIER HISTORIES

The setting—the World's Columbian Exposition in Chicago on a steamy July afternoon in 1893; the dramatis personae: members of the American Historical Association congregating at their annual meeting; the final speaker: Frederick Jackson Turner, a professor of history at the University of Wisconsin; the topic: the significance of the frontier in American history.

Although nothing at the Chicago conference, or anything immediately thereafter, indicated it to be so, Turner was about to deliver what would become the most famous and important essay in the course of American historical writing. Within a generation after its presentation, Turner's pathbreaking essay became the primary interpretation of the American past, hailed as a fresh and convincing framework for understanding American history. The Turner or frontier thesis came to dominate American historiography during most of the first half of the twentieth century. Although the thesis suffered something of a decline during the 1930s, it bounced back after World War II until large numbers of historians challenged it again during the 1960s. At present, even though few American historians explicitly follow the frontier thesis, it remains the single most-discussed theme of American historical writing.

Frederick Jackson Turner was, and is, the central figure in the frontier interpretation of American history. Ironically, both at the beginning of his career and now, a century later, his views have been oversimplified, leading first to an overly enthusiastic acceptance of his generalizations and, more recently, to a too-quick dismissal or refusal to examine several of his major ideas.

In fact, there were several Turners, and comprehending them is important to understanding his role as the pivotal figure in the frontier interpretation of the American West. Like so many pathbreaking figures, Turner first pointed out the shortcomings of previous interpretations of American history even as he argued for his frontier and later sectional/regional hypotheses. At the same time, he broke from many of his contemporaries by calling for analytical and interdisciplinary approaches to the study of the frontier. To overlook any of these contributions, even while noting Turner's limitations and mistaken notions, is to underestimate his premier importance.[1]

From his earliest writings Turner wanted to reorient contemporary American historiography. Among the first professional frontier historians, he pondered more deeply than others *what* ought to be written about the frontier and *how* these writings should bear on what other historians of the time were writing about the American past. Indeed, Turner's observations about historical methods and approaches during the 1890s supply a useful introduction to the first stages of western historiography.

From the outset Turner was convinced that historians on the Atlantic Coast knew little about the trans-Appalachian frontier, an oversight that skewed their vision of the American past. Even before Turner published his first substantive essays, he wrote to his mentor, William Allen, at the University of Wisconsin to criticize the graduate offerings in American history at Johns Hopkins University, where he had enrolled for his doctorate. "The great lack of it all," he told Allen, "is in getting any proper conception of the Great West. Not a man here that I know of is either studying, or hardly aware of the country beyond the Alleghenies." Moreover, as he revealed years later to his well-known student Carl Becker, his pathbreaking essay on the importance of the American frontier "was pretty much a *reaction*" to what he considered the mistaken notions of his Hopkins mentor, Herbert Baxter Adams, who told his students that "American institutional history had been well done. That we would better turn next to European institutions!" "Due to my indignation," Turner added, he determined to show others the significance of the frontier.[2]

At the same time that most American historians overlooked the central importance of the frontier, they also placed too much stress on other topics. Using the writings of Hermann von Holst as an example, Turner asserted that von Holst and other historians of his persuasion were too tied to the issues of slavery and the Civil War and had "lost sight of the fundamental, dominating fact of United States history, the expansion of the United States from the Alleghenies to the Pacific." Further, von Holst should have dealt with larger constitutional issues rather than focusing so narrowly on slavery in discussing the Civil War. Nor had previous historians sufficiently emphasized European backgrounds and the peopling of the New World. "How shall we understand American history," Turner asked, "without understanding European history? The story of the peopling of America has not yet been written. We do not understand ourselves." Earlier historians had stressed politics and the scientific method, but economic history now needed more attention. And, finally, historians must remember that "each age tries to form its own conception of the past." Well before advocates of the New History surfaced during the Progressive Era, Turner asserted: "Each age writes the history of the past anew with reference to the conditions uppermost in its own time."[3]

But Turner did not expend all his critical darts on European and eastern historians; he saved some of his sharpest barbs for earlier and contemporary interpreters of the West. If others were caught up in writing about sectional conflicts between the North and South and thereby overlooked the West, too many writers treating the West had fallen victim to excessively romantic narration, stultifying antiquarianism, and overemphasized detail. If the frontier and the West were to be treated thoughtfully, these historiographical pitfalls had to be avoided.

Who were these misguided historians of the West, and what specific evidence was there of their mistakes? Here Turner was less ready to name names, but his later private correspondence and his early book reviews clarify his discontent with previous interpreters of the West. In 1922, Turner succinctly summarized what was being written about the frontier when his career began: "I began my publication when [Theodore] Roosevelt and [Justin] Winsor were active, and my colleague, [Reuben Gold] Thwaites soon took up his editorial work. Roosevelt, though with a breadth of interests, was more concerned with *men* than with *institutions,* and especially with the strenuous life, and more particularly, the fighting frontier. Winsor approached the West as a cartographer and librarian. Thwaites' instincts were toward the romantic side, and toward editorial publication."[4] Even though Turner's reviews of these three men's major works, as well as those of Francis Parkman, are generally positive, he clearly expresses his dissatisfaction with their interpretations of the frontier. While saluting the pathbreaking, literary, and lively qualities of Roosevelt's multivolume work *The Winning of the West*, Turner also believed that the author should have been more interested in institutional development on the frontier, that area's influences on the East, and the "later history of the events in the areas across which the waves of pioneers have passed." Granted, Roosevelt went beyond previous local historians in mining several American archives and in embedding his narrative in broader international perspectives than they had considered, but he was not "disposed . . . to devote as much attention to social and economic aspects of the [westward] movement as the student of the period would like to have him give." Moreover, Roosevelt's work leans "to the romantic side" of his subject, with sometimes too much emphasis on the heroic, derring-do of individual frontier leaders.

Turner had much less to say about Justin Winsor, the librarian, cartographer, and historian of Harvard. In reviewing Winsor's *Westward Movement* (1898), Turner praised the author's thoroughness and breadth as well as his factualness. If Roosevelt was intrigued with the picturesque, vivacious leaders, and stirring campaigns, Winsor was more interested in exhaustively detailing his stories. "He knew the uses of the card catalogue," Turner wrote, and "loved an abundance of facts." Still, he lacked the "artistic instinct" and "historical imagination" to give framework and meaning to his mountains of "classified cards." In short, *The Westward Movement* is a "thesaurus of events for the student, rather than a history for the general reader." Missing here, Turner seems to conclude, is the interpretive design that would suffuse Winsor's indefatigable labors with the conceptual power and larger meanings that frontier history needed.

Of Reuben Gold Thwaites, his Wisconsin colleague, and Francis Parkman, one of his schoolboy favorites, Turner was less critical. He commented on Thwaites's tireless and immensely successful editorial work and his large contributions to the study of the West, although he seemed to admit that Thwaites might have made even more significant contributions if he were less romantic and less tied to stories of exploration. Meanwhile, in reviewing a new edition of Parkman's works in 1898, Turner applauded the Boston historian's "correct scholarship, fidelity, graphic power, and literary beauty," but, he added, Parkman was "not so skilful in exposition of the development of institutions," thus making some of his volumes less "satisfactory to the critical historian." Since Parkman loves the romantic, dramatic, and picturesque, he tends to skip over less lively details, indicating that he might be less "preeminent in other fields of historical research" that treat less theatrical topics. Turner concluded that, in the end, Parkman's "work will live because he was even greater as an artist than as a historian."[5]

So if American historians such as James Ford Rhodes and Hermann von Holst erred badly in overemphasizing slavery and overlooking the signal importance of the frontier and the West in American history, those writers who had turned their attention to the frontier had not yet provided satisfactory models for others wishing to specialize in the West. Some, like Roosevelt and Parkman, tended to be too romantic, and others, such as Winsor, bordered on fact-ridden antiquarianism. None had asked the questions about significance that had so interested Turner throughout his career.

Meanwhile, in addition to pointing out some of the limitations in earlier and contemporary American historical writing, Turner was gradually formulating his own views about the frontier. In several respects, his emphasis on the frontier West arose naturally from his own life and early training. Within the first decade of his scholarly career, in the 1890s, he gradually advanced his notable views about the central importance of the frontier to a new and enlarged understanding of American history.

Born in Portage, Wisconsin, on November 14, 1861, and reared in that frontier town of 4,000 inhabitants until he enrolled at the University of Wisconsin in the fall of 1878, Turner relished the small-town, outdoor environment and the rapidly changing social patterns that characterized his boyhood years. Sensing the diminishing presence of Native Americans and the mushrooming numbers of newly arrived European immigrants, Turner experienced these changes firsthand as well as through the pages of his father's newspapers. Additionally, Turner enjoyed nature through hikes and fishing expeditions to nearby woods and streams. As his biographer has written, near Portage "the wilderness was not quite subdued, and young Turner felt its influence."[6]

Once at Wisconsin, Turner was undecided about a major until his junior year and his first courses with a remarkable professor, William Francis Allen. Thereafter, through his remaining undergraduate and master's work, Turner willingly and joyfully became Allen's admiring disciple. Trained in Germany in the new scientific history, Allen urged his students to immerse themselves in documents, published and in manuscript, and to produce class reports and research papers reflecting the latest techniques in comparative and analytical methods. Traditional methods of rote memorization and an emphasis on military and political history played little or no role in Allen's classes. Moreover, Allen stressed the evolutionary nature of society, telling his students to examine closely the steps through which institutions and cultures evolved. Allen's problem-centered instruction, in contrast to the narrative and chronological approach of most of his colleagues, deeply impressed Turner. It became central to his views of the frontier.

Completing his master's degree at Wisconsin under Allen and promised a position at Madison if he completed a doctorate in history, Turner headed off to the Johns Hopkins University in 1888. In Baltimore he fell among a group of gifted instructors, such as American historian Herbert Baxter Adams, colonialist Charles M. Andrews, medievalist Charles Homer Haskins, and visiting lecturer Woodrow Wilson. Of these, Adams had the largest impact on the twenty-seven-year-old Turner. Schooled in Europe and a devotee of the application of scientific and evolutionary principles to the study of history, Adams preached the doctrine of the "germ theory" (the conviction that institutional "germs" from Europe spawned New World institutions such as New England towns) with the enthusiasm of a committed evangelist. Adams's clearest influence surfaced in the opening chapters of Turner's dissertation where he traced Middle Eastern and European precedents of the fur trade in frontier Wisconsin. At the same time, the germ theory furnished a target against which Turner soon launched his own counterinterpretation: the frontier as the major source of American exceptionalism.

Turner's thesis was soon to come. In fact, within the next decade he wrote a series of provocative essays that laid out the larger dimensions of the frontier thesis, and in 1906, in the only book he completed during his lifetime, *Rise of the New West, 1819–1829*, Turner furnished an example of how the thesis might be applied to one decade of American history. By that time the Turner thesis had become the accepted view of the frontier among most professional historians.

If too many disciples of Clio were overlooking the molding influences of the great West, Turner pondered at the end of the 1880s, how could their mistaken ways be mended? He would show them—by admonition and by example. When he wrote his dissertation in 1889–90 and his first essays in the early 1890s, Turner practiced what he was preaching in his concurrent reviews and letters, treating the Wisconsin fur trade with Indians in broad perspective and noting frontier topics that merited attention. In his published dissertation, *The Character and Influence of the Indian Trade in Wisconsin: A Study of the Trading Post as an Institution* (1891), Turner zeroed in on "the entry of the disintegrating and transforming influences of a higher civilization," in which successive floods of European traders, breaking the "cake of custom" on New World frontiers, thoroughly disrupted Indian culture and redirected previous contacts between natives and earlier traders. His was not a study of Indian-white military skirmishes but of conflicting cultures, out of which conflict, in Turner's view, a "higher" culture replaced a "lower civilization."[7] In his first major publication, then, Turner demonstrated how historians might deal with a series of evolutionary cultural and economic contacts on the frontier, how these contacts paved the way for later settlements, and how these frontier topics might be treated analytically rather than romantically. At this stage, he stressed the shaping power of an invading European culture; within four years his emphasis had reversed, with the new frontier gaining the upper hand against the invaders.

In the same year, at the request of the president of the University of Wisconsin, Turner published the brief essay "The Significance of History" to help popularize history courses offered through the university's extension division. Although Turner focused primarily on topics other than the frontier, most of his major statements were apropos to his views of the frontier and acceptable writing about it. Historians must trace more of the direct lines between past and present, Turner declared, because "the present is simply the developing past, the past the undeveloped present." They must also avoid the narrow provincialism of too much historical writing: "Local history must be viewed in the light of world history." Equally important, histories that emphasized literary qualities—sprightly writing, apt turns of phrase, and lively vignettes—were acceptable as long as the "truthfulness of substance rather than the vivacity of style be the end sought." In the past, historians had overemphasized politics and the scientific method; now they needed to pay more attention to economics and to tell "the story of the peopling of America."[8]

One year later, in "Problems in American History," Turner sounded the tocsin for frontier history, sentence after sentence foreshadowing his famous essay of the next year. He argued that writers must turn to the central theme of American history, "the expansion of the United States from the Alleghenies to the Pacific," since "the true point of view . . . [was] not the Atlantic coast . . . but the Mississippi Valley." In addition, Americans must learn that the "ever retreating frontier of free land [was] the key to American development." Not until we traced and analyzed the stages of this moving frontier would we realize that it, more than any other experience, shaped our history and culture. Nor had students of the past paid sufficient attention to the environment:

"There is need for thorough study of the physiographic basis of our history," Turner wrote. And, of course, "native populations" had also been "determining factors in our development" since their existence influenced the physical, economic, and cultural ingredients of our history. Without being very specific, Turner added that the Indian presence also impacted our political institutions, since the "earliest colonial unions were in a large measure due to the need for a concerted Indian policy."

Then Turner traced the frontier across the country, noting how westward-moving lines of settlement left behind nascent sections (regions) gradually developing their own identities. Foreshadowing his later pioneering interest in regionalism, these abbreviated comments illustrate again how, early on, Turner was aware of ideas that others took decades to understand and utilize. "The real lines of American development," he continued, "the forces dominating our character, are to be studied in the history of westward expansion." Already in 1892, Turner pointed to the central importance of the frontier experience, which included contacts with new environments and unique native peoples that were important in defining American character. Not satisfied with the clear, straightforward quality of these expository assertions, Turner closed his piece with one of his characteristic rhetorical flourishes: "What the Mediterranean Sea was to the Greeks, breaking the bond of custom, offering new experiences, calling out new institutions and activities, that the ever retreating Great West has been to the eastern United States directly, and to the nations of Europe more remotely."[9]

Within less than a year, Turner climbed back into his historiographical pulpit, this time to present in Chicago the most significant sermon on American history any historian has yet to deliver. Seen as a continuation of his previous ideas, "The Significance of the Frontier in American History" becomes part of his agenda to reorient historical writing about the United States, to counter earlier antiquarian and romantic works on the West, and to provide a brief analysis of the notable impact of the frontier on American life and culture. He makes these points at the onset, suggesting that "when American history comes to be rightly viewed it will be seen that the slavery question is an incident" and that too much "has been written about the frontier from the point of view of border warfare and the chase, but as a field for the serious study of the economist and the historian it has been neglected." And in as succinct and direct a definition as Turner ever produced, he asserted that the frontier defined American history: "The existence of an area of free land, its continuous recession, and the advance of American settlement westward, explain American development." Prefiguring the sentiments of the essay "The Evolution of the Cow-Puncher" (which Owen Wister wrote but to which Frederic Remington contributed both ideas and illustrations), Turner argued that to study the frontier advance, "the men who grew up under these conditions, and the political, economic, and social results of it, is to study the really American part of our history."[10]

Turner practiced what he preached in emphasizing an analytical approach to understanding the frontier. His research revealed, he noted, that the open frontier encouraged democracy and individualism, nourished nationalistic ties between the West and the central government, and helped bring about a "composite nationality," a melting pot, although Turner did not use the phrase. Beginning with the "Indian Trader's Frontier," Turner progressed through the successive groups that moved to the frontier and asked his listeners to consider carefully the large impact these experiences had on American history and character. Lest anyone misapprehend his goal, he intended his essay "to call attention to the frontier as a fertile field for investigation, and to suggest some of the problems which arise in connection with it." Finally, in a footnote, Turner obviously parted company with western popularizers, dime novelists, and others hyping a Wild West: "I have refrained from dwelling on the lawless characteristics of the frontier," he wrote, "because they are sufficiently well known. The gambler and desperado, the regulators of the Carolinas and the vigilantes of California, are types of that line of scum that the waves of advancing civilization bore before them, and of the growth of spontaneous organs of authority where legal authority was absent."[11]

Seen from this perspective, Turner's famous essay could have been titled "Research Opportunities in Frontier History." Why didn't he set out quickly to take advantage of several of these research opportunities? Prince of procrastination that he was, Turner made handfuls of promises, signed more contracts than a clutch of ambitious historians could have completed in several years, and already showed signs of the occupational hazard plaguing many academics, then and since: he spent more time in explaining missed deadlines and incomplete projects than in finishing them. By the late 1890s he was already behind in several of his promises.

Still, the one book that Turner completed during his lifetime illustrates the several Turners laboring to clarify the concept of the frontier and how that idea could be used to illuminate all of American history. Indeed, *Rise of the New*

West, 1819–1829, in theme and form, illustrates much of what Turner had asserted earlier about the frontier. Beginning *in medias res,* Turner describes the northeastern, middle, and southern frontiers that gradually evolved into states and sections and then devotes four chapters to the West (more space than he gives to the other regions combined). In three of these chapters, he deals with the colonizing process, the socioeconomic, commercial, and urban transformations of the expanding frontier and section between the Alleghenies and the Mississippi, but in the fourth chapter he treats the trans-Mississippi frontier, including early contacts with Indians and the exploration of the Oregon Country and the Rocky Mountains. Taken together, these discussions, along with the early sections on New England, the Middle Region, and the South, serve as frontier and regional backgrounds on which Turner builds the next eleven chapters, which deal with important political, economic, and constitutional events and trends of the 1820s. Along the way, he also tries, briefly, to point out some of the frontier's large influences his previous essays had mentioned. Among these comments were such memorable sentences as "the wilderness ever opened a gate of escape to the poor, the discontented, and the oppressed." Even more so, "Western democracy was no theorist's dream. It came, stark and strong and full of life, from the American forest."[12]

Turner's first essays, his *Rise of the New West,* and the essays collected in *The Frontier in American History* (1920) won early and wide acceptance for his views of the frontier. This favorable reception, although experiencing various ups and downs, continued into the 1960s. Since that time, however, outspoken revisionists have often dismissed Turner and his views, arguing they have little if any relevance for understanding the frontier or the American West. Such views carry considerable validity. Like most of his contemporaries, Turner overlooked the importance of Indians, other minorities, and women and families, although he paid more attention to Native Americans than did most contemporary American historians. Likewise, he overstated frontier influences on democracy and nationalism. Generally, he boldly advanced the central importance of the frontier to American history without supplying detailed studies of those influences. And, similar to many Americans between the 1890s and the early 1920s, he suffered from an excessive nationalistic spirit; thus he was too inclined to assert that the frontier was *the* key to understanding American exceptionalism. In the three generations since Turner's death, many historians have shown that most of these emphases lack sufficient empirical evidence.

Yet to dismiss Turner because of these limitations is to take too narrow a view of his understanding of the frontier and his influence. As William Cronon has noted recently, despite the limitations of his frontier thesis, Turner still supplies the most useful plot line for narrating the story of American history: a series of contacts between European invaders and new lands and peoples eventuated in a society and a culture different from those coming from Europe.[13] Additionally, Turner successfully broke from the stultifying historiographical paradigms of his time, avoiding excessive emphases in American historical writing on slavery and history as merely past politics and in addition demonstrating to specialists in western history that they must break free from the dime novel Wild West and the romantic and antiquarian interests that infected too much frontier historiography. Finally, as much as anyone of his times, Turner called for analytical history that demonstrated the shaping power of the past on the present. When linked to his writings on the frontier, this stress urged historians to examine the powerful influences of the frontier on *all* of American history and to see that molding power in conceptual, not purely romantic, terms.

At this point one must ask: Since Turner dealt primarily with eastern frontiers, from the East Coast to the Mississippi, did his interpretations hold up when applied to the trans-Mississippi West? He thought so, as did most of his contemporaries. As convinced of this conclusion as a fundamentalist is convinced of scriptural inerrancy, Turner asserted that the democracy, individualism, nationalism, and mobility he discovered in the East were also characteristic of life in the Southwest, the Rockies, and the Pacific Coast. In his earliest writings, Turner sided with those pointing to the coercive force of nature, thus ensuring similar pioneer experiences throughout all American frontiers. Few of his contemporaries disagreed. Not until after the regionalists emerged following World War I, especially in the works of writers like Walter Prescott Webb and James C. Malin, did historians question the suitability of Turner's frontier thesis for new kinds of frontiers or subregions west of the Mississippi.

Overall, Frederick Jackson Turner was probably the most powerful figure to bring the frontier image to the forefront of American thought. First, his writings gradually won over historians writing about national and regional history; then scholars in other fields; and, by the 1920s, other writers and much of the general public. If recent students of the frontier and the West single out the limitations of Turner's views, his contemporaries were generally blind to those shortcomings. They so quickly and thoroughly accepted his position on the frontier that by the Depression he had become the most influential writer on American history. In one area, however, Turner and his acquaintances recognized a serious lack in his career. He had never produced an overview of the frontier's impact on American history and culture. That notable achievement was left to others, particularly to Frederic Logan Paxson.

After Turner, no historian specializing in western history did more to spread the frontier gospel in the first decades of the twentieth century than did Frederic Logan Paxson. As Turner's replacement at the University of Wisconsin in 1910, Paxson was the author of several important books and essays about the frontier and mentor to more than two hundred master's and doctoral students during his nearly fifty-year teaching career. Indeed, next to Turner, Paxson was perhaps the most significant teacher and writer of frontier history in the first half of the twentieth century.

Paxson's background would not suggest, however, that he would quickly become one of the nation's leading scholars in western history. A Quaker, Philadelphia-born and reared, with undergraduate and graduate degrees from the University of Pennsylvania, Paxson traveled a route to the frontier markedly different from those of most frontier specialists. Indeed, until he took his first full-time college teaching post at the University of Colorado in 1903 he knew much more of Europe than of the American West. But once isolated from the sources for his earlier diplomatic work and urged to offer courses in Colorado and frontier history at Boulder, Paxson quickly nourished his newfound fascination.[14]

Writing to friends about the "extremely pleasant" and "excellent outlook" of his new position at Colorado, Paxson immediately plunged into his frontier work. Stealing a now-familiar refrain from Turner's revisionist song, Paxson decried previous historians' overemphasis on slavery and their failure to address such topics as "the problem of the expansion of the agricultural West, the settlement of new areas and the providing of adequate institutions of government for citizens of the frontier." Here and in a handful of other essays on Colorado and the frontier, Paxson gradually moved beyond local history to set his western research in a larger interpretative framework. As Turner wrote in response to Paxson's article "Historical Opportunity in Colorado," Paxson evidenced a "grasp of the significance of western history" and an ability "to handle a problem." In the initial essays, two ingredients of Paxson's views about the frontier West are as clear as his limpid prose: he argued, along with Turner, that historians ought to show how the West shaped American society and also that, in the fashion of the New History, they should demonstrate how the past illuminates and guides the present.[15]

Paxson's talents and tireless research soon catapulted him out of Boulder and on to the University of Michigan, where he taught from 1907 to 1910. During his stint at Ann Arbor, Paxson wisely abandoned a book he had begun on Colorado to incorporate that material into his first and more broadly based book on the West, *The Last American Frontier,* which appeared at just the right moment in Paxson's career.[16] Intended more for students and general readers than for scholars, Paxson's volume illustrates his major emphases and evinces the strengths and limitations of his writings about the frontier. As a gifted writer with obvious strengths of synthesis, Paxson presents a readable overview of several aspects of frontier history from roughly 1821 to 1885, but in the first chapter, he also essays to cast his story in a Turnerian framework, to demonstrate the molding power of the frontier on American history. In retrospect, Paxson provided a useful, readable overview, but he failed to achieve his goal of conceptualization and analysis.

In the opening chapter of *The Last American Frontier* Paxson strikes notes already familiar to western specialists early in the twentieth century. Declaring that "the greatest of American problems has been the problem of the West" (p. 1) and that "the influence of the frontier has been the strongest single factor in American history" (p. 3), Paxson suggests, in terms reminiscent of Turner, that his work will demonstrate the dramatic role of the frontier in determining American culture and character. But, for the most part, his volume does not follow these promising remarks. Instead, it moves toward a more popular stance, emphasizing the wavelike movement of pioneers westward and their continued conflicts with Indians, especially in the Great Plains and Rocky Mountains.

More than other contemporary frontier historians and more than in his own later writings about the West, Paxson here devotes extraordinary attention to conflicts between Indians and settlers. That emphasis cuts two ways: modern readers are likely to see primarily the ethnocentric nature of Paxson's conclusions, whereas his contemporaries were struck with his lengthy discussions of Indians. Throughout his volume, Paxson seems sympathetic to the plight of Native Americans and critical of pioneers for the way in which their juggernaut steamrolled natives along the frontier. But he also concludes that "the conflict . . . could not have ended in any other way than that which has come to pass" (p. 15). Labeling Indians as "wild beasts," as savage and yet childlike innocents, and as an "inferior race," he also depicts whites as rapacious and selfish but still a "superior" and "stronger" race. Paxson seems to think that the government and the country's institutions had been fair in their attitudes toward and treatment of these "savages," but he scored most Anglo-Americans as usually unwilling to oppose grasping and greedy frontiersmen bent on gobbling up Indian lands.

Attempting to cover more than six decades of frontier history and a host of new topics forced Paxson to center on a few subjects and to exclude many others. In addition to focusing on clashes with Indians, he places notable stress on the roles that means of transportation—particularly overland trails, stages, and railroads—played in closing the frontier. After devoting several chapters to these topics, Paxson concludes that the meeting of the Central Pacific and the Union Pacific at Promontory Point in 1869 was profoundly significant— "for the immediate audience, or for posterity"—as a symbol of the "struggle for the last frontier" (pp. 337–38). The railroads not only hauled in hordes of new settlers; they also provided the lasso that intrepid pioneers, with the aid of the army, threw around the Indians, pulling them onto reservations. In providing these mental maps of the swiftly closing frontier, Paxson also depicts the iron horse as a wedge, a spearhead for the forces dividing and then encircling the final frontier.

Squeezed for space, Paxson failed to push much beyond these extended sections on transportation and conflicts with Indians and two or three chapters on mining rushes and mining camp life. Probably much more than he intended, Paxson's narrator seems situated on the eastern slopes of the Rockies, watching white settlers flood past the "bend of the Missouri," pressuring and supplanting Indians, skirting the mountains, and moving toward the Pacific Northwest and California. Three generations of frontiersmen flow westward to the Rockies and Great Plains, but Paxson follows few of them past the ridge of the mountains.

Paxson's book is also restricted in another way. Following the perspectives of most western historians before regionalists began publishing in the 1930s and 1940s, Paxson does not deal with changes over time *within* the West. Although he follows settlers into or toward Oregon, California, and Utah during the 1840s, he overlooks sociocultural, economic, and political occurrences within these newly settled areas during the two generations after the first arrivals. Instead, he joined his contemporaries in emphasizing new contacts with the land and Indians, not the social organization and institution making that followed those initial years of cultural contact and confrontation. But we must not downplay how much Paxson accomplished in such a short time. In a few years he mastered enough western history to produce a more-than-satisfactory popular introduction to the nineteenth-century frontier.

For Paxson, the volume appeared at an opportune moment. Late in the fall of 1909, a few months before *The Last American Frontier* was published, Frederick Jackson Turner unexpectedly resigned from the University of Wisconsin to take a chair in American history at Harvard. The best-known professorship of western history in the country became vacant just as Paxson was seeing his first western book through the press. In January, Turner asked to see page proofs. Serious negotiations began soon thereafter, and by late spring Paxson had joined the Wisconsin fold. He must have been euphoric; in seven short years he had leaped to the top of the "western men."

Over the next twenty-three years (1910–1932), Paxson solidified his status as a leading western historian even while he wrote several other books, dozen of essays, trained many graduate students, and held administrative posts and national offices in historical organizations. Most remarkable of all, Paxson rapidly expanded his career into a new field, modern American history, and soon published pioneering textual overviews on that subject. Then, in the early 1920s, realizing that Turner would probably never write his overview of the West, Paxson decided to move ahead with his. While participating actively in all aspects of a busy teaching and writing career, Paxson completed his 575-page book in less than two years.

No one should approach Paxson's *History of the American Frontier, 1763–1893* (1924) as a revisionist study of the frontier. Just as Theodore Roosevelt had noted earlier that Turner had pulled together many ideas that were "in the air" in his famous frontier essay, so one might have observed that in his Pulitzer Prize–winning volume Paxson synthesized and reflected many widely held conclusions concerning the American frontier experience. It is a thorough, readable overview of contemporary research and judgments about the significant shaping power of the frontier on American history. As the author points out in one of his typically terse prefaces, "the time is ripe for this synthesis, in which an attempt is made to show the proportions of the whole story," proving "that the frontier with its continuous influence is the most American thing in all America."[17]

The contents of Paxson's second book about the West reflect how much his thinking and reading had expanded in the decade and a half since the publication of *The Last American Frontier*. Dealing with a greater expanse of place and time in his second volume, Paxson still hesitates to treat the colonial frontier that so intrigued Turner and many of his followers. If fully two-thirds of *History of the American Frontier* traces the westward movement from the eastern frontiers to the ninety-fifth meridian and in doing so introduces new material on the eighteenth century and on eastern frontiers in the first half of the nineteenth century, the sections on the trans-Mississippi West both follow and break away from similar coverage in *The Last American Frontier*. Both books emphasize what happened as the frontier moved west but elaborate little on the significance of these happenings. Conflict with Indians is still a major theme in the second volume, but here native peoples are not "beasts" or "savages" innocent of rational thought or learning. Rather, they are barriers, as they were for most Turnerians, to the inexorable movement of pioneers and the civilizing process they embodied, pushing them westward. Clearly, the tone and point of view of Paxson's observations about Indians are greatly moderated and more balanced than those of fourteen years earlier. Paxson likewise continues to stress state making and railroad building, as well as other transportation means and routes, in his later volume. In fact, throughout his writings on the frontier, Paxson used clashes with Indians, the coming of railroads, and the organizing of new states as major symbols of a closing frontier.

Contrasts between the two books are equally evident. Perhaps remembering the omissions reviewers pinpointed in *The Last American Frontier*, Paxson provided new sections on land policies, economic problems, the cattle country, and Texas and the Mexican War. Unlike other frontier historians, Paxson omits mention of the rise of Populism as a symbol of a closed frontier. Indeed, why Paxson stopped with 1893 is unclear. Was it because of the Panic of 1893, because of Turner's speech, or for other reasons? In fact, the final chapters, like too many chapters in Paxson's books, are grab bags of several topics. Most notable of all, even though he promised to do so, Paxson does not show how frontier experiences molded America and made it significantly different from earlier European cultures. Granted, he points out unique experiences west of the Mississippi, but he fails to demonstrate how these events and resulting ideas redirected the history of the country.

Paxson's contemporaries found little to criticize in his *History of the American Frontier*, however. Most seemed to think his work deserving of the Pulitzer Prize; reviewers particularly praised it as the much-needed overview of the

American frontier. And for professional historians the book furnished just the text they needed for their classes. Less clear to Paxson's contemporaries was the position of his 1924 volume in the development of frontier historiography. No one in the 1920s noted that his book placed him more in the camp of western historians stressing *process* (to-the-West) over *place* (in-the-West). Like most of his contemporaries, Paxson charted the successive tides of westward-moving people through a series of floods, but unlike later historians such as Webb, Malin, and Paxson student Earl Pomeroy, Paxson was much less interested in showing change over time and institution building within a specific region or section. In pitching his tent with historians who emphasize *process,* Paxson joined the largest and most influential group then interpreting the West. Not until the 1960s would regionalists or in-the-West historians vie on nearly equal terms with scholars of the frontier school, in which Paxson early became and remained a proponent.

Although Paxson produced no full-length volume on the frontier West after the mid-1920s, he did publish a collection of lectures and a few scattered essays before the end of his career — alongside a continuing flood of major publications on modern American history. *When the West Is Gone* (1930), which consists of three lectures Paxson delivered in 1929 at Brown University, is a disappointing volume because the author draws too heavily on his previous work, avoids speculating on the meaning of the frontier, and fails to discuss the twentieth-century West.[18] Only in commenting on the Populists and their defeat in 1896 as a sign of a vanishing frontier does Paxson move beyond his earlier frontier interpretation. He speculates here neither about frontier and western influences on women's suffrage, labor activism, and conservation policies — influences he noted in histories of modern America — nor about the events of western history between the late 1890s and the 1920s. The lectures seem more like warmed-over observations from previous writings than stimulating new insights into a society and culture bereft of a frontier.

Once Paxson moved to the University of California, Berkeley, in 1932, where he joined his longtime friend Herbert Eugene Bolton, he wrote little about the frontier. But late in 1932, after Turner's death the previous March, Paxson presented the first article-length discussion of Turner's historiographical legacy: "A Generation of the Frontier Hypothesis: 1893–1932." After examining Turner's generalizations about frontier influences on democracy, individualism, and nationalism, Paxson concludes that the Turner thesis "stands today as easily to be accepted as it was when launched." Perhaps, he adds, in a ringing conclusion, we can "account for the weakness of the straggling attack upon his hypothesis by the inherent weakness of the case against it."[19]

In several ways, Frederic Logan Paxson was a loyal Turnerian. He not only championed Turner's frontier thesis of 1893; he repeatedly urged his colleagues and students to rewrite American history, emphasizing the paramount importance of the frontier in shaping the country's past and present. In all his writings about the West, Paxson never broke markedly from what Turner had to say about the frontier.

But from other perspectives Paxson differed a good deal from Turner. He betrayed little interest in Turner's concept of section, was less intrigued than Turner with "significance" (analysis), and except for minor census and map research, was less fascinated than Turner with the application of social science techniques to the study of history. Yet Paxson finished his projects. He produced two influential syntheses of frontier history, something Turner often promised but was unable to accomplish. And his amazing productivity carried over into other areas. During his nearly forty-five years in the classroom, he lectured to thousands of students in frontier history courses and trained more than two hundred master's and doctoral students, including such well-known western historians as John D. Hicks and Earl Pomeroy. Through his teaching and writings Paxson preached the frontier gospel to many willing converts.

In addition to asserting boldly the molding power of the frontier on American democracy, individualism, and nationalism in his famous frontier essay, Frederick Jackson Turner also opened and closed his pathbreaking piece with another arresting image that dominated western historiography, fiction, and art in the first three or four decades of the twentieth century. Quoting the now familiar words of the census of 1890 in the first sentence of his essay, he then added: "this brief official statement marks the closing of a great historic movement." Even more powerful was Turner's closing sentence: "And now, four centuries from the discovery of America, at the end of a hundred years of life under the Constitution, the frontier has gone, and with its going has closed the first period of American history."[20] Like a skillful orator and fiction writer recognizing the importance of a unifying theme, Turner ended where he had begun, with the riveting idea of a vanishing frontier as the end of the central theme of American history.

The concept of a closing frontier was central to Turner's thinking, as it was to most historians writing about the West before 1930. Whether as professional historians like Turner and Paxson, as generalists like Theodore Roosevelt and Woodrow Wilson, or as literary historians like Hamlin Garland and Emerson Hough, these writers, along with a host of novelists and artists, were intrigued with the frontier's end. The fascination is not surprising considering how much shaping influence these and other historians assigned to the frontier. Since they argued that the frontier, more than any other force, had molded American society and culture during the previous three centuries, what would happen now that the frontier was gone, or was quickly disappearing over the horizon? As historian David M. Wrobel has shown in his stimulating study *The End of American Exceptionalism: Frontier Anxiety from the Old West to the New Deal* (1993), professional historians like Turner and Paxson were but a small group among the host of American intellectuals, journalists, and other writers who worried about the closing of the frontier and the impact of these events on the country's future. So anxious were these Malthusian alarmists that, pointing to a closed frontier, they also predicted overpopulation, inadequate land for immigrants, and a diminishing food supply for all Americans. "We are heading toward a crisis," one alarmist wrote, whereas others spoke of the United States as experiencing a turning point or being subject to the law of diminishing returns.[21] If many historians and other observers still spoke of an open and available frontier in the 1880s, within the next generation they exhibited a growing anxiety about a frontierless America. For these writers, images of hordes of incoming immigrants, crowded landscapes, and an inadequate land base displaced earlier images of a free frontier in which newcomers from Europe and the American East encountered new lands and peoples. Whatever the facts of the matter — that more homesteads were established after 1900 than before, for example — the image of a closed frontier dominated the minds of many historians who wrote about the West in the early twentieth century.

Even Turner fell in with some of the pessimists, although he avoided bundling with the most naysaying alarmists. At first convinced that the legacy of a pioneer spirit of competition and individualism would buoy citizens in a frontierless America, Turner became less certain. By the 1920s he was wondering whether a rising urban-industrial United States with mounting bureaucratic centralization had broken loose from its frontier moorings, like many European nations, to drift on a gray sea of increasing loss of identity and meaning. Privately, he collected the writings of the alarmists, agreeing with some of their laments, but he was too buoyant and optimistic to embrace their cynicism and occasional despair. For Turner, and for like-minded historians, the impact of a closing frontier was two-pronged: not only had the experiences they considered the most beneficial and powerful in shaping American history and culture disappeared from the scene, but the positive legacies they ascribed to those experiences—democracy, individualism, and a composite nationality—also seemed to be falling before a new juggernaut of change. For Frederick Jackson Turner, between the 1890s and the 1920s, a much-loved frontier vanished, to be replaced by a new America bereft of its nourishing and positive frontier legacies.[22]

Meanwhile, ironically, other interpreters of the frontier were beginning to calculate its large impact on American culture just as Turner worried most about the loss of frontier influences and moved in other directions. Indeed, by the early 1920s, Turner's frontier thesis had become the most widely accepted interpretation of American history. In history textbooks, in monographs in the humanities and social sciences, and in the writings of dozens of journalists and other generalists, the frontier was named as the most important shaping force in American history. Pulitzer Prizes for Turner's first collection of essays, *The Frontier in American History* (1920), and Paxson's *History of the American Frontier* (1924) were clear evidence of the widespread popularity of the frontier thesis in the 1920s.

Throughout that decade, and into the 1930s, scholars in several fields, including those emphasizing western subjects, frequently used the frontier as *the* cohering concept for their monographs and syntheses. For instance, no field in the 1920s was more rife with frontier interpretations than the emerging field of American literary criticism. Along with the first issue of *American Literature* (1929), on whose masthead Turner was listed as an editor, came such notable volumes as Ralph L. Rusk's *The Literature of the Middle Western Frontier* (2 vols., 1925), Dorothy Dondore's *The Prairie and the Making of Middle America: Four Centuries of Description* (1926), and Lucy Lockwood Hazard's *The Frontier in American Literature* (1927), all of which owed much to Turner's frontier and emphasized writers and works that stressed European contacts with new lands and peoples. Although slower than historians to emphasize the shaping power of the frontier, many students in the new field of American literary history were obviously in the frontier camp by the end of the 1920s. Indeed, as the noted literary historian Norman Foerster pointed out, by 1928 the frontier had been "strangely exaggerated." No doubt the appearance of the important volumes by Rusk, Dondore, and Hazard between 1925 and 1927 helped lead to this conclusion. Other pioneering scholars in American litera-ture supported the increasing attention paid to the impact of the frontier on American literature, even calling for additional scrutiny of this central topic in the pathbreaking volume *The Reinterpretation of American Literature* (1928).[23]

Yet other signs, still vague in the mid-1920s, hinted that not only were some scholars dissatisfied with frontier interpretations, but they were also beginning to move toward new ways of describing and analyzing the American West. In the first decade after World War I, a few reviewers concluded that Turner stressed the frontier too much and that other ingredients, including the con-tributions of immigrants and ethnic groups, the persistence of European and eastern cultural legacies, and the influence of economic clashes deserved more emphasis. As the distinguished historian Charles Beard noted in his review of Turner's collection of frontier essays published in 1920, Turner made too much of frontier influences without noticing the large impact of concomitant experi-ences. Chief among these, Beard argued in 1921 and again in 1928, were other economic forces such as industrialism, labor-capitalist clashes, transportation, banking and credit, and slavery and the plantation system.[24]

Turner himself added to the decreasing stress on the frontier as the only his-toriographical interpretation of the West. Beginning early in his career and in-creasingly after 1910 he urged historians to study "sections," the term he used for postfrontier areas that developed after earlier frontiers had moved farther west. As we shall see in chapter 5, Turner was in the vanguard of historians urging the study of the West as a developing region. He thus led the way for historians like Webb, Bolton, and Malin, who moved from viewing the West as a frontier to studying it as an emerging region.

So in slightly more than three decades Frederick Jackson Turner burst on the scene with his frontier thesis, oversaw its acceptance among most Ameri-cans interpreting the West, and then, in the mid to late 1920s, witnessed the frontier interpretation undergoing its first major challenge. Despite this chal-lenge, however, at the end of that decade most essays and books still viewed the West as a frontier, even if it was a frontier that had vanished. These his-toriographical trends clearly paralleled similar transformations taking place among writers who set their novels in the West. In a similar fashion, the 1920s were a decade of transition from frontier to region among large numbers of painters who emphasized the American West.

Chapter 3

FRONTIER ART

At the turn of the century, artists portrayed the American West through a rich variety of paintings about the region. Soon after the Civil War, the popularity of earlier portraits of Indians and mountain men by George Catlin, Karl Bodmer, and Alfred Jacob Miller precipitously declined in the face of the gigantic, colorful landscapes of Albert Bierstadt and Thomas Moran. A generation later, in the 1890s, when Owen Wister and Frederick Jackson Turner were calling the nation's attention to the impact of the frontier on American and western literature and history, a new crop of artists abandoned the huge, romantic scenes of Bierstadt and Moran to focus again on Native Americans and also on frontier soldiers, cowboys, and other pioneer figures. Among these newcomers, Frederic Remington and Charles Russell painted dramatic Indian, military, and cowboy scenes, while a coterie of eastern artists who settled in Taos and Santa Fe focused on ethnic groups and the arid, brightly colored spaces of the Southwest. Meanwhile, in the 1880s and 1890s in the Pacific Northwest, Mary Hallock Foote produced a series of revealing domestic scenes.

No painters in the past century have done more than Remington and Russell to dramatize the artistic vision of the West as frontier. What Wister and Grey achieved in their fiction, and Turner and Paxson accomplished in their histories, Remington and Russell executed in their art: the depiction of the West as a large, open frontier peopled with Indians, cowboys, and other pioneer worthies but also a frontier quickly disappearing. Of conflicting backgrounds and temperaments, the two painters nonetheless portrayed a West more similar in subject matter and theme than the works of most other leading artists of the time. A New Yorker who ventured west for a short time in the 1880s and on brief jaunts during the 1890s, Remington drew on his experiences and readings to create a cast of vibrant and courageous characters whose lives epitomized much of what he saw as lacking in eastern society. Concurrently, Russell fled his midwestern home to become an adopted—and then lifelong—westerner. Yet for Russell, as for Remington, the frontier, especially Montana, remained a vivacious and sustaining setting, a society that offered an alluring and refreshing alternative to turn-of-the-century eastern America.

Frederic Remington's upbringing, as well as a series of traumatic experiences he underwent at the turn of the century, markedly influenced his first reactions to the West. The death of his supportive father in 1880, pressure from his intractable mother, his inability to find a suitable career, and the rejection by his sweetheart of a proposal of marriage all conspired to drive Remington west in the 1880s to find himself. As it was for Wister and Roosevelt, the frontier became an arena in which Remington experienced ordeals that led to manhood. Remington was a troubled young man when he arrived in Montana in the early fall of 1881. But within a half dozen years he had chosen his career and married and had already become a well-known illustrator. Central to this rapid rite of passage is, in the apt phrase of one critic, "Remington's use of the West to define himself."[1]

If Remington's first trip west came at a crucial juncture in his own life, he also encountered a frontier that was itself rapidly changing. Twenty-five years later, he recalled a moment of epiphany beside a Montana campfire where he discovered a West in transition. A lonely old freighter told the traveler, not yet twenty-one, that "there [was] no more West." These words, the artist asserted, drove him "to try to record some facts . . . without knowing exactly how to do it," about "the wild riders and vacant land [that] were about to vanish forever."[2] Undoubtedly overly dramatized and colored by a memory bent on linking a disappearing frontier with the genesis of his artistic career, Remington's recollection nonetheless represents the essence of his introduction to the West. Here in the Rockies, escaping the complexities of his life, he encountered a frontier that was free (he thought) from a storied past, alive with rambunctious cowboys inhabiting landscapes that faded into faraway horizons. It was a mind-stretching canvas on which to etch a life, and Remington took to the task with the enthusiasm of a schoolboy on the first day of summer vacation.

Remington's next act, as was so often the case, preceded—indeed, flew in the face of—reflection. Paying out a large portion of his inheritance for an unseen Kansas sheep ranch and innocent of even the barest details of ranching or raising sheep, he soon lost most of his investment. Then he bought into a Kansas City saloon and saw the rest of his patrimony disappear to skillful shysters. By the mid-1880s, and now married, Remington had squandered his inheritance and seemed without an occupation.

Then his luck swiftly changed. Good fortune, previous connections, and serendipity raised their heads. While in the West, Remington had traveled to the Southwest, sketching desert scenes, soldiers, and Indians; and when Geronimo escaped in 1885 and the army pursuit of him captured newspaper headlines and filled magazine pages, the artist's "portfolio was to prove to be filled with gold."[3] New York magazine editors snapped up his southwestern scenes and commissioned him to illustrate several stories. Ten of his illustrations appeared in early 1886 in the influential *Harper's Magazine*, others in *St. Nicholas* and *Outing Magazine*. Visiting the *Outing* office, Remington discovered by chance that his Yale classmate Poultney Bigelow was editing the journal. Quickly examining Remington's paintings, Bigelow immediately recognized them as the real thing; "genius was in those rough drawings," the editor later recalled.[4] The next year *Harper's* took twelve and *Outing* seventy-one of Remington's illustrations. A year later the illustrator hit the jackpot, placing more than a hundred illustrations in *Harper's*, *Outing*, and *Youth's Companion*. Even the lordly *Century Magazine* bought sixty-four Remingtons.

By the end of the 1880s, having already placed more than four hundred illustrations in about four years, Remington ranked at the top of the list of illustrators focusing on the West. Readers and editors, praising his authenticity, his vigorous style, his attention to detail, saluted his documentary treatment of a vanishing mode of life, particularly his depictions of Indians, explorers, mountain men, soldiers, and cowboys. In his illustrations for Elizabeth Custer's *Tenting on the Plains* and Theodore Roosevelt's *Ranch Life and the Hunting-Trail* and in such paintings as *Indian Scouts on Geronimo's Trail* (1886), *A Fight in the Street* (1888), and *A Cavalry Man's Breakfast on the Plains* (ca. 1890), Remington impressed observers with his knowledge of horses, horsemen, Indians, and other frontier types. Art critic Royal Cortissoz hit upon what many others have praised Remington for: his illustrations proved him the master of "the swift notation of the movement which lies somehow at the very heart of wild Western life."[5]

Frederic Remington, *A Dash for the Timber*, 1889. (Oil on canvas, Amon Carter Museum, Fort Worth, Texas, 1961.381)

A Dash for the Timber (1889) is a particularly impressive example of Remington's early artwork. Commissioned by the well-to-do inventor E. C. Converse, this four- by seven-foot oil depicts a dramatic chase in which eight riders at full gallop, shooting over their shoulders and urging on their foaming horses, try to elude closely pursuing Apaches. Carefully detailing the riders' mounts, saddles, boots, and other paraphernalia, infusing the action with spectacle, and supplying the desired "stirring frontier scene," Remington obviously provided his patron with the "monumental canvas depicting a life struggle on the frontier" that Converse had requested.[6] Further, the grand confrontation between cowboys and Indians takes place in an arid, dusty West with the horsemen attempting to escape into a small stand of timber nearby. Here was a revealing sample of two of Remington's self-proclaimed understandings of the frontier: "he knew the horse," and he dealt with "men with the bark on."

In the mid-1890s, Remington's and Wister's careers converged in an illuminating moment for the two easterners, as well as for the imagined frontier they helped create. For two years Remington had importuned Wister to tell the story of the cowpuncher, sending the novelist dozens of letters jammed with anecdotes, bits of historical background, and sketches of cowboy dress and poses. At the time, Remington knew more details than Wister, but because the artist seemed unable to treat the topic with its merited significance, he urged Wister to tell the story.[7]

When Wister's essay "The Evolution of the Cow-Puncher" appeared in *Harper's Monthly* in September 1895, five of Remington's illustrations accompanied it. Of these, *The Last Cavalier, What an Unbranded Cow Has Cost,* and *The Fall of the Cowboy* revealingly illustrate Remington's views of the frontier. The most nostalgic of the three, *The Last Cavalier* portrays a cowpuncher riding from left to right against a backdrop of mounted men of the past. Like them, Remington's cowboy seems to be slowly riding out of the picture, the last of a series of sturdy horsemen that Remington so admired. More complicated and freighted with greater significance, *What an Unbranded Cow Has Cost* pictures a cowboy near the end of a disastrous shootout, surrounded by dead or gravely wounded men, and possibly himself soon to become the target of a nearby marksman. The recumbent men and animals, dead or badly injured, represent Remington's vision of the frontier as an arena of masculine courage — and violence.

Even more revealing for understanding Remington and his West is *The Fall of the Cowboy,* one of the classics of frontier art. In several ways the archetypal portrait of a closing frontier, as were Wister's *The Virginian* and Turner's "Significance of the Frontier" essay, Remington's well-known oil displays two weary cowboys and their humped-up horses pausing before a pole gate. Their footprints paralleling the barbed-wire barrier, the somber mood and color of the setting, and the fence itself suggest the end of an Old West, the close of an open-range bonanza that Wister chronicled in his accompanying essay on the rise and fall of the cowboy. Neither entirely tragic nor elegiac in tone, *The Fall of the Cowboy* displays a bleak, snowy, and cold frontier, far removed from the romantic West that inhabited so many other paintings by Remington and Russell. Above all, this memorable work illustrates Remington's lifelong fascination with a closing frontier that intrigued his contemporaries.

In the first decade of his career, then, Remington produced many of the Wild West images for which he is best known. In these works, Remington deemphasized the gigantic spaces of Bierstadt and Moran, stressing instead rugged individuals contesting with new lands and peoples. As one historian has pointed out, "the western experience implied to [Remington] the presence of man in potentially hostile natural surroundings."[8] Relishing, too, the cult of masculinity that fired writers like Roosevelt, Wister, London, and Turner, Remington was little interested in picturing women or minorities, except Indians, in his frontier paintings. Sometimes Remington treated Indians as if they were part of the hostile environment with which explorers, soldiers, and cowboys contested. On other occasions, such as in *Crow Indians Firing into the Agency* (1887) and *An Indian Trapper* (1889), he handled Native Americans more sympathetically, as victims of complex cultural confrontations or as important agents in frontier economic activity. Most often, however, Indians were opponents, challengers to the masculinity and daring of the frontiersmen the artist so admired. Unfortunately, on still other occasions Remington's ethnocentric views, already deeply rooted, flowered into repugnant racism. In 1893, for example, he displayed his virulent xenophobia in writing to a friend: "Jews, Injuns, Chinamen, Italians, Huns — the rubbish of the Earth I hate — I've got some Winchesters and when the massacring begins, I can get my share of 'em, and what's more, I will."[9] Most of the time Remington reined in such excesses, but he was convinced that the frontier was a harsh, demanding place where a man had to learn to take care of himself.

Meanwhile, the restless and indefatigable Remington began to move in new directions that reoriented his contacts with, and views about, the West. Although some critics of the time affirmed that, by the early 1890s, Remington had scaled Parnassus and become the best-known illustrator in America, the artist himself was less certain of his success. Dissatisfied with being lionized primarily as an illustrator, Remington hungered and thirsted after a reputation as a major American artist. When he failed to garner such attention, he turned to sculpting and produced, in 1895, his first bronze, *The Bronco Buster*. The two-foot-high statuette represented what Remington aimed for in all his art: "excitement, realism, fluid motion, and perceptive handling of equine anatomy."[10] Some observers wondered if the bronze, so different from his flat-surfaced sketches, was but one more example of Remington's need for self-testing. Did the rider's precarious pose on the bucking bronco, one boot slipping from a stirrup and one hand clutching the mane, symbolize more than a momentary exhibition of dexterity? Even if the horse and rider hardly illustrated a "wild diabolism" or a "single bolt of energy gone crazy,"[11] were they metaphors for the frontier competitiveness that Remington exalted and that might be disappearing? Could *The Bronco Buster* stand for a West already vanished and now reemerging as myth?

Other happenings in Remington's life suggest this may have been the case. In the early 1890s he plunged into New York social and cultural life and seemed much less inclined to revisit and renew his ties to the frontier. Bit by bit he internalized his view of the frontier, accepting its cowboy martial spirit as an alternative to the urbanization, immigration, and industrialization he saw overrunning the American East. A heightened belligerency and an exaggerated masculinity flowed from his letters and his other comments, perhaps as he saw frontier life passing from view. Ironically, even while his chauvinistic western spirit intensified, he remained absent from the West, making no extensive trips there after the late 1890s. It was as if, once separated from his western experiences of the 1880s, he replaced that documentary West with a new mythic and legendary one that powerfully controlled his emotions for the last fifteen years of his life.

In the mid-1890s Remington turned to writing, producing several short-story collections and a novel in a half-dozen years. In such anthologies as *Pony Tracks* (1895), *Crooked Trails* (1898), *Sun Down Leflare* (1899), and *Men with the Bark On* (1900), and in the novel *John Ermine of the Yellowstone* (1902), Remington dealt with East and West as conflicting cultural symbols and value systems, ideas that replaced his previous attempts at realistic narrative portraits of the West. The white hero raised among Indians in *John Ermine*, published the same year as Wister's *Virginian* but ending much differently, dies tragically, unable to understand or adapt to eastern-spawned class and social distinctions. This protagonist, like other Remington figures of the late-1890s, was more symbol than fact, suggesting that the artist and fiction writer had internalized an imagined frontier increasingly divorced from his earlier West.

The Spanish-American War changed Remington in still other ways. Intrigued since boyhood with wars and the unbridled actions they often generated and longing for a military conflict in which he could participate, Remington nonetheless quickly lost his militancy in the quagmires of Cuba in 1898. Bureaucratic foul-ups, debilitating diseases, and violent deaths crushed his untested romanticism. Despite Remington's earlier bellicosity, his praise for Roosevelt and American servicemen, and his own Hearst-like bombast, the horrors of what he saw in Cuba destroyed his idealism about war and forced him back to his western focus—but to a West different from what he had portrayed twenty years earlier. Briefly visiting Colorado and the Southwest in 1900, he wrote his wife that the Indians he saw were vastly different from those of the frontier period. The Utes were too "far on the road to civilization," he observed, and the Pueblos did not appeal to him because they were "too decorative—and too easily in reach of every tenderfoot." Then, echoing the laments of Roosevelt and Wister, Remington added that he would "never come west again—It is all brick buildings—derby hats and blue overhauls—it spoils my early illusions—and they are my capital."[12]

Not surprisingly, these experiences transformed Remington's vision of the West even as he experimented with new techniques. Once freed from financial necessity by a generous contract with *Collier's* to furnish several years of illustrations, Remington returned to his western work with characteristic enthusiasm. Although he chided Impressionists by joking that his two maiden aunts could knit better than they could paint, the Impressionists' use of bright colors and light particularly attracted him. Abandoning what art historian Brian Dippie describes as "the crisp, linear illustrative style"[13] of his earlier paintings of the frontier, Remington experimented with new combinations of impressionistic light and color, especially brilliant sunlight and light-and-dark moonscapes. These rich, pathbreaking colorations allowed Remington to suggest fresh poetic and mysterious meanings for his western scenes.

Shadows, complexities, and less unrestrained exuberance mark much of Remington's final work on the West. For example, in *A Taint in the Wind* (1906), *Downing the Night Leader* (1907?), and *The Luckless Hunter* (1909), he employed shadowy scenes, ghostly figures, and spooky settings to introduce another West, one much less heroic, adventuresome, and violent than in his first frontier artworks. His oils, such as *The Unknown Explorers* (1908) and *The Buffalo Runners, Big Horn Basin* (1909), are explosions of the bright colors and expansive spaces of the Impressionists. In both paintings the dazzling sunlight and rich, varying colors and contrasting shadows revealingly demonstrate how much Remington's art had changed. As Brian Dippie has said of *The Buffalo Runners,* "it is a highpoint in his hard-earned transformation into an American impressionist."[14]

Equally clear were Remington's amended notions about the West. In 1907 he wrote that he was no longer interested in the West because it was, he said, not "my West." "What he called 'my West,'" Ben Merchant Vorpahl explains, "was not a place where he had once been but a condition he presently imagined."[15] Like many writers and artists of his time, Remington began his career celebrating the West as an inviting but demanding frontier wilderness, distant physically and socially from eastern society and civilization. Over time, his views of the West became increasingly nostalgic, romantic, and mythic. Part and parcel of the most popular conceptions of the West during his times, Remington first worshipped the West as an Eden where individualism was tested and masculinity put on display. Like his friends Roosevelt and Wister and similar to Grey and Turner, he lamented the passing of the frontier in the 1890s, but he too was unable to think of the West as gradually becoming a region with its own cultural identity.

When Charlie Russell landed in Montana in March 1880, he came as an idealistic fifteen-year-old Huck Finn, intending to "light out for the Territory ahead." Fleeing his middle-class St. Louis home, Charlie hoped to experience firsthand a Wild West just four years beyond Custer's debacle at the Little Big Horn. Already chock-full of frontier stories from his mother's family, which included the fabled Bent brothers of Colorado and New Mexico, Charlie took to Montana and the frontier West like a hungry trout chasing a new lure. Quickly becoming a westerner — in dress, occupation, and outlook — Russell hunkered down in Montana, where he stayed for half a century, increasingly loving a frontier West and loathing people and institutions that tried to move that West toward a postfrontier society and culture.[16]

On a superficial level, similarities between Russell and Remington seem more significant than differences. Not so, however. In background, in personality, in temperament, in intensity of contact with the West, and in ideology the two artists diverged profoundly. True, both loved the Wild West, lamented the vanishing frontier, and focused primarily on a masculine setting of cowboys and Indians, but in the long run the parallels are less noteworthy than the dissimilarities.

Indeed, in the drama of frontier culture between the 1880s and the 1920s, no figure more closely and intensely identified with that culture than Charlie Russell. If Roosevelt, Remington, and Wister passed through the West on the way to national reputations in politics, art, and fiction, if Zane Grey and Jack London were cheerleaders for a masculine, outdoor, twentieth-century West, and if Willa Cather and Mary Austin recognized the emerging regional West during these decades, Charlie Russell wore the Old West like a highly favored, if well-worn, sombrero. More than that, he came to identify with the rangeland West — its ways of life, its values, and its perspective on other regions. Even in physical appearance he became western. His wife Nancy recalled decades later her first impressions of Charlie, which were remarkably similar to those of other observers: "The picture that is engraved on my memory is of a man of little above average height and weight, wearing a soft shirt, a Stetson hat on the back of his blonde head, tight trousers, held up by a 'half-breed sash' that clung just above the hip bones, high-heeled riding boots on very small, arched feet.

His face was Indian-like, square jaw and chin, large mouth, tightly closed firm lips . . . straight nose, high cheek bones, gray-blue deep-set eyes that seemed to see everything, but with an expression of honesty and understanding."[17]

In his first half-dozen years in Montana, Charlie went through jobs like an uncertain customer picking through a display of hot potatoes. Hating sheep, he was, first of all, a failure at herding. "I'd lose the damn things as fast as they'd put 'em on the ranch," he told an acquaintance. Next he partnered with a backcountry hunter for two seasons before landing a job as horse wrangler and, later, another position as a nighthawk, looking after herds in their bedding grounds.[18] Fretting little about making a living, Charlie floated from outfit to outfit, not much of a rider but a man who could make friends easily, a young man observing, mimicking, and sketching the grizzled riders and cowmen who became his friends and bosses. But Charlie's bachelor days ended swiftly after he met Nancy Cooper in 1895. They married the next year, and Nancy, the daughter of divorced parents with double doses of determination and ambition, put her cinch on Charlie, limiting his drinking and partying with the boys and encouraging him to make a profession of his artwork. Afterward, Charlie sometimes grumbled about his wife's bossing and expressed astonishment at the prices she asked — and got — for his paintings, but for the rest of his life he also credited her with his financial success.

Before Nancy helped midwife Charlie into a career as a successful artist, he did little to further his career financially, choosing to trade his sketches and early paintings for drinks or to give them to friends. Yet one unusual circumstance attracted immediate attention to Charlie's art and helped him to understand a frontier West that was rapidly disappearing. When a Montana ranchman asked his foreman how the herd was making it through the vicious winter of 1886–87 (a disaster later known as the Great Die Up), Charlie, almost without thinking, sketched a lone, gaunt steer about to lose out to skulking coyotes. His 2" by 4" watercolor sketch, *Waiting for a Chinook* (1886; later retitled *Last of the 5,000*), when reproduced in several Montana newspapers, immediately caught on and made Charlie a celebrity among livestock people and Montana townsmen alike. In 1886 he exhibited a painting of a cow camp (*Breaking Camp*) at the St. Louis Art Exposition and two years later placed *Caught in the Act*, a bleak portrait of western Indian life, in *Harper's*. Then, in 1890, a privately published collection of twelve of Charlie's sketches became his first book.[19]

Charlie's experiences in his first decade in Montana and the material he drew from pioneer stories became the central emphases of his first paintings and remained his major themes for the next thirty-five years. Clearly, Russell loved the Old West and refused to accept its passing even though by the early 1890s he had seen the coming of railroads, the end of much open-range ranching, and the arrival of thousands of newcomers. Between the Custer incident and 1900, Montana moved from frontier status to statehood and beyond, with Russell viewing firsthand most of the transformation. But like Remington and Roosevelt, Charlie closed his eyes to the future, refusing to face forward. Instead, he turned to the past, nostalgically holding on to the earlier years and freezing those times in his thousands of paintings of the frontier.

Russell's loving attachment to the "old times" emerges most often in his depictions of people competing with a demanding setting or with other people, or their involvement in perilous occupations. In his early oil *Lost in a Snow Storm—We Are Friends* (1888), Russell depicts two cowboys, lost in a blinding blizzard and befriended by a handful of Indians, who through sign language tell them of their compatriots on the other side of the mountain. Six years later, in another rather unpolished oil, *Buffalo Hunting,* Russell portrays an Indian dangerously riding alongside a galloping buffalo, ready to drive his arrow into the beast's vitals. Concurrently, he completed *For Supremacy* (1895) and *Bested* (1895), which, respectively, dealt with a dramatic battle between the Piegans and Crows and a group of horse thieves surrendering to pursuing vigilantes. In both paintings a wide-angle frontier serves as a stage for furious confrontations between "savage" opponents.

More often than not, Russell depicted his Old West through hundreds of portraits of Native Americans and cowboys. As for Indians, Charlie was more interested in and knew more about them than did most other novelists, historians, and artists during the period from the 1890s to the 1920s. In fact, during his lifetime and since, Charlie has gained a large reputation as a friend of the Indians—most of it well deserved. Much more than Remington and most artists of the early-twentieth-century West (with the possible exception of Joseph Henry Sharp) Russell knew Indians firsthand. Although he early gained a book knowledge of Indians and had studied paintings by artists such as Karl Bodmer, Charles Wimar, and Frederic Remington, he was also personally acquainted with Indians, having lived for a few months with the Bloods in Canada in 1888 and maintaining friendships with other natives in western Montana. Often called "the cowboy artist," Russell did even more artwork about Indians, throughout his career painting hundreds of scenes about Native Americans.[20]

Not surprisingly, given Russell's love affair with an open frontier, most of his paintings about Indians deal with earlier buffalo days or initial contacts with whites. *Squaw Travois* (1895) and *Indian Hunters' Return* (1900), for example, realistically depict Indian camps, the return of hunters, the roles of women in these camps, and specific details of families, hunting techniques, tepees, and the seasonal cycles of Indian life. Another series of paintings deals with Indian contacts with Lewis and Clark, sometimes from the native viewpoint. Whether treating meetings with the Mandans, the Sioux, the Shoshone, or the Chinook, Russell filled his paintings with revealing ethnographic detail gathered from his readings, his scrutiny of other art, and his conversations with Indians.

When Russell stressed conflict between Indians and whites or intertribal warfare, he did so with more variety than did Remington or the southwestern artists. *Attack on the Wagon Train* (1904), a dramatic oil painting of an Indian attack on immigrants, depicts the conflict from an Indian perspective. The viewer sees the scene over the shoulders of the attackers as they fire on the white-canvassed wagons. The spectacular encounters between perhaps a Piegan and a Crow in *Duel to the Death* (ca. 1891), *For Supremacy* (1895), and *When Blackfeet and Sioux Meet* (1908) attest to the artist's ability to depict violent clashes between heroic representatives of conflicting native groups.

On other occasions when Russell dealt with contemporary Indian experiences, he did so with empathy and humor. In *Matters under the Skin* (1900) he contrasts a gowned white woman lounging in the shade of a tree before her attractive home, her cradled child and blooded dog nearby, with a foregrounded Indian woman, her blanketed child on her back and followed by her mongrel dog, representing natives lacking a homeland. This empathetic perspective parallels the attitudes Russell expressed in his writings about Indians, in which he encouraged fellow whites to be more understanding of the social and economic precariousness of Indians and of the traumatic changes forced on native society and culture. Sometimes the contrasts are presented humorously, as in *Skunk Wagon* (1907), a watercolor showing an Indian man and woman riding by two white couples, whose touring car is bogged in a mud hole. The caption, "White man's skunk wagon no good, heap lame," reflects not only Russell's sympathy for the Indian perspective but also his own reservations about the technological invasion of the West.

Charlie Russell, *Bronc to Breakfast*, 1908. (Watercolor, Montana Historical Society, Mackay Collection, X52.01.06)

If one follows the conclusion of the distinguished ethnologist John Ewers, the oil entitled *Charlie Russell and His Friends* (1922) represents the painter's respect and admiration for Indians. Mounted and atop a grassy knoll, Charlie points with his sweeping left hand to an approaching group of Indians riding toward him with their greeting, set against an eye-stretching Montana background. As Ewers concludes, in this appealing scene Russell rounds up his "favorite subjects . . . Cowboys, Indians, and Montana." [21]

Russell's hundreds of paintings about cowboys and the cattle country also allowed him a lifetime of demonstrating his emotional attachment to a frontier West. Among his first oil paintings, *Breaking Camp* (1885) and *Cowboy Camp during the Roundup* (1887) were apprenticeship works on roundup crews working near Utica, Montana. Intrigued with documentarylike reproductions of the lively lives of cowpunchers, Russell tried to cram recognizable likenesses of all his cronies into these cow camp paintings. His friends thought them marvelous art because Charlie depicted their bucking, crow-hopping mounts and clearly identified cowboys well known to Judith Basin residents. Still in his early twenties, Charlie seemed satisfied with these rather primitive attempts at realism.

Gradually over time, possibly because he could sell standard cowboy pieces more readily than innovative scenes, Charlie devoted increasing numbers of cowboy paintings to rather stereotypical action scenes.[22] None of these are more typical than *Bronc to Breakfast* (1908) and *In without Knocking* (1909). Both illustrate Russell's fascination with horsemen frozen in vignettes of violent activity. In the former, a bronco, out of its rider's control, crashes through the campfire, destroying the cowboys' breakfast and scattering the riders gathered nearby. The distraught cook threatens the horse and rider with his butcher knife, and other cowboys leap out of the way or grab the bridles of their jittery mounts. For Russell, this scene of campfire confusion seemed to epitomize an untamed West, full of surprises and pleasing disorder, one that he captured in similar fashion in *Bronc to Cow Camp* (1897) and *Camp Cook's Troubles* (1912), and in his bronze *A Bronc Twister* (n.d.)

Frenetic action also dominates *In without Knocking*, based on an incident Charlie had heard about twenty-five years earlier. Five pistol-shooting cowboys, still mounted, try to ride their horses through the door of the Hoffman Hotel in Stanford, Montana. One rider ducks through the door, another spills off his fallen mount onto the board sidewalk, and the others charge the doorway. A swirling maelstrom of dust, smoking pistols, scattered cards, and several tense horses thrown against the facades of the jerry-built cowtown add much to Russell's picture of a raw, uncivilized frontier. Praised by participants in these and other parallel incidents as authentic to the smallest detail, these paintings are even more significant as revealing examples of Russell's persisting celebration of an untamed Wild West.

If growing numbers of Russell's customers favored his stock Indian and cowboy paintings, they also seemed drawn to his memorializing of a passing frontier. Often easterners are depicted humorously as a species of dudes unable to handle the demands of the frontier. In a series of pen-and-ink and watercolor paintings in 1907 (*A Touch of Western Highlife*; *Dance, You Shorthorn, Dance*; and *When East Meets West*, for example) Russell, with tongue in cheek, depicted easterners as greenhorns, as victims of western violence, as butts of western humor, or as over-dressed women and objects of western scorn. They stand out as foolish, weak, or misguided examples of a regional culture out of place and unable to withstand the practical demands of a frontier West.

Charlie began to eulogize the Old West well before the final years of his career, however. In fact, by the late 1880s and early 1890s, just as he was ending his days as a working cowboy and trying to become a full-time artist, he commenced to speak of the old days now gone, took as his personal insignia a buffalo skull symbolizing the closure of that earlier era, and he participated in the cultural *ubi sunt* of the 1890s that mourned the passing of the West Out There. That is, early on, and throughout his career, Charlie Russell, while glorying in and celebrating the Old West, also elegized its ending.[23]

Two sketches Charlie completed in the late 1890s (*Dame Progress Proudly Stands* [1898] and *The Last of His Race* [1899]) explicitly reveal Charlie's requiem for the past. In the first of the pen-and-ink drawings, the figures of Civilization and Father Time—backed by symbols of contemporary religion, technology (a bicyclist and a belching smokestack), and sophisticated society —seem to be banishing from the scene representations of the Old West— Indians, cowboys, trappers, outlaws, and bullwhackers. At the feet of the representations of progress is a casket on which is written "Wild West, Loved by All Who Knew Her."[24] Above the Old West types, in the hazy clouds, are signs of older times: Indians hunting buffalo, a cowboy and steers, and a careening stagecoach. Much the same imagery appears in *The Last of His Race,* with a more pronounced negative tone. An old Indian, kneeling near a roadway and leaning against his staff, stares into the past while a stylishly dressed young woman rides a bicycle past him, headed in the opposite direction in which he gazes. She pedals toward fences and telegraph lines, and in the background a smelter stack belches smoke. Immediately above the gigantic chimney, in the heavens, ghostly figures of Indians pursuing buffalo symbolize an Old West now gone. Paeans to Charlie's beloved early Montana, these sketches illustrate his lifetime veneration of times past.

By midcareer Charlie had become known nationally—even internationally—as the artist of the Old West. Exhibitions in New York City, Calgary, and London between 1911 and 1914 advertised him as one who painted "the West that Has Passed." At the same time he told a prospective customer that the country from the Yellowstone to the Saskatchewan, once Blackfeet territory, was today "fenced and settled by ranch men and farmers with nothing but a few worn trails where once walked the buffalo."[25] As he wrote on another occasion, "the West is dead," and then added: "You may lose a sweetheart, / But you won't forget her."[26]

Charlie's pent-up nostalgia and melancholy often burst out in correspondence with lifelong friends. One of them was Teddy Blue Abbott, a well-known cowboy Charlie first met in his Judith Basin days in 1886. More than thirty years later in a letter to Abbott, Charlie remembered a revealing conversation: "I remember one day we were looking at buffalo carcus and you said Russ I wish I was a Sioux Injun a hundred years ago And I said me to Ted thairs a pair of us I have often made that wish since. . . . Old Ma Nature was kind to her red children and the old time cow puncher was her adopted son. . . ."[27] Two years later he lamented: "the long horned spotted cows that walked the same trails their humped back cousins made have joined them in history and with them went the wether worn cow men. They live now only in books. The cow puncher of Forty years ago is as much history as Parkmans Trapper."[28]

Throughout his career, Russell produced dozens of sketches, oils, and water-colors that were mournful memories of the glorious early days, but as he grew older that tendency increased. *Men of the Open Range* (1923), for instance, brims with melancholy for the era before barbed wire enclosed the range. As Brian Dippie points out, "there is a pervasive nostalgia in this picture. It is daybreak, but the mood is sunset . . . a tribute to youth in full vigor recollected in old age."[29] *Laugh Kills Lonesome* (1925) carries a similar feeling. An iris-like technique focuses the viewer's attention on a cluster of cowboys around a nighttime campfire. The night rider lingers in the glow of the warmth of the fire and his companions' conviviality, reluctant to move on. Again, Russell's melancholy invades his work, celebrating his attachment to a now-vanished cowboy West.

In the closing years of his life, Russell, like Remington, increasingly infused his artwork with a revived spirit. But unlike Remington's partial conversion to Impressionism, Russell chose to enlarge and deepen his previous emphasis — his nostalgic treatment of the Old West — for which he was already known by the outbreak of World War I. Writing to acquaintances throughout the late teens and early twenties, Charlie lamented how many of their mutual friends had journeyed to the other side, how much Montana had changed, and how little of the God-created West survived man's innovations. Significantly, just as Mary Austin and Willa Cather were discovering a new West with emerging subregional cultures, Charles Russell was attempting to hold on to a frontier West he had fallen in love with in the 1880s and with which, emotionally, he had lived for more than forty years. If the 1920s were for many others a divid-ing point between the West as a vanishing frontier and as a surfacing region, Charlie refused to recognize the transition to a New West, choosing instead to champion an Old West that he knew and embraced. To Charlie, the frontier West was the real West, the only valid West. Agreeing with Roosevelt and Remington, with authenticists like movie star William S. Hart and humorist Will Rogers, and with later literary aficionados such as Eugene Manlove Rhodes, W. H. Hutchinson, and Louis L'Amour, Charlie believed in his West and persistently, lovingly, depicted that frontier in his thousands of paintings, illustrations, bronzes, and illustrated letters.

Although Remington and Russell were by far the most influential individual artists in molding opinion about a frontier West during their lifetimes — and since — they by no means represent the full picture of painterly treatments of the West from the 1890s to the 1920s. Dozens of other artists, particularly those who flocked to the nascent art colonies in Taos and Santa Fe illustrated other divergent views of the West. They too were intrigued with landscapes, particularly the arid terrain, bright colors, and large skies of the Southwest; and they were especially drawn to the Indian and Hispanic cultures of the area.[30]

At the turn of the century and in the next decade, such artists as Ernest L. Blumenschein, Bert Geer Phillips, Joseph Henry Sharp, E. Irving Couse, Oscar E. Berninghaus, and W. Herbert ("Buck") Dunton visited or moved to Taos and established the Taos Society of Artists in 1915, which lasted until 1927. Later, painters like Walter Ufer, Victor Higgins, E. Martin Hennings, Kenneth M. Adams, Catharine Carter Critcher, and Julius Rolshoven became active members of the society. Meanwhile, an equally large contingent of painters were discovering the canyons, mesas, and caminos surrounding Santa Fe.

Nearly all these artists were easterners, had been trained in Europe at the famed École des Beaux-Arts and Académie Julian in Paris or in art schools in New York City and Chicago, and had considerable experience as illustrators or artists prior to moving west before World War I. Their coming, like that of many other emigrants, resulted from several push-pull factors. Similar to Remington, Russell, and Wister, they felt vaguely hemmed in, overrun with alienating urban-industrial-immigrant cultures, and in need of novel settings with new materials. Ironically, the arid Southwest — dismissed as backward, isolated, and unpromising economically by earlier developers and politicians — was just the place to attract artists discontented with their surroundings and in search of settings less settled and boisterous. The Southwest to which they became emotionally and professionally attached exhibited the isolation, the cultural primitiveness, and the novel terrain they sought.[31]

These interests markedly shaped what subjects appealed most to the migrating artists, what attitudes they would take toward these subjects, and which techniques they would employ in their art. Several of the painters had been exposed to the new trends in modern art, especially those on display in the studios of Paris and New York City and represented in the avant-garde Impressionist and Cubist works that startled Americans in the pathbreaking Armory Show in 1913. One might therefore have expected that the newcomers would employ these experimental techniques in the Southwest. But that proved not to be the case. Most of the first-generation Taos–Santa Fe painters endeavored to present realistic representational portraits of the Southwest, albeit in romantic moods and tones; more innovative trends characterized only their later paintings. Similar to tourists or sojourners, the painters seemed so taken with the new landscapes and peoples they encountered that, like local-color writers, they devoted their attention primarily to describing the settings and societies before them rather than to analyzing how these cultures had evolved over time, as later regionalists would.

Early on, unique southwestern landscapes captured the emotions of the newcomers. After just a few days in New Mexico, a smitten Ernest Blumenschein wrote: "No artist had ever recorded the New Mexico I was now seeing. . . . The color, the effective character of the landscape, the drama of the vast spaces, the superb beauty and serenity of the hills, stirred me deeply."[32] What Blumenschein experienced in 1898 foreshadowed a similar moment of epiphany for D. H. Lawrence three decades later. "The moment I saw the brilliant, proud morning shine high up over Santa Fe," Lawrence wrote, "something stood still in my soul, and I started to attend. . . . In the magnificent fierce morning of New Mexico one sprang awake, a new part of the soul woke up suddenly, and the old world gave way to the new."[33] Under such provocative emotional stimulation the landscapist urge, dormant for nearly a quarter century among many American artists, awoke in the sun-baked, richly hued Southwest.

Nearly all the Taos–Santa Fe painters sought to catch the size and scale of the novel, spectacular scenery of the region. On occasion, those goals seemed beyond them. Emil Bisttram, who arrived in the 1930s, undoubtedly spoke for others when he wrote of his difficulties: "whenever I tried to paint what was before me I was frustrated by the grandeur of the scenery and the limitless space."[34] Walter Ufer's spectacular oil *Where the Desert Meets the Mountain* (before 1922) captures the spaciousness of the Southwest by situating a small wagon in the immense terrain stretching from the green-and-tan sagebrush foreground to the distant, dark mountains. The scene reminds one of the lone, diminutive stagecoach passing through the gigantic setting in John Ford's classic film *Stagecoach*. Eye-stretching landscape spaces also fill Dunton's *Horse Wrangler* (ca. 1928), in which a mounted cowboy pasted against an immense, clouded blue sky looks down over his shoulder at the remuda grazing nearby in an area extending endlessly to the faraway shadowy mountains. The best-known of the southwestern artworks that utilized this expansive setting is Blumenschein's *Sangre de Cristo Mountains* (1925), in which the rounded backdrop mountains "are echoed in the bowed and blanketed processional figures and adobe buildings" in the foreground.[35]

In none of these paintings does nature threaten or even frown. Unlike the vicious, numbing storms that invade Remington's and Russell's canvases, climatic changes in southwestern paintings come in without a bang. In *Winter Funeral* (1931) and *Storm Approaching Adobe* (ca. 1920s), by Victor Higgins, the snowy landscape and approaching storm clouds illustrate the varied but predictable faces nature wears, not the bludgeoning, cruel visages depicted by the northern artists.[36]

These scenes of nature's timelessness and placidity are often linked to southwestern artists' depictions of Native Americans. No doubt the painters' desire for peaceful lives, coupled with their conviction that serene scenes were antidotes to the ills of American society, attracted them to the Indians of New Mexico. The initial reactions of the artists to the region's Native Americans evidenced that they had found a new, invigorating culture replete with models for harmonious social organization, as well as abundant material for fresh artistic renderings.[37]

Taos–Santa Fe artists painting between 1900 and the beginning of the Depression were fascinated by what they perceived to be picturesque and tranquil Indian life. *Sunset Dance-Ceremony to the Evening Sun* (1924), by Joseph Henry Sharp, and *Pueblo of Taos* (before 1927), by Victor Higgins, are revealing examples of the societal congruity southwestern artists imposed on Native scenes. In both paintings of Indians gathered in their pueblos, the elements of color, lighting, natural settings, and the placement of people gave a strong impression of harmony between people and nature, as well as order within the native communities. By superimposing patterns of unity on the foregrounded human figures and suggestions of their oneness with the distant mountains, southwestern artists depicted both the societal and environmental tranquility they wanted so much to discover. As the art historian William Truettner has discerningly noted, this "sense of order and harmony" was particularly revealing: "no image could more effectively demonstrate the view of Pueblo life held by the Anglo painters."[38]

But the artists chose not to see other facets of Indian life in the Southwest. In doing so, they demonstrated their differences from Remington and Russell as well as their limitations as students of Pueblo history. No evidence of competition or conflict complicates the works of the Taos–Santa Fe painters; nor are there depictions of the poverty and health problems that troubled some pueblos. Finally, these artistic works freeze the Indians in time; they are unthreatened with the social, economic, and technological changes that novelists, historians, and other artists used to depict a closing frontier and its often traumatic impact on Indians.

Southwestern artists were slower to deal with Hispanic traditions, perhaps because Indian life seemed somehow more wonderfully strange, but they eventually succeeded in capturing a good deal of the Spanish presence in the Southwest. Repeatedly they painted Spanish adobe churches, homes, and other buildings; they likewise betrayed a strong interest in Hispanic handicrafts and arts. As with Indians, they attempted to showcase unities within Hispanic communities, religious practices, and families.[39] Only on a few occasions were artists critical of Hispanic life and culture.

Hispanic art and architecture especially interested southwestern artists. Painting parish and pueblo churches, *moradas* (Penitente meeting places and churches), and *santos, bultos,* and *retablos* seemed almost *de rigueur* for southwesterners, much as buffalo hunts and bucking broncos were for Remington and Russell. Nearly always their paintings of churches, as in Ufer's *Oferta para San Esquipula* (1918) and Kenneth Adams's *The Mission Church* (before 1925), and numerous depictions of religious edifices at Ranchos de Taos and Chimayó suggest the congruence among churches, believers, and settings, almost as if the adobe churches had emerged naturally from their backgrounds. Even though most immigrant southwestern painters were neither Catholic nor religious, they seemed to respect Hispanic religious objects as symbols of a simple, pious faith grounded in the land, work, and communities that had appeared during three centuries of settlement in the Southwest. *A Shrine to St. Anthony* (1917), by Victor Higgins, *Still Life with Santo* (ca. 1930), by B.J.O. Nordfeldt, and *New Mexico Bulto* (ca. 1924), by Bert G. Phillips, are sympathetic portrayals of Hispanic faith as reflected in art and objects. Other artworks emphasized

Los Penitentes or Los Hermanos (the Brothers) whose independent, pious rural religious ways were unique among American Catholics. Their Easter processions, dramatizing the agonies and Crucifixion of Christ, were the subject of memorable paintings by Phillips (*Penitente Burial Procession,* n.d.), and Willard Nash (*Penitentes,* ca. 1930). Along a similar line, several of the southwestern artists helped foster a revival of Hispanic artisans by encouraging the teaching of courses on Hispanic arts and crafts, the renovation of several adobe churches, and the support of Hispanic wood sculptors such as Patrocino Barela and Celso Gallegos.

The strength and endurance of Hispanic individuals and families also mark dozens of southwestern paintings. The elderly Hispanic in Hennings's *The Goatherder* (ca. 1925), the craftsman in Phillips's *The Santero* (ca. 1930), and the elderly woman in Bisttram's *Comadre Rafaelita* (1934) celebrate these heroic laborers. In a similar vein, Phillips's oil, *Our Washerwoman Family—New Mexico* (ca. 1918), focuses on the work ethic and endurance that the elderly washerwoman and her husband will bequeath to their daughter and grandchild. For southwestern artists these Hispanic workers exuded a strength and perseverance missing from the sweatshops, factories, and settlement houses crowding European and eastern cities.

One notable painting, Blumenschein's *Jury for the Trial of a Sheepherder for Murder* (1936), provides an unusually revealing example of social comment in southwestern art. Seated among eleven roughly dressed Penitente brethren in the jury box (a twelfth behind thick glasses peeps over the edge of the enclosure), a young Hispanic herder is tried for the unpremeditated murder of an intruder who suddenly appeared in his sheep camp. As the herder sits bewildered, ill-at-ease among his peers and watched over by George Washington's portrait among the vigas overhead, he represents one cultural tradition being overtaken and controlled by another. An Anglo court demands justice (the herder was convicted of second-degree murder) based on its new system, one at odds with an earlier tradition. In suggesting the closing of one cultural frontier and the emergence of another, Blumenschein proved an exception in explicitly noting cultural change and by furnishing social commentary often missing from the work of his contemporaries.

Were the southwestern artists, who did so little with pioneer images and seemed so uninterested in a closing frontier and yet captured the varied cultural roles of Indians and Hispanics in New Mexico, abandoning the camp of frontier image-makers to pitch their tents with the regionalists? Not quite.

They were at best reluctant regionalists. Too tied to picturesque, romantic images of Native Americans and cowboys, painters such as E. Irving Couse, Oscar E. Berninghaus, and Buck Dunton often refused or were unable to move beyond static, two-dimensional scenes and figures. Thus they were unable to achieve the central goal of the regionalists: demonstrating how, over time, physical and cultural environments shaped character and outlook.

Another pressure, primarily financial, militated against more probing portraits of the Southwest. As the Atchison, Topeka and Santa Fe Railroad purchased increasing numbers of illustrations to help sell the region to tourists, the influential patron encouraged artists to paint placid, even romantic, depictions of southwestern landscapes and Native Americans and discouraged artwork that suggested any ambivalent dimension to life in the Southwest.[40] When coupled with the artists' initial reluctance to move beyond narrative, descriptive presentations of the Southwest, this pecuniary pressure proved decisive. Most southwestern artists before 1920 seemed satisfied to continue producing portraits of a romantic Southwest of placid Native Americans and Hispanics.

When New Yorker Mary Hallock Foote came west in 1876 as a new bride at twenty-eight, she had already launched a successful career as a book illustrator. During the next quarter century, largely spent in western mining camps and small towns, Foote turned out dozens of illustrations despite her role as a mother and eventually duties as bread-winner that assaulted her Victorian sensibilities and threatened her eastern soul. Gradually leaving off work on classic or eastern American literary works, she turned to sketches and woodcuts of California and Rocky Mountain scenes.[41] Her earliest frontier art reflected her tentative, romantic reactions to this strange new West, but bit by bit, although she was never much at home in the region before the 1890s, her artwork included more probing depictions of the West she was beginning to comprehend. More than anything else, Foote's treatment of women and families suggested how much the Wild West imagery of artists like Remington and Russell omitted.

Understandably, Foote's first treatments of the West betrayed her recent arrival. Her initial local-color descriptions of California, Colorado, and Mexican scenes (the Footes traveled briefly to Mexico in 1881) emphasized the exotic landscapes and romantic characters of these locations and hinted at their origins as illustrations for Foote's sketches and stories in magazines such as *St. Nicholas, Scribner's,* and *Century*. Gradually moving beyond the Bret Harte–

like illustrations of *The Water Carrier* and *The Mexican Camp* in 1878 and a picturesque Rocky Mountain scene, *At the Foot of the Pass,* in 1882, Foote produced her most notable series, *Pictures of the Far West,* in *Century* magazine in 1888 and 1889.[42]

The eleven sketches of the series showcase Foote's premier talents as woodcut illustrator and reveal her changing attitudes about the frontier West as well. A former teacher, evaluating these and the remainder of Foote's sketches, saluted her as the "best of our designers on the wood," whereas another critic praised Foote as "the dean of women illustrators," and still another concluded "she is the only woman who can claim company among the men in the field of Western picture."[43] Foote's realism in the series, her fresh material, and her steady, probing insights helped elicit these positive reactions.

Individual illustrations in *Pictures of the Far West* signify, in addition, much about Foote's West. For instance, although the subjects treated in *The Sheriff's Posse, The Last Trip In, Looking for Camp,* and *The Winter Camp* allowed for romantic or sensationalized glimpses of a Wild West, none of these works contains the shootouts, dashing horsemen or teamsters, or vicious winter weather so common in Remington or Russell. Instead, the sleeping girl in *Afternoon at a Ranch* or the serenading young woman in *The Pretty Girls in the West* reflect a gentle if isolated rural West.

Even more significant are those illustrations focusing on women. In *The Orchard Windbreak,* an attractive female serves as middle ground linkage between the wild (a fawn) and civilization (a background orchard), whereas in *The Coming of Winter* a young mother holding her baby provides domestic balance to her rifle-toting husband about to discharge his weapon. The domestic West becomes even more explicit in *The Irrigating Ditch* through the image of an aproned mother with her babe in arms standing between a full irrigation ditch and a row of sheltering trees. Altogether she symbolizes fruitfulness, settlement, and a woman's West. None of these illustrations hints of a frenetic Wild West; rather, the places and inhabitants Foote utilizes portray a West of hard work, endurance, solitude, domesticity, home, and family.[44]

Two other illustrations, *The Engineer's Mate* and *Between the Desert and the Sown,* embody Foote's most intriguing ideas about the West. The former, which appeared in *Century* magazine in 1895, centers on a stylishly dressed (probably eastern) young woman who has just arrived at an isolated railroad station. No one awaits the engineer's wife and her pile of luggage, although a young cowboy at the end of the platform stares over his shoulder at her

Mary Hallock Foote, *The Engineer's Mate.* (*Century Magazine* 50 [May 1895]: 90)

while laboring with a heavy trunk. She's alone, isolated, and separated from her cultural origins. Perhaps Foote is reiterating here the East-West conflict at the heart of so much of her fiction or commenting on the difficulties facing a young woman newly come to the West. There is also a hint of irony and mockery beyond mere physical separation.

Between the Desert and the Sown likewise overflows with cultural significance. It illuminates Foote's enlarged understanding of changes within the West and suggests how her vision, if more widely known, could have amplified understandings of the frontier. To give physical and symbolic meaning to her landscape, Foote employs a diagonal irrigation ditch to divide her scene into irrigated and arid sections. Below the ditch, next to a dark, tree-dotted sown area, stands a handsome, well-dressed young woman glancing toward a horseman to the northeast. He and his mount stir up desert dust in the distance. The cowboy represents the sole human presence above the ditch, whereas collectively the young woman, the irrigated farmland, and the homes in the lower background signify a settled West below the ditch. As the loyal wife of a hard-pressed irrigation engineer who tried to make "the desert blossom like a rose," Foote's support for reclamation projects and irrigated farming is overwhelmingly clear. Even more significant, when linked to her other portraits of the 1880s and 1890s, *Between the Desert and the Sown* indicates how much her conception of a settled West revolved around women and family. In those emphases, she moved well beyond many artistic renditions of the West created between the 1880s and World War I.

For Mary Hallock Foote, the West as frontier was significantly different from that portrayed in the artwork of Remington, Russell, and the southwestern artists. Heroic Indians and dashing cowboys are missing from her illustrations. Indeed, at the very time Wister and Remington were teaming up to trace the evolution of the cowpuncher as the central figure in frontier history, Foote filled her woodcuts with images of women, families, and irrigation ditches. Hers was a domestic, settled (albeit isolated) West much at odds with an Old West peopled with Indians, cowboys, Hispanics, and other frontier worthies such as explorers, mountain men, and prospectors. An important women's perspective too little recognized then or since, her point of view serves as an alternative to a purely masculine Wild West even while it prefigures the important perspectives of Mary Austin and Willa Cather, whose regional writings began to appear just as Foote retired from the field as an illustrator of the frontier West.[45]

II

THE WEST AS REGION

INTRODUCTION

I n the same decade that Ernest Hemingway, F. Scott Fitzgerald, and other Lost Generation writers were seeking European solace and rejuvenation for their personal and cultural dislocations resulting from World War I, hosts of other American writers and artists turned inward to search for answers to these nagging dilemmas. All across the United States, but particularly in the West and South, novelists, poets, and other intellectuals looked to their own regions and locales for remedies to postwar ills. Urges similar to those that motivated literary southerners to organize the Fugitive and Agrarian literary movements and to publish the regional cultural manifesto *I'll Take My Stand* (1930) encouraged many westerners to find parallel solutions within their region.

Other intraregional concerns ate at westerners. Throughout the early twentieth century, waves of immigrants poured into the West, redirecting its social patterns adding mainly to its urban populations but also disrupting nonurban patterns of pioneer life. If novelists, historians, and artists responded to these floods of newcomers between 1890 and 1920 by lamenting the passing of the frontier, writers and painters after World War I began to ask if the American West had not entered a new postfrontier or regional stage.

During the 1920s and 1930s, increasingly responding to this growing sense of region, editors of several literary magazines and writers like Willa Cather, H. L. Davis, and John Steinbeck probed their experiences in the Midwest, the Pacific Northwest, and California in important regional fiction. Walter Prescott Webb, Bernard DeVoto, and James C. Malin did much the same for Texas, the Rockies, and Kansas in their regional histories. Meanwhile, the midwestern artists Thomas Hart Benton, Grant Wood, and John Steuart Curry mined their Missouri, Iowa, and Kansas backgrounds in dozens of regional paintings.

Nearly all these regionalists were intrigued with several questions. How, for example, did the dynamic interplay between the physical environment and human residents spawn unique regional or subregional identities? Were westerners different from other Americans, and if so, how had those differences come about? Some regionalists, such as editor B. A. Botkin of Oklahoma's *Folk-Say* and the southwestern novelist Mary Austin, argued that the investigation, analysis, and celebration of regional folk traditions were necessary antidotes to the disorienting social and psychological changes of the 1920s. Others, like historians Webb and DeVoto, urged westerners to understand their regional birthrights and to protect them from eastern imperialists. For many others, regionalism was a satisfying credo by which to order their personal and public lives.

Gradually in the interwar years, then, the American West was reinvented. Many westerners adopted an *in*-the-West perspective on their region. Examining changes over time *within* the West rather than focusing on newcomers to-the-West, they discovered, to their satisfaction, that the West had moved beyond a frontier of cowboys and Indians. It was in the process of establishing a new cultural identity that they should not only understand but also, perhaps, champion.

Chapter 4

REGIONAL NOVELS

I n the early fall of 1927, the publication of a privately issued pamphlet in The Dalles, Oregon, dramatically illustrated a watershed in western literature, signaling that frontier literature, at least that of the Wild West variety, was under vigorous attack. Cobbled together by Northwest authors H. L. Davis and James Stevens, *Status Rerum: A Manifesto, Upon the Present Condition of Northwestern Literature, Containing Several Near-Libelous Utterances, Upon Persons In the Public Eye* harpooned several Northwest editors and professors, simultaneously ridiculing literary efforts in the region. Instead of turning out good books, Davis and Stevens asserted, western writers were producing an "interminable avalanche of tripe." Even worse, Col. E. Hofer's periodical *The Lariat* (a little magazine published in the Pacific Northwest) was little more than "an agglomeration of doggerel," displaying "colossal imbecility," "preposterous bathos," and "metrical ineptitude." The Northwest had not escaped its share of "mental weaklings, numskulls, and other victims of mental and moral affliction," and too many had taken up the teaching of short-story writing, especially in the universities of Washington and Oregon. These "posers, parasites, and pismires" had produced a "devastating flood of imbecility." Now was the time for "the young and yet unformed spirits, to cleanse the Augean stables which are poisoning the stream of Northwestern literature at the source." Those redeemers had not yet appeared, but Davis and Stevens "had a vision" and were certain that redemption was drawing nigh.[1]

Within a few weeks of the appearance of *Status Rerum*, H. G. Merriam, the indefatigable editor of *The Frontier* at the University of Montana in Missoula, transformed his campus literary magazine into a full-fledged regional journal with a new subtitle, *A Magazine of the Northwest.* Celebrating the publication of Davis and Stevens's inflammatory pamphlet, Merriam called for an outpouring of northwestern regional literature in his lead-off editorial, "Endlessly the Covered Wagon." If the Northwest had shown it was "industrially alive and agriculturally alive," Merriam wrote, it now needed to prove it was "spiritually alive" by refusing to continue to turn east for its cultural cues and by avoiding "uncourageous, unindigenous 'literary' expressions of writers too spiritually imitative and too uninspired." Merriam was convinced that an emerging critical spirit, encouraged by such outlets as *The Frontier* promised to be, could produce the kind of regional literature the Northwest needed.[2]

These two events in the fall of 1927, tucked away in the far northwestern corner of the West, symbolize major cultural shifts then taking place throughout the region. Together they illustrate a new way of interpreting the West that novelists, historians, and artists increasingly embraced during the interwar period. Along with Davis, Stevens, and Merriam, these spokesmen for a new regionalism not only pointed to the inadequacies of earlier frontier interpretations but also trumpeted the greater realism and relevance of a regional West. From the mid-1920s to the late-1930s, many interpreters of western culture leaped on this regional bandwagon.

Behind all its bombast and parody, *Status Rerum* had a serious and pointed purpose, one with which Professor Merriam and hosts of other editors and writers heartily agreed. Northwest teachers and writers, Davis and Stevens asserted, had prostituted their regional birthrights by straitjacketing regional materials within the demands of popular commercial fiction. This formula fiction, tied to the editorial demands of pulp and slick magazines, such as *Western Story Magazine, Adventure, Collier's,* and the *Saturday Evening Post,* too often overemphasized Wild West adventure, romance, and sentimentality. Unless Northwest writers were able to avoid these commercial and nostalgic traps, their fiction would remain lifeless and dull.

If *Status Rerum* provided a biting criticism of what Davis and Stevens considered the dramatic shortfall in the teaching and writing of Northwest literature, editor Merriam, while also pointing out the inadequacies of the earlier literature, furnished a brief agenda for a much-needed new regional literature. Merriam said that, beginning in 1927, *Frontier* would be a "pioneer endeavor to gather indigenous Northwest material." His journal would encourage authors "turning their gaze upon the world that makes comparison of near and far-off matters and conditions." The key to first-rate regional literature was a new "critical attitude" that allowed talented writers to understand the uniqueness of the Northwest even while they comprehended how that region participated in national and international cultural currents. Merriam added: "We in this territory need to realize that literature, and all art, is, if it is worth anything at all, sincere expression of real life. And the roots for literature should be in our own rocky ground, not in Greenwich Village dirt or Mid-west loam or European mold or, least of all, in the hot-house sifted, fertilized soil of anywhere."[3]

In the next few years, Merriam formulated a more specific definition of regionalism. When he broadened the scope of *The Frontier*, several doubters warned him that the only subjects in the region worth writing about were Indians and pioneers and that they had been buried in the dust of the past. But Merriam responded that that was a misguided approach to regional writing. Authors interested in writing regionally had to realize that these figures, their actions, and the ideas they represented were *not* buried in the past; instead they were the "inworked substance" of contemporary times. The term *inworked substance* defined regionalism for Merriam. Like the later western novelist and biographer Wallace Stegner, Merriam came to believe that writers had to understand both the past and the present in order to comprehend how the past shaped and became the inworked substance of the present. Rather than emphasizing a to-the-West approach that centered on early contacts with new lands and new peoples, regionalists had to adopt an in-the-West perspective, seeing how the interplay over time between people and the environment spawned a unique culture that defined its region. Unless aspiring writers understood this dynamic relationship between past and present, they would fail to give a full picture of a regional culture. For Merriam, *The Frontier* and other similar journals had to encourage authors to take on this broader view of their province.[4]

But, of course, H. G. Merriam was not working in a vacuum. Several earlier westerners — and, as we shall see, many of Merriam's contemporaries — were similarly intrigued with the West as region. As early as the 1860s and throughout the Gilded Age, for instance, local-color writers such as Mark Twain, Bret Harte, Joaquin Miller, and Mary Hallock Foote wrote dozens of novels and hundreds of short stories and poems describing the surface details of a frontier West. These writers emphasized vernacular speech patterns, varieties of dress, and stereotypical characterizations of miners, prospectors, engineers, prostitutes, and a wide assortment of other frontier "toughs." Description, often of picaresque figures or of provincial incidents, powered this fiction and poetry. Yet Harte and the other local-color writers, while calling attention to the varied new settings on the western frontier, were rarely interested in trying to show how a cultural environment shaped well-formed characters or spawned specific ideas.

A few predecessors of the 1920s regionalists, however, moved beyond local colorists in analyzing a developing regional culture. Of these regionalists, the nineteenth-century Californian Josiah Royce was the most noteworthy. Reared in a California mining camp and later a professor of philosophy at Harvard, Royce in the late 1880s wrote a history and a novel about his home state, both of which illustrated his thorough understanding of the unique provincial culture that had evolved in California following the Gold Rush. In *California, from the Conquest in 1846 to the Second Vigilance Committee in San Francisco: A Study of American Character* (1886) and *The Feud of Oakfield Creek: A Novel of California Life* (1887), plus a series of essays about the Far West written during the 1880s and 1890s, Royce castigated the materialistic, nativistic, and egocentric strains of California culture even while he suggested the best remedies for curing these ailments. To counter these fragmenting and destructive societal tendencies among Californians, Royce recommended a new sense of loyalty to place or community, a "wise provincialism." This cohering sense of community, this regionalism, would serve as a balance against an excessive centralizing force that threatened to homogenize all Americans. As he wrote in 1902 in his essay "Provincialism": "[I]n the present state of the world's civilization, and the life of our own country, the time has come to emphasize, with a new meaning and intensity, the positive value, the absolute necessity for our welfare, of a whole provincialism, as a saving power to which the world in the near future will need more and more appeal."

For Josiah Royce, California of the 1890s was significant not because it had once been a frontier and had reverted to primitivism in its early years but because over time it had forged a regional identity through the interplay of geography, people, and social and economic experiences. Royce was much interested in an evolving regional character and a unifying sense of community. Intrigued with what California had become in the 1890s, his excursions into state history and culture examine how the outlook of Californians had developed through the generations. Writing at about the same time as Turner, Royce chose not to spend most of his energies on the early frontier but to use those experiences as a preface to understanding California's provincialism of his day. In this respect, Josiah Royce was an important forerunner of those thinkers who were more interested in the West as a region than as a frontier.[5]

Less cerebral and far more romantic, the easterner Charles Fletcher Lummis served as another forerunner of the regionalists. His 3,500-mile walk across the country from Ohio to Los Angeles in 1884 symbolized the energetic ebullience of the man. At first a gatherer of anecdotes, a popularizer, and a describer of exotic southwestern scenes and cultures, particularly those of Indians and Hispanics, Lummis matured into a more discerning student of regional ethnic cultures. Transitioning from explorer and onlooker to participant evaluator of the Southwest, Lummis clearly moved from viewing the West as a strange frontier to seeing it as a region whose cultures needed to be understood and appreciated.

Lummis's deepening understanding of his adopted home was reflected in his wide-ranging activities. Perhaps the first to use the term "the Southwest" in referring to the region, he became a zealous investigator of the region's archaeology, architecture, language, and literature. Even more influential was Lummis's editorial work. As the editor of *Land of Sunshine/Out West,* he dragooned contributors into dealing with the history and culture of the Southwest, and in the process he became the midwife to a heightened regional consciousness. As an editor and author himself, Lummis moved beyond the local-color mentality of Bret Harte to something far deeper. And in encouraging such writers as Joaquin Miller, Sharlot Hall, and Eugene Manlove Rhodes, Lummis helped to promote a more penetrating treatment of southwestern cultures. Through his editorial work, writes his biographer, Lummis "was teacher and interpreter, and he sought to instruct . . . readers in many aspects of the Southwest—its scenic wonders, its climate, its business opportunities, its cultural potential, and its rich and romantic archaeological and historic past."[6]

Another author whom Lummis encouraged to become a notable voice in championing regionalism was Mary Austin. An Illinois native who moved to southern California at age twenty in 1888, Austin soon experienced a series of disappointments in her new home. When an unhappy marriage, the birth of a mentally disadvantaged child, and conflicts with her mother and other acquaintances complicated her life, Austin turned to her natural surroundings for renewal. After failures in farming and teaching, she resorted to writing, barely able to support herself. Gradually she discovered a sense of place and community in her relationship with the desert country. Walking throughout southern California, leisurely studying and reflecting on the links among people, animals, and the land, she developed a mystical vision of mind and nature that, she was convinced, would spawn a new culture. For Austin, as for Lummis, the desert Southwest became a restorative region to be zealously embraced.

Austin's land-based ethic infuses her best-known early work, *The Land of Little Rain* (1903). This rather loosely coordinated collection of nature sketches resembles the works of John Muir and Joseph Wood Krutch. Sensing the mutual influences of land and people — the folk wisdom that allowed accommodating residents to survive in these demanding settings — Austin foreshadowed the later regionalist stress on the shaping power of landscape. But such relationships were to be understood only after concentrated, demanding effort. Seasons, passing time, the diurnality of movement — all these must be watched carefully if one were to experience "deep-self," Austin's term for the revivifying juxtapositions of observer and surroundings. These sudden moments of epiphany would occur only after the onlooker had realized and understood her unity with the seemingly ordinary, barren landscape.

Austin's keen interest in a new appreciation of physical and cultural environments carried over into her fascination with Indians and Hispanics in the Southwest. Once she moved to Santa Fe in the early 1920s, she turned enthusiastically to supporting — and sometimes leading — efforts to protect Indian land and water rights and to sponsoring the production and sale of Indian and Hispanic arts and crafts. These actions, she argued, were part of her regionalist credo. It was not enough for the regionalist merely to deal with correspondences between people and the environment; committed regionalists must also endeavor to understand the rhythms endemic to their area and encourage residents to so adapt themselves "regionally that in the place where we live we [can] achieve a continuous process of living and expressing, neither of which [can] be mistaken for living and expressing in other localities." Self-assured, imperious, and sometimes bossy, Mary Austin was often a difficult friend, as several acquaintances have recalled; yet she never wavered in her appeals for regionalism, particularly that which "expressed in ways of living and thinking, . . . the mutual adaptations of a land and a *people*." In her books, in her support of southwestern magazines and authors, and in her call for a nurturing marriage between environment and resident, Mary Austin was a significant forerunner of the redolent regionalism that surfaced all over the West in the 1920s and 1930s.[7]

Even though such writers as Royce, Lummis, and Austin were important stimuli for discussions of regionalism, more influential were a half-dozen or so western literary magazines that commenced publication between World War I and the beginning of the New Deal. Paralleling the appearance of similar regional magazines in other sections of the country, such journals as the *Southwest Review* (from the *Texas Review*), *The Midland* (Iowa), *The Frontier* (Montana), *Prairie Schooner* (Nebraska), *Folk-Say* (Oklahoma), and *The New Mexico Quarterly* urged writers and readers not only to abandon earlier Wild West images of a frenetic frontier but also to embrace a new regionalism that included more truthful treatment of slowly emerging sectional identities. Located in university communities and edited by tub-thumping regionalists, these new journals became outlets for prose and poetry, forums for discussions of regionalism, and bulwarks against what many westerners considered the excessive influence of Europe and the American East on the West. No force was more instrumental than these journals in fostering new discussions of western regionalism during the 1920s and 1930s.

The most influential of the magazines was the *Southwest Review*. Launched in 1915 as the *Texas Review*, its name was changed in 1924 when the journal moved from Austin to Dallas. In its first decade the journal avoided a pronounced regional focus, hoping to supply an outlet for writers in the region (and outside Texas) without excessively "reeking of the soil." But when Jay B. Hubbell, later the editor of *American Literature*, assumed editorship in 1924, he decided that the *Southwest Review* would be most successful when it adapted "to the *milieu* from which it springs." Although the review would be "national in its outlook," it would "especially encourage those who [wrote] on Western themes." In the next three years, Hubbell and his staff dramatically expanded the number of subscribers; published the work of regionalists like J. Frank Dobie, Mary Austin, George Stewart, and Stanley Vestal; launched a series of essays on southwestern cities; and enlivened the journal's pages with illustrated essays and articles on southwestern art.[8]

When Hubbell abandoned Southern Methodist University for Duke in 1927, John H. McGinnis—a journalist, professor of English, and tireless editor— took over the *Review* and served until 1943. During his reign the *Review* became the best-known western regional magazine, saluted for its increasingly sophisticated and comprehensive coverage of the literature, history, art, and other cultural activities of the Southwest. While soliciting from authors who ranged from Mississippi to California, placing more stress on New Mexico, especially its painters, and initiating a series of essays on southwestern naturalists, McGinnis also emphasized the ethnic Southwest, with several publications on Indian and Hispanic cultures. Under his editorship, the journal became the outlet for a virtual who's who among southwestern writers, including historians, novelists, and critics like Walter Prescott Webb, Mody Boatright, Howard Mumford Jones, and Tom Lea. As Henry Nash Smith, chief assistant to McGinnis, has noted, even though the *Review* never "produced a theology of regionalism" and was "unsystematic and inconsistent," it was always "fertile and open to new ideas."[9] Realizing which topics interested readers and being acquainted with the writers best qualified to furnish those essays, McGinnis jawboned authors into producing timely and revealing articles for the *Review*. As editor, as superb student of clear and lively writing and thinking, and as a man of ideas committed to a balance between universal concepts often clothed in regional settings and forms of expression, John McGinnis was the most influential editor of the leading western regional magazine between the two world wars.

Launched in the same year as the *Texas Review*, *The Midland* was the outstanding regional magazine of the Midwest until its demise in 1933. Edited by John T. Frederick and located primarily in Iowa City, Iowa (before its removal to Chicago in 1930), *The Midland* championed a more explicit brand of regionalism than the other western magazines. As the editors wrote, "'We have found . . . that the Middle West possesses a regional consciousness. . . . The Middle West exists as a unit of life in the world.'"[10] Although Frederick never furnished a brief definition of regionalism, he agreed with much of what other regionalists were arguing. New York City dominated too much of American thought and culture, allowing East Coast editors to control what was published about the United States. Too often these media moguls were uninterested in midwestern writing. As a result, *The Midland* had to be the voice of the Midwest, as other journals were of their regions. Still, Frederick would not publish just anything about the region; his journal would take only the best writing, a literature that reflected a close acquaintance with the Midwest.

Influenced by Josiah Royce's call for a higher or wiser provincialism, Frederick labored for nearly two decades to keep *The Midland* alive and open to midwestern regionalism. He cajoled the region's best-known writers, such as

John G. Neihardt, Ruth Suckow, Loren Eiseley, Howard Mumford Jones, and Frank Luther Mott, to publish with him. Frederick was especially drawn to writing about the rural Midwest, and *The Midland* reflected his bias with heavy doses of farm fiction and more than a bit of hostility toward cities. A modest, unpretentious man of rural background, Frederick rarely encouraged experimentalism, preferring prose and poetry conservative in point of view, subject matter, and style. But Frederick eventually ran into the major problem facing most regional magazines: if they were not closely tied to a university, they often were in financial difficulties. When the independent-minded Frederick severed ties with the University of Iowa in 1930, he soon realized he would be unable to keep the journal alive. In 1933 he telegrammed H. G. Merriam in Missoula, requesting the Montana editor to link *The Midland* with Merriam's *The Frontier*. Although the union spelled the end of Frederick's journal, he had achieved a good deal. No less a pundit than H. L. Mencken declared *The Midland* to be "probably the most influential literary periodical ever set up in America."[11]

Meanwhile, as we have seen, Merriam had transformed *The Frontier* in 1927 from a campus literary magazine into a full-fledged regional journal. Actually, the transformation was not as abrupt as Merriam suggested. By the mid-1920s, *The Frontier* was already a regional magazine, publishing work by such authors as Dorothy Johnson, A. B. Guthrie, Jr., Oliver Wendell Holmes, Howard McKinley Corning, Norman Macleod, Frank Bird Linderman, and John K. Hutchens — all of whom either already had or would establish notable careers as western authors. Moreover, the later content mix of *The Frontier* — a balance of regional prose and poetry, selections of western history, and reviews of western books — was evident well before 1927.

The Frontier reached the apex of its significance as a regional magazine between 1927 and 1933, after which its marriage to Frederick's *Midland* diluted Merriam's regional focus and caused other problems that eventually led to its demise. Securing short stories, essays, and poems from writers like H. L. Davis, James Stevens, and Vardis Fisher during these halcyon years, Merriam was unable to attract these authors or others of superior achievement after the mid-thirties. In addition, he never enjoyed office help or aid from colleagues, which both the *Southwest Review* and the *New Mexico Quarterly* profited from. In 1931, for example, Merriam alone read through 1,100 manuscripts from more than 500 writers. In addition, the University of Montana refused to consider his editorship as part of his academic load, so at times Merriam taught fifteen hours per week, chaired the English Department, and edited *The Frontier* all at the same time. In fact, stung by administrative criticism of the time he spent as an editor and his failure to gain a terminal degree, Merriam returned to Columbia University to complete his Ph.D.—even while he kept up his horrendous load of other duties.

But despite all these major problems, *The Frontier* folded at the end of the 1930s probably for a different reason, one that Merriam had gradually come to understand several years earlier. Quite clearly, then as now, northwesterners seemed to lack the same sense of region that southwesterners, midwesterners, and southerners exhibited. When he began *The Frontier* and his other regional projects, Merriam wrote in 1934, he wanted "to make readers and writers of this region conscious of its literary achievement . . . [and to] join with efforts of other workers toward articulate expression of Northwest life, ultimately to an unmistakable regional movement." Although he detected "some consciousness of the region," there were "no signs . . . of a concerted movement."[12] Merriam was correct in this observation. The Pacific Northwest lacked a Mary Austin, a J. Frank Dobie, or a Walter Prescott Webb to champion its regional literary or historiographical efforts. In retrospect, one can recognize that Merriam's battle was a losing one: if he could not enlist the support of Seattle or Portland or the leading regional universities, he could not keep his regional boat afloat. And despite all his enthusiasm, hard work, and valuable service in encouraging a regional renaissance, Merriam lost out because the Pacific Northwest lacked a strong regional consciousness.

The most short-lived but perhaps the most boisterous of the regional magazines was *Folk-Say,* edited by B. A. Botkin at the University of Oklahoma. At first celebrating the lore of "the folk" and urging authors to collect, comment on, and assimilate folk life and legend into their writings, Botkin later cast a wider net to include more than folklore in his definition of regionalism. Published early in his career, the four volumes of *Folk-Say* (1929–32) reflected Botkin's infectious enthusiasm for folklore, on which he eventually became a nationally known authority. For Botkin, if southwesterners—indeed, all Americans interested in the New Regionalism—were to achieve a more realistic, revealing understanding of themselves and their cultural landscapes, they would have to escape from misleading Wild West images and the numbing sentimentalism of the local-color writers, which were evidence of a sense of "threatened Westernism" that regionalists needed to eradicate from their consciousness. A few years later, Botkin, although still holding to the importance of folklore, enlarged his purview. He wrote: "The conception of a regionally differentiated and interregionally related culture has something to offer to literature, namely, a subject matter (the physical and cultural landscape, local customs, character, speech, etc.), a technique (folk and native modes of expression, style, rhythm, imagery, symbolism), a point of view (the social ideal of a planned society and the cultural values derived from tradition as 'the liberator, not the confiner')." [13]

Although journalist Carey McWilliams was mistaken in pointing to Botkin and his *Folk-Say* as the chief Pied Pipers of the new western regionalism, he was correct in noting that in 1930 Botkin was a notable force in challenging regionalists to pay more attention to folk cultures so as to achieve a newer, more comprehensive understanding of their region. After he left his editorship in 1932, Botkin continued as a regional chauvinist, but on a broader, less intense, basis. [14]

The last of the major western regional journals to appear was the *New Mexico Quarterly*, which began publication in 1931. At first wobbling uncertainly between a journal of general intellectual substance for New Mexico authors and readers and a journal for regional writing, the quarterly began to find its regional focus when Professor T. M. Pearce of the English Department of the University of New Mexico (who had been an undergraduate with H. G. Merriam at Montana) became editor in 1932 and steered the journal toward the regionalist camp. Inspired by the example of the *Southwest Review*, buoyed by the encouragement and suggestions of Mary Austin and Henry Nash Smith, and supported by President James Zimmerman (who saw the *Quarterly* as one part of his plan to make the University of New Mexico a citadel for regional studies), Pearce included sections on southwestern history, folklore, and literary gossip. Not particularly innovative and no champion of the avant garde, Pearce, listening to the advice of his friend Mary Austin, made the *New Mexico Quarterly* into a prime outlet for regional writers, particularly those focusing on the Indian, Hispanic, and Anglo cultures of New Mexico. Networking with Botkin, Merriam, and the editors at *Southwest Review*, Pearce sponsored several conferences on regionalism in the early 1930s, which included such participants as Arkansan John Gould Fletcher and southerner John Crowe Ransom. Although Pearce's journal did not capture as much national attention as *The Frontier* and *The Midland*, by the end of the 1930s it was increasingly being mentioned as an important regional magazine; it eventually outlived both *The Frontier* and *The Midland*.

These magazines and their editors did not march to an explicit, well-ordered credo of regionalism, but they did agree on several points. Picturing the West solely as an adventuresome or vanishing frontier was insufficient; frontier legacies must illuminate the present so that emerging regional cultures could be described and evaluated. Further, ethnic cultures must be dealt with in the way that Frank Bird Linderman in the Northwest, John G. Neihardt in the Midwest, and Mary Austin and J. Frank Dobie all treated Indian and Hispanic peoples. These emphases on regional matters were both culturally and psychologically significant. Westerners needed to counter New York–centered cultural tendencies and to realize that America boasted a mosaic of cultures rather than a single culture. These were the goals, often understated and frequently shifting, that western regional magazines sought to achieve in the 1920s and 1930s.

By the early 1930s, then, a number of trends converged to help spawn new regional interpretations of the American West. While writers such as Josiah Royce, Charles F. Lummis, and Mary Austin were furnishing influential early examples of regionalism and a clutch of regional magazines were serving as outlets for regional writers, other developments were stimulating regionalism in complementary ways. In the mid-1920s, H. L. Mencken's popular journal, *American Mercury,* through issues devoted to the prose and poetry of western states, encouraged regional writers. In the South, the earliest publications of two literary groups, the Fugitives and the Agrarians, and the electrifying manifesto *I'll Take My Stand: The South and the Agrarian Tradition* (1930) provided similar spurs to western regionalists. All over the United States—and in Italy, France, and other parts of Europe, in fact—regionalism was in the air.[15] Indeed, the burgeoning interest in regionalism in the 1920s paralleled similar nationalist and regionalist outpourings that flooded the United States after the Revolutionary War, the War of 1812, the Civil War, World War I, and the Vietnam War. Throughout their history, Americans have often taken refuge in such movements after the trauma of war. So it was after World War I, with many disappointed Americans retreating from President Woodrow Wilson's flawed internationalism, the failed armistice, and the dissatisfying 1920s and taking refuge in what many considered the safer and more orderly havens of the local and regional. Cultural historians often give Lost Generation authors top billing in literary histories of the twenties, but regionalists merit more attention because their numbers and influence eventually proved more significant and enduring. Among western regional novelists of the interwar years, none were more noteworthy than Willa Cather and John Steinbeck. As the Alpha and Omega of western literary regionalism, representing the high points of its early and later years, these writers also illustrate its important subregional diversities. Nor should one overlook the differences between Cather's guarded optimism and Steinbeck's palpable pessimism. Unfortunately, as their places in the American literary canon grow more secure, their stock as major western regional literary figures has fallen. Such oversight, however, overlooks the full significance of Cather and Steinbeck.

Even before the full flower of regionalism blossomed in the 1920s, Willa Cather had turned out several notable western novels. Among these *O Pioneers!* (1913) and *My Ántonia* (1918) are splendid examples of western regionalism. Born in Virginia, Cather moved with her family to Red Cloud, Nebraska, in 1883. Eventually she took a degree from the University of Nebraska and produced a book of poems (*April Twilight*, 1903), a collection of short stories (*The Troll Garden*, 1905), and her first novel (*Alexander's Bridge*, 1912) before she turned to her Nebraska heritage for fictional material. In depicting the transition from frontier to region in south central Nebraska in *O Pioneers!*, a decade after Owen Wister's *Virginian* and a year after Zane Grey's *Riders of the Purple Sage*, Cather differed from these frontier writers in two ways. Rather than placing her greatest emphasis on newcomers battling new lands and peoples or on a vanishing frontier, she stressed the development of communities and the growing sense of place among several of her characters.

O Pioneers! covers roughly two decades in which the Nebraska setting and society are transformed from a pioneer to a settled community. The first of the novel's five sections, "The Wild Land," depicts German, Scandinavian, and Bohemian immigrants as a pitiful force against a blunt and demanding landscape. The land, Cather writes, "seemed to overwhelm the little beginnings of human society that struggled in its sombre wastes." Against such a forceful opponent, the men "were too weak to make any mark." The jerry-built hamlets the pioneers throw up before these obdurate forces lack "any appearance of permanence, and the howling wind blew under them as well as over them." Only the sturdiest, most insightful, and committed newcomers, like the most indefatigable and courageous of Thomas Hardy's protagonists, are a match for this raw environment.

Alexandra Bergson is such a person. Through a series of buffeting challenges to her heroine, Cather pictures her Swedish protagonist as the only character able to withstand the coercive physical and psychological experiences confronting settlers on the Nebraska Divide. Alexandra's victories carry many costs, however. She gathers several tracts of land, works them successfully, and symbolizes progress and advancement to her neighbors, but she does so at the expense of alienating two brothers, of seeing her favorite third brother murdered by a jealous neighbor, and of being separated for nearly twenty years from Carl Linstrum, her loyal admirer. Despite these disappointments and tragedies, Alexandra endures, and it is she whom Cather apostrophizes in the novel's title, with its reference to poet Walt Whitman's exuberant celebration of westward-moving pioneers.

Cather reflects the views of most western regionalists in her celebration of the beneficial results derived from the settling and cultivating of the Great Plains. Cather's heroine is neither selfish, greedy, nor wasteful in her taming of the land, helping it to blossom with wheat, orchards, and pioneer families, towns, and institutions. As the foresighted, ambitious, and level-headed daughter of her dying father, Alexandra works in tandem with the land, carefully and lovingly applying new scientific techniques as well as employing Old World agricultural practices to nurture the land for its own benefit and for the benefit of those who wish to farm it.

Cather expresses no reservations about these agricultural practices, nor is she uneasy about the society that emerges on the Divide as a result of the diligent work of Alexandra and other immigrants. Cather is notably positive in describing these changes: now "telephone wires hum along the white roads," the countryside is dotted with dozens of "gayly painted farmhouses," windmills "vibrate in the wind," the Divide "is now thickly populated," and the rich soil yields "heavy harvests." Among the sturdy tillers of the soil, ambitious Alexandra stands out. "Any one thereabouts would have told you," Cather writes, "that this was one of the richest farms on the Divide, and that the farmer was a woman."[16]

Cather's premier talents in sifting, arranging, and blending her personal experiences, her reading, and her research—all in a disarmingly straightforward style—are also clearly evident in *My Ántonia*. Here too appealing characterizations, penetrating portraits of place, and a strong awareness of historical continuities power her regional fiction. Ántonia Shimerda, the novel's memorable heroine, radiates regional energy. Even as a teenager fresh from the Old World and thrown into the maelstrom of a challenging new setting and society, Ántonia overflows with land-based strength—and innocence. As the novel progresses, she exudes an expanding sense of attachment to the land, a nourishing reciprocal relationship interrupted and coming temporarily to grief when she is uprooted, becomes a hired girl in a nearby town, and is seduced by an egocentric male symbolic of nonagricultural forces invading and corrupting the territory. Later, Ántonia redeems herself, marries, and returns to the land to become the fertile earth mother of a rambunctious brood of children, who illustrate the vivaciousness, tenacity, and fecundity of their mother and the Nebraska plains.

Jim Burden, the novel's other major character and its narrator, represents the person alienated from the shaping and restorative powers of the region. Cut off from what supports Ántonia, Jim is isolated from the land, the sustaining agricultural labor, and the cultural legacies that restore Ántonia and the other immigrant girls. He illustrates the powerlessness of a life made solely of memories. He recalls his boyhood and his early friendships with farm girls, but he cannot translate these memories into meaningful links to his surroundings, into a successful occupation (like those that sustain Tiny, Lena, and the Bohemian Marys), or into the reinvigorated vitality that drives Ántonia, reunites her with the land, and ties her to her flock of happy offspring.

Cather's characters in *O Pioneers!*, *My Ántonia*, and nearly all her other western writings act out their stories on carefully created regional stages. Employing apt descriptions of seasonal changes closely coordinated with major plot shifts pitting town against country and portraying the traumatic influence of historical change over time, Cather suffuses *My Ántonia* and her other regional fiction with an extraordinary sense of place. Her settings—sometimes broad expanses of landscape, sometimes pinpointed hamlets and homes—are much more than simple fringes on her fictional tapestries; they are a richly imagined and transcribed substances of the Great Plains (and less often the Southwest), shaping the lives of Cather's characters and enriching her plots, and thus expanding the meaning of her first-rank fiction.

Cather also greatly enlarges the significance of her regional settings through her apt use of history. In *My Ántonia*, through asides, through appealing vignettes, and through symbolic scenes, the author juxtaposes the Old World backgrounds of Mr. Shimerda, the Russian immigrants Peter and Pavel, and other newcomers with the new circumstances of pioneer Nebraska, demonstrating how these varied people react to the novel situations. If Shimerda, Peter, and Pavel cannot adjust and eventually succumb to the raw forces, others, like Ántonia and Alexandra, acclimate themselves and eventually win out in spite of their initial difficulties. Through these links between the Old

World and the New West, between past and present, as well as through the passing of time, Cather not only moves beyond the static settings of so many frontier writers but also illustrates the ever-changing complexities of history and culture that were so intriguing to regionalists. She demonstrates that regional identity results primarily from persisting cultural processes within a place and that these processes produce an identity often unique to that place and its residents despite the diversity of their experiences. Like Hardy, William Faulkner, and other notable regionalists, Cather proves that setting and character cannot be divorced; one pollinates the other. Understanding this important marriage — and building on it — Willa Cather produced the most forceful and memorable western regional fiction of the early twentieth century. But by the 1920s and early 1930s, at the same time that historians and artists were discovering a regional West, other novelists in several subregions of the West were beginning to produce notable regional fiction.

In the Pacific Northwest during the interwar years, the frontier tradition in western literature remained widely popular in the historical romances of Eva Emery Dye and B. M. Bower, and increasingly so in the popular Westerns of Ernest Haycox, Frank Richardson Pierce, and Robert O. Case. But by the 1930s, regionalist fiction had gained much attention in the Far Corner, particularly in the logging novels of James Stevens, the Idaho backcountry and Mormon fiction of Vardis Fisher, the wheat ranch settings of Nard Jones, and the proletarian stories and novels of Robert Cantwell. But the most significant of the Northwest regionalists was H. L. Davis, whose Pulitzer Prize–winning *Honey in the Horn* (1935) remains the most impressive example of Northwest regional fiction.

The son of southerners with strong Confederate sympathies, H. L. Davis grew up in a well-educated but impecunious family of wanderers. His one-legged schoolteacher father moved his wife and children throughout central Oregon, unable to stay in one spot until they landed in The Dalles in 1908. Davis matured into a loner, a standoffish and morose man and a voracious reader who impressed others with his knowledge of world literature, his skillfully composed poems, and his obvious desire to be left alone. When he came to write his first novel in the early 1930s, he drew heavily on his firsthand acquaintance with rural Oregon, laboring and migrant peoples, and a remarkable range of other rural types.

In several ways Davis achieved what many regionalists called for in literature about the West. His *Honey in the Horn,* brimming with pungent descriptions of settings and lively characterizations, is a sprawling picaresque work, revealingly portraying the Oregon countryside and overflowing with the full gamut of rural people. Taking a longer view than frontier writers like fellow Oregonian Ernest Haycox, Davis shows how experiences over time have shaped — even skewed — the lives, communities, and work patterns of Oregonians in the early twentieth century. The author sends out a young couple suffering from the bittersweet pangs of inexperienced love to wander over much of interior Oregon, where they encounter a panoply of provincial character types. Telling his yarn in a rich, racy vernacular, shot through with humor, tall tales, and more than a few dashes of exaggeration — thereby following the stated agenda of regionalists like H. G. Merriam and especially B. A. Botkin — Davis betrays his strong ties to Mark Twain, the southwestern humorists, and the cultural influences of H. L. Mencken.

A few years later, Davis made even more explicit the failures of early writing about the Northwest and the way a regionalist perspective can overcome those limitations. Poets, novelists, and journalists alike, Davis asserted, had turned cheerleader, picturing the northwest country as facing "an agricultural future second to that of no section in the world. It would become the granary of America, and all Hell could not stop it." Most of this writing, he continued, was "feeble-minded puling," falsely picturing pioneers as heroic, progressive, and community loving. Instead, newcomers to Gros Ventre (Davis's thinly disguised hometown of The Dalles) had "succeeded in whipping out of its corporate limits" enough "devilment and cussedness" to "line Hell a hundred miles." More often than not, however, pioneers to Oregon were nomadic immigrants living off the country's abundance rather than thrifty, hardworking ranchers and farmers starring in frontier stories about the Pacific Northwest. Put more succinctly, the difference between the rich regionalism Davis advocated and the stylized, "rip-roaring type of conventionalized fantasy" that dominated too many western stories was "the difference between tradition and illusion. Tradition is what a country produces out of itself; illusion is what people bring into it from somewhere else. On the record, the illusions have considerably the better of it. People keep bringing them in."[17] For Davis — as well as for his regional sidekick James Stevens, and for *Frontier* editor H. G. Merriam — a new literary reconnaissance had to be launched, re-examining the past, avoiding the stereotypical illusions of popular Westerns, and rediscovering western legacies that continued to shape regional life in the 1930s and 1940s.

In the Midwest, several fiction writers besides Cather, some of whom clustered around the regional journals *Midland* and *Prairie Schooner,* illustrate other achievements in western regionalism. Even before 1920 *Midland* editor John T. Frederick and his friend the poet John G. Neihardt were championing new emphases on regional subjects, with several midwesterners taking up these challenges between the 1920s and the end of World War II. Not surprisingly, regionalists of the Midwest addressed topics different from those in many novels of the Pacific Northwest. If Lewis and Clark, loggers, ranchers, Mormons, and the Columbia River were familiar subjects in Northwest fiction, midwesterners often peopled their stories with European immigrants, small-town residents, and increasing numbers of Native Americans. But primarily they turned to agriculturalists as subjects, thereby producing a more bountiful crop of farm novels than elsewhere in the West.

Building on the earlier interests of Hamlin Garland and other novelists of the late nineteenth century and the encouragement of John T. Frederick and *The Midland* to deal with the rural life of the Midwest, a host of midwestern writers turned out dozens of farm novels between 1920 and the end of World War II. Such writers as Bess Streeter Aldrich, Paul Corey, Herbert Krause, Herbert Quick, and Sophus Keith Winther attracted wide attention with their farm fiction. Nor should one overlook the work of Ole E. Rölvaag, whose trilogy *Giants in the Earth* (1927), *Peder Victorius* (1929), and *Their Father's God* (1931) illustrate the pronounced emphases midwesterners (including Willa Cather) placed on European immigrants and farmers in their fiction. Moving beyond the frontier depictions in Garland's best-known short stories, Rölvaag's stark and sometimes tragic accounts of Scandinavian newcomers to the bleak upper Great Plains are not limited to initial contacts between setting and pioneers. Garland's shorter fiction centered on such conflicts and the westward movement, whereas Rölvaag's novels illustrate the regionalist's attempt to present a longer, larger view of these relationships. Sketching in the biographical and sociocultural backgrounds of his two major figures, Per and Beret Hansa, and skillfully delineating the demanding new landscapes that challenge their European heritage, Rölvaag dramatizes the physical and cultural conflicts that define their lives and those of their offspring in his three novels.

Iowan Ruth Suckow likewise dealt with immigrants and agriculture. In her first novel, *Country People* (1924), a long line of German immigrants is traced from their initial settlements in the Midwest through the complexities of community building and their traumas during World War I. Impelled by materialistic motives, these German Americans discover the meaningless nature of their lives once they achieve their economic goals and retire. The wives seem particularly adrift, unable to relinquish their Old World attachments but also unable to feel comfortable as Americans. Conflicts between continuity and change also power Suckow's later novel, *The Folks* (1934). Here the controversial social changes that pervaded the United States in the 1920s and 1930s assault the Ferguson family, "the folks," to bruise and sometimes destroy family traditions as father and mother try to bequeath their values to their four children. As in other regional fiction, Suckow emphasizes change over time within a given place, trends in regional cultural identity that evolve as varied ethnic and social heritages meet, conflict, accommodate, and continue to re-form.

Meanwhile, in the Southwest, the *Southwest Review* and the *New Mexico Quarterly* were notable outlets for regional writers as well as for commentaries on the nature of regionalism. Concurrently, clusters of writers congregated around Austin, Dallas–Fort Worth, and Taos–Santa Fe, sparking a burgeoning interest in things regional. Historians, folklorists, and painters like Walter Prescott Webb, J. Frank Dobie, Alexandre Hogue, and Peter Hurd emerged as regional aficionados. And, more than any other writer, Mary Austin encouraged writers to produce stimulating, probing literature about the Southwest, including its Indian and Hispanic peoples. These groups and individuals in Texas and New Mexico challenged those in the Pacific Northwest and Iowa as the most active regional literary centers.

Even though no single writer in the Southwest emerged as the region's leading literary light, as Cather did in the Midwest and John Steinbeck did in California, several southwestern fiction writers labored to treat the region realistically. Mary Austin wrote a series of novels and books of nonfiction that illustrated her maternalistic and reformist energies aimed at "saving" Indians and Hispanics and at promoting her strong interest in folklore and feminism. In addition, Harvey Fergusson produced a series of novels — including *The Blood of the Conquerors* (1921), *Wolf Song* (1927), and *In Those Days* (1929) — that dramatized the history of the Southwest over time, illustrating the conflicts, conjunctions, and convergences that both identify and obscure the region's identity. Dissatisfied with studying the past for only the past's sake, Fergusson traced historical change over time from Spanish and Anglo entrances and tried to depict the results of these cultural conflicts and unions.

Frank Waters also focused on Hispanic and Indian cultures in his southwestern novels. *People of the Valley* (1941) and his highly regarded *The Man Who Killed the Deer* (1942) illustrate well Waters's attraction to non-Western cultures. The former novel deals with María del Valle, an ancient earthmother mestiza who utilizes her folk traditions to fight against impinging bureaucratic policies. The hero of *The Man Who Killed the Deer*, Martiniano, attempts to retain his land-based mysticism in the face of encroaching Anglo rationalism. More than most regionalists, Waters was drawn to a synthetic consciousness similar to Indian attachments to land and at odds with Judeo-Christian traditions that urged pioneers to subdue the land and to be fruitful and multiply.

Of all the subregions of the West, California was least caught up in the regionalist movement that swept across the country between the wars. Perhaps California writers, beginning with the local colorists and other contributors to the *Overland Monthly*, and later with the realists inhabiting the Bay Area and Carmel, had already experienced a nascent regionalism before the 1920s. Possibly the hundreds of thousands of newcomers who invaded California, especially the Los Angeles area, in the 1920s undermined any developing sense of area kinship. Whatever the reason, California failed to launch a notable regional magazine during the interwar years and seemed more interested in nonregional themes than were other westerners. Still, by himself John Steinbeck more than balanced the lack of regional interest among his contemporary California writers.

If Willa Cather represents an early high point in western literary regionalism, Steinbeck illustrates its full flower at the end of the 1930s. Born, reared, and educated in California, Steinbeck published several noteworthy fictional portraits of the Far West during the Depression Era, but it was for his Pulitzer Prize–winning novel *The Grapes of Wrath* (1939) — one of the half-dozen or so most notable novels written about the West — that he is deservedly best known.

Although much of Steinbeck's premier fiction deals with California and although he displayed an intimate and probing understanding of many of the sociocultural currents and conflicts that buffeted California from World War I to the 1960s, most literary historians discuss him as an author of historical, social, or proletarian fiction rather than as a regional writer. Truth to tell, Steinbeck early on became a regional writer and continued to be a regional author for most of his career. Gradually, he turned toward fictional portraits of California workers, farmers, and migrants, especially those from Oklahoma that he encapsulated in the Joads, archetypal regional migrants of the 1930s.[18]

Even before the publication of his premier work, Steinbeck proved more attuned to class differences in the Far West than were other regional novelists. In his first well-known novel, *Tortilla Flat* (1935), Steinbeck recorded the bittersweet lives of the *paisanos* of Monterey. Dreaming of successes well beyond their means or ken, Danny and his cronies are innocent vagabonds in a coercive world. Similar idealistic dreams drive Mac, the Communist labor organizer, throughout *In Dubious Battle* (1936), but he too illustrates the unrealistic, chaotic social and economic worlds Steinbeck invented for California in the 1930s. In these two novels, as well as in most of his longer works, Steinbeck recognized the conflicts among owners, investors, ideologues, working stiffs, and wage slaves—conflicts absent from most frontier or regional fiction.

Especially significant for understanding Steinbeck's views about a closing frontier and its impact on a regional West is his best-known short story, "The Leader of the People." Structured around the boy Jody's gradual perception of what his grandfather represents, the story speaks often of "westering." As grandfather says, the movement west was a " 'whole bunch of people made into one big crawling beast,' " and then he adds: " 'it wasn't getting here that mattered, it was the movement and westering.' " When Jody speaks of wanting to become a leader like his grandfather, the old man replies: " 'There's no place to go. There's the ocean to stop you. There's a line of old men along the shore hating the ocean because it stopped them.' " Lamenting the passing of the Old West, grandfather pushes on to a larger truth: " 'No place to go, Jody. Every place is taken. But that's not the worst—no, not the worst. Westering has died out of people. Westering isn't a hunger any more. It's all done. . . . It is finished.' " [19]

Grandfather implies that even though the frontier is gone physically, the spirit of the frontier—that is, westering—need not have died. As he tells his grandson, " 'I tell those old stories, but they're not what I want to tell. I only know how I want people to feel when I tell them.' " [20] What the old man wants, of course, is for *all* his listeners to understand and to act on the spirit of westering. For him, a strong link exists between the past and the New West, through the adventuring spirit that impelled people to lead others and that drove entire groups across the country. Does Steinbeck agree with grandfather that no one comprehends this possibility, and thus a powerful contribution of the frontier to the regional West has been lost? He seems to, and, interestingly, it is just this spirit of advancement and achievement that upset so many revisionists among the later postregional writers.

In *The Grapes of Wrath* Steinbeck provided his fullest picture of the economic and social eruptions that altered the Southwest during the late 1930s and that explosively transformed the region in the war years and later. He portrayed the emergent California as the economic behemoth of the West, and thus the journey of the Joads, resulting from their being tractored out of Oklahoma and being drawn down Route 66 by the images of Eldorado and the pot of gold at the end of the California rainbow, typified a regional transformation that Steinbeck realized owed as much to myth as to fact. The Golden State was arising as the new pivot of the modern West, a dramatic series of occurrences that Steinbeck portrayed in much of his best regional fiction. He also understood, well before many historians and other writers, that California was rapidly becoming a new cultural citadel on the West Coast. Depicting the class, subregional, and ethnic diversity (his Okies seem as much a separate ethnic group as do others who exhibit class and geographical coherence) that have flavored as well as divided modern California, Steinbeck proved to be a discerning regional and cultural historian well before journalists, scholars, and other California watchers described the state as a barometer of American ethnic and racial diversity—Los Angeles as the new Ellis Island of the United States.

If Steinbeck treats the Joads and other migrants as products of their Oklahoma experience, he also implies, perhaps unknowingly, how imported sociocultural backgrounds might fare in later California. True, the Joads, especially the men, seem defeated one by one in a new society that calls for social organization, economic and technological knowledge, and cultural understanding well beyond their experience or training. Yet in the final scene when Rose of Sharon breast-feeds a starving man after she has lost her own newborn child, Steinbeck suggests that a persisting courage and humanitarianism among the Joads, particularly that which the daughter inherits from Ma Joad, insures the perilous continuity of family and culture. In this regard, *American Exodus,* James Gregory's provocative examination of Okie cultural legacies in modern California, furnishes an intriguing substantiation of persisting sociocultural trends at which Steinbeck only hinted in his premier regional novel.[21]

Finally, *The Grapes of Wrath* not only reveals dramatic social and economic trends transforming the Southwest, it also illustrates new attitudes toward California lurking on the ideological and historiographical horizons. Steinbeck's novel serves, in this regard, as an exemplar of western regional fiction but also, as we shall see, as a forerunner of the postregional West that arose after World War II and during the 1960s.

By the end of the 1930s, writers scattered over the American West, having experienced the singular histories of their subregional Wests, were producing fiction dramatizing these unique experiences. Rather than treating the West as Wister, London, and writers of Westerns had, as a new frontier arena of contact and perhaps conquest, the regionalists, from Willa Cather to John Steinbeck, tried to show how a regional West through time had produced new character types and mentalities. Many regional historians and painters came to similar conclusions, but their routes of discovery often differed from those the regional novelists pioneered.

Chapter 5

REGIONAL HISTORIES

In 1929 when the first national history conference to study the trans-Mississippi West convened in Boulder, Colorado, it gathered in the midst of a regionalist revival. Called together two years after the publication of *Status Rerum* and Willa Cather's *Death Comes for the Archbishop* and one year after the appearance of Thomas Hart Benton's painting *Boomtown* and John Steuart Curry's canvas *Baptism in Kansas,* the historians at Boulder reflected the transition from frontier to region already underway in western historiography.

Although ill health kept Frederick Jackson Turner, the titan in the field, from attending, his presence shadowed many of the sessions. Indeed, several of his former students, including Herbert Eugene Bolton, Colin B. Goodykoontz, Archer B. Hulbert, and Joseph Schafer, were present, as were others like Frederic Logan Paxson and Percy Boynton, who illustrated the suasive power of Turner's frontier interpretations of the West.

Concurrently, the historians at Boulder represented important changes invading western historical writing. At the same time that magazine editors, novelists, and painters were plumping for regional perspectives on the West, increasing numbers of historians were also realizing that the western past was much more than a frontier now vanishing over the horizon. At Boulder, Walter Prescott Webb presented an overview of his regional approach, which appeared in expanded form in *The Great Plains* two years later; geographer Carl Sauer argued for a cultural landscape perspective on western history;

and Bolton urged listeners to follow a Borderlands schema in writing about the West. These regionalists at Boulder in 1929, as well as others like Bernard DeVoto and James C. Malin, supplied another vista by which to define the West: as a region or group of subregions that were developing their own separate identities. In the 1920s and 1930s, and even well past World War II, these historians furnished a new regional interpretation of the West that jostled with the earlier and persisting view of the West as frontier.[1]

Even though Frederick Jackson Turner exhibited a lifelong interest in regionalism and spent more time and energy working on sections than on frontiers, he is rarely recognized as a founding father of western historical regionalism. In truth, however, his frontier and sectional ideas were linked from the time of his first publications and remained so until the end of his career.

Turner's earliest essays carry glancing references to sections or sectionalism, and both of his books are rightly considered regional studies; but he did not devote extensive discussion to the nature of sections until midcareer. In "Problems in American History" (1892), for example, he urged historians to study sections or regions of the East Coast and the "extension of these sections, with their conflicting characteristics, toward the West." Even in his monumental essay "The Significance of the Frontier in American History" (1893) Turner spoke briefly of the regions left behind as frontiers opened up, developed, and then moved on west. Through its democratizing and nationalizing tendencies, Turner was convinced, the westward-moving frontier would keep older sections from the divisive competition that had led to the Civil War. As Fulmer Mood concluded, Turner's famous essay "is not only a plea for the study of the West; it is also, though to a smaller extent, a plea for the study of the other three historic sections that had grown up on the Atlantic Coast."[2]

Turner's interest in sectionalism and regionalism did not emerge in a vacuum. Students of American geography and demography, writers such as John Wesley Powell and Josiah Royce, Turner's mentor William Francis Allen, and dozens of European scholars were clearly intrigued with studying American history regionally. Yet Turner seemed several steps ahead of these commentators, especially his American colleagues. When the editor of *The Atlantic* proposed a series of essays "report[ing] civilization" in three or four American regions, Turner replied with a lengthy, provocative letter outlining the possibilities for studying American regions. "This [letter] is," wrote Mood, "the high-water mark for the nineteenth century, of serious thinking on the nature and utility of the concept of the section in American history."[3]

As always, Turner's enthusiasm outran his ability to complete his projects. He made promises to undertake essays or books on regional topics, but other promises, family responsibilities, and fishing trips delayed or derailed his intentions. As he told one editor, "I can't teach and write at the same time." Still, at midcareer and later Turner turned out several essays that focused explicitly on regional topics, including "Is Sectionalism Dying Away?" "Sections and Nations," "Geographical Sectionalism in American History," and "The West– 1876 and 1926: Its Progress in a Half-Century." Obviously differing in approach and content, these articles nevertheless emphasized the essential ingredients of Turner's ideas about regionalism: sectionalism or regionalism resulted primarily from the interplay between physiographic places (topography) and the incoming peoples who entered and inhabited them. From this marriage of varied places and varied ethnic and racial stocks came recognizable regional identities. In Turner's words, "the earth's surface is divided into geographic entities, regions, where the relations of environment and peoples, resources, position, resulting economic, social, political and cultural phenomena, have affected the history of civilization and the burning questions of contemporary diplomacy and government."[4]

Much of Turner's thinking about sections appears in capsule form in his key essay "The Significance of the Section in American History," which he read before the State Historical Society of Wisconsin in 1924, the year he retired from Harvard. Here Turner summarized how sections arose as a result of unique mixes of "physical geography and the regional settlement of different peoples and types of society," reminding his listeners too that these emerging sections had eventually turned the United States into a mosaic of pulsating, influential regions. Now that the frontier had closed, Americans needed to take more cognizance of these persisting sections, realizing that sectionalism gone wrong could lead to civil wars, but as his Harvard colleague Josiah Royce pointed out, regionalism, when understood and nourished, was a positive, sustaining ingredient of American history and culture.

Not satisfied simply to point out how regionalism had shaped the American past, Turner turned to the present and future significance of the country's regions. Voting patterns, economic competition, and numerous other rivalries continued to stem from this "geography of culture." Like the good New Historian he was, Turner reminded his audience, as he had in his first essays thirty years earlier, that every generation had to rewrite its history in light of present-day concerns. Politicians, economists, and custodians of American culture who failed to understand and take into consideration the powerful ongoing influences of regionalism overlooked one of the molding forces of the past and present. Turner was also convinced that "sectional self-consciousness and sensitiveness" were likely to increase when "crystallized sections [felt] the full influence of their geographical peculiarities, their special interests, and their developed ideals, in a closed and static nation." Perhaps Turner overemphasized the future significance of regionalism, but he stood on surer ground in his closing argument that "national action" of the future could not overlook "the fact of a vast and varied Union of unlike sections."[5]

If these essays summarized Turner's ideas about regionalism, his two book-length studies illustrated how historians might use a regional approach to the American past. Too many followers of Turner (and his critics) overlook the organization of *Rise of the New West, 1819–1829* (1906) and the posthumously published *The United States, 1830–1850* (1935), in which he traced developments in the North, South, and West in their progress from frontier to region. Moving beyond the emphases of frontier historians (including, sometimes, himself) on the period of initial European or American contact with new lands and new peoples when frontiers first opened, he treated postfrontier eras in which institutional and sociocultural developments evolved from nascent gatherings into regional communities. Devoted primarily to eastern sections of the country, these two books provided paradigms that western historians, often calling themselves Turnerians, have been slow to follow. In his writings on regionalism, Turner clearly went beyond a to-the-West approach to portray neither process nor place but process *within* place. Turner opened both of his books with overviews of America's major regions and then attempted to show how these regional experiences helped to influence the subsequent events and policies of the periods covered. Toward the end of his career, Turner wondered whether he had made these regional emphases sufficiently clear, or whether he should have been a more enthusiastic cheerleader for a regional perspective. Perhaps, but Turner, though an ardent advocate for his views, was rarely a regional chauvinist. That posture more naturally suited Walter Prescott Webb and Bernard DeVoto, who took up the cudgels of regionalism with an enthusiasm — and pugnaciousness — that Turner avoided.[6]

Of all the western regionalists, Walter Prescott Webb was the most spirited — and perhaps the most defensive. Westerner and southerner, dirt farmer's son and university professor, Texan and Oxford lecturer, Webb's life embraced a series of contradictions that powered and peppered his regionalism with a conflicting sense of place and intellectual insecurity. Throughout his life Webb battled a searing inferiority complex, even after he had climbed to the very apex of his profession. In his autobiography, Webb succinctly summarized his life: it had been a series of " 'deep humiliations and pleasant surprises.' " [7] Not surprisingly, his writings repeatedly betray these ambiguous impulses.

In the same year that Turner published his regional essay "Sections and Nation" (1922), Webb discovered, in a rainy moment of epiphany, the central idea of his career. In a flash of insight he realized that his region, the Great Plains, with its arid, treeless terrain, allowed for some kinds of activity and not others. His burst of illumination was, of course, the crux of regionalism: regional identity emerged over time within a specific place as a result of the mixing of environmental and cultural forces. Like so many other westerners in the 1920s, Webb sensed that the national culture and literature of that era did not reflect the experience of westerners. Concurrently, they realized that the frontier was gone even though little writing about the West dealt with a postfrontier era.

Specific personal and cultural forces further shaped Webb's career in the 1920s. Realizing he would need a doctorate in order to keep his position as a history professor at the University of Texas, Webb went north to the University of Chicago to take his degree. When he attempted to sit for his comprehensive exams before finishing his first year of residency, however, he failed. Instead of admitting that he might be rushing things, Webb convinced himself that his Yankee instructors were demanding procedures and accomplishments inconsistent with his career, that his eastern and northern professors were bent on dismissing his regional background and interests. When he returned to Austin without a Ph.D., a spirit of revenge seems, in part, to have driven him to write a book that would both defend his region and background and prove his abilities as a scholar. Eventually, *The Great Plains* was Webb's answer to those Chicago "folks" whom he considered supercilious and insensitive in their attitudes toward Texans and graduate students in general. [8]

Meanwhile, other intellectual sources had been at work on Webb. Although he probably underplayed Turnerian influences on his thinking, his pathbreaking conceptions about the Great Plains seem to have derived more from his own life and distinctive patterns of learning than from the Turnerian heritage that so shaped contemporary thinking about the West. For Webb, the ideas of Lindley Miller Keasbey, a controversial University of Texas professor of economics, and, later, institutional history, were paramount. Keasbey's teaching and thinking, Webb wrote much later, influenced everything he wrote, for he gave Webb "a method of investigation and thinking I have never found in any other teacher." That method was the study of the crucial and ever-changing relationship between the environment and human institutions. Webb's notes from Keasbey's lectures are a revealing introduction to much of what Webb wrote for the next fifty years.[9]

These strains of experience and conviction converged in the mid-1920s, when Webb embarked on what he always considered his most important project, the writing of *The Great Plains*. Gathering materials from a plethora of sources, Webb began to write in 1927 and finished a draft in five months of Herculean effort, ten-to-twelve-hour days of two-fingered typing. He later recalled the effort as like "the feeling and the exultation of an explorer who was charting a new course into a wild, new, and intellectually little known country. I loved the task passionately and touched depths I never dreamed I possessed — depths of subconscience [*sic*] — in its construction."

Reviewers nearly unanimously saluted *The Great Plains* as a brilliant new interpretation of American history. Both published reviews and private correspondence praised Webb for his innovative research, his clear approach, and his provocative conclusions. As an example, Frederic Logan Paxson, winner of the Pulitzer Prize six years earlier for his frontier overview, hailed Webb's *magnum opus* as "the most useful book on the West that has appeared in many years, doing for one of Turner's sections or provinces what no writer has yet done for any other."[10]

Paxson's astute observation hit dead center. What the novels of Willa Cather and John Steinbeck did for western literary regionalism and what the early paintings of Thomas Hart Benton, Grant Wood, and John Steuart Curry did for western regional art, Webb's *Great Plains* did for western regional historiography. In fact, Webb — more explicitly than most regionalists — prefaced his pathbreaking work with a useful definition of regional culture: "the Great Plains environment . . . constitutes a geographic unity whose influences have been so powerful as to put a characteristic mark upon everything that survives within its borders." He then proceeded to show, beginning with the powerful Great Plains landscape, how that area had acted upon (and was acted on by) a series of invaders.[11] Like an observant cultural geographer (geographers and anthropologists markedly influenced Webb), he provided illuminating analyses of successive cultural landscapes being laid down one on another to form

Mysteries of the Great Plains

Literature of the Great Plains

New laws for land and water

The search for water

Transportation and fencing

The cattle kingdom

The American approach

The Spanish approach

The Plains Indians

The natural environment

↓

Mysteries of the Great Plains
Literature of the Great Plains
Laws for land and water
The search for water
Transportation and fencing
The cattle kingdom
The Americans
The Spanish
The Plains Indians
The natural environment

↑

The Great Plains

A separate culture

In *The Great Plains*, Walter Prescott Webb sought to show how many distinct influences were compressed and bound together to form a regional identity that was, like a laminate, stronger than its individual parts.

a Great Plains identity. Webb accomplished what no previous western historian had attempted; he clearly traced the historical development of a regional culture rather than merely describing a series of movements into the region. To illustrate this newly formed regional culture, Webb summarized and evaluated the literature of the Great Plains in his penultimate chapter, suggesting that the plains were truly a separate, identifiable region because they had produced their own literature (see flow chart).

Webb explored the major themes of *The Great Plains* throughout his career, but in his third book, *Divided We Stand: The Crisis of a Frontierless Democracy* (1937), Webb took a sharp new turn. Convinced early on that the North (those states supporting the Union in the Civil War) had invaded and conquered the South and was now duplicating those conquests in the West, Webb returned to this thesis in *Divided We Stand,* producing a manifesto whose theme was "the economic imperial control by the North over the South and the West." At the same time, he made clear his bonding with the regionalists when he wrote that "the time has come to define the West as a region, and not as a movement or a direction."[12]

Webb pointed to several blatant examples of northern hegemony over the South and West. He argued at length that the West and South had become colonies, that they lagged behind the North because that overbearing region used the tariff, Civil War pensions, and patent monopolies to strangle regional competition. When Webb's publishers tried to get him to soft-pedal some of his assertions, he accused them of censorship and bias. More outspoken and vociferous — and perhaps more defensive — than most other western regionalists, Webb asserted that the economic depression in the West and South resulted in large part from a century-long domination by outside (northern) interests. Similar to the southern Agrarians and the outspoken contributors to the southern regionalist tract *I'll Take My Stand* (1930), Webb called for the recognition and then defeat of these alien influences. In *Divided We Stand*, Webb likewise followed the path of the southern sociologist Howard Odum, who urged the careful, systematic application of regionalism to current socioeconomic problems.

Among the other western regionalists, Bernard DeVoto most closely paralleled Webb. Born in Utah of a Mormon and Catholic heritage, DeVoto lived out a life of dramatic tensions: West and East, novelist and historian, and enthusiastic and encouraging friend and savage critic. His biographer, Wallace Stegner, encapsulates DeVoto in a memorable one-sentence profile: "flawed, brilliant, provocative, outrageous, running scared all his life, often wrong, often spectacularly right, always stimulating, sometimes infuriating, and never, never dull."[13]

The widely read essays DeVoto produced about the regional West in the 1930s and 1940s vied with Webb's *Divided We Stand* as the most influential statement of the West-as-colony-of-the-East leitmotif. Although they differed in approach and conclusions, DeVoto and Webb nonetheless shared the pronounced conviction that most westerners — and many other Americans as well — little understood the recent West and the pressures on it, and they were certain that they should provide those others with much-needed information and instruction on the dilemmas of the contemporary West.

DeVoto wielded his lively and sometimes acid pen in *Harper's* for more than a generation, lashing out at cattlemen, legislators, and easterners for not protecting the West from grasping corporations and politicians. His point of view was nowhere clearer than in his notable essay "The West: A Plundered Province" (1934). Depicting the West as a victim of selfish investors and insipid policy-makers, DeVoto emphasized the theme of western colonialism so prominent in later writings about the West. Like Webb in *Divided We Stand,* DeVoto stood convinced that the East (for Webb, the North) so dominated the West that it had plundered the newer region, exploiting its natural resources, passing inapplicable land legislation for its arid lands, and generally caring little about its future. But DeVoto also noted that the West had learned valuable lessons—in particular, individualism did not work in the West; cooperation and careful planning were necessary to overcome the difficult barriers westerners faced. These lessons, DeVoto asserted, easterners and many legislators had not learned. The West must teach them.

A dozen or so years later, while repeating his criticisms of eastern mistreatment of the West, DeVoto turned to a new foe: greedy interests within the West itself. His earlier criticisms of eastern investors and bureaucrats were light jabs compared to the knockout blows he rained on western livestock men and politicians who, he was convinced, were willing to sell off the western domain and relentlessly exploit its resources. These "Western despoilers," DeVoto charged in "The West Against Itself," were "hellbent on destroying the West," liquidating "all the publicly-held resources" of the region. Their ambivalent platform amounted to simply telling the government, "Get out and give us more money." This western paradox, calling for the end of eastern economic domination and yet displaying a shameless willingness to trade away a resource birthright for a brief and uncertain future, became DeVoto's new target. If westerners were unwilling to protect their land, lumber, and wilderness areas, DeVoto vowed, others would have to do it for them. Beginning as a regionalist of the Webb camp, attacking easterners as the evil invaders who forced an economic colonialism on the West, DeVoto now turned his big guns on westerners too driven by greed to understand the need for regional cooperation and a sense of community.[14]

Another regionalist, Kansas historian James C. Malin, a contemporary of Webb and DeVoto, shared their tendency to harpoon opponents, but his interests, his foes, and his historiographical approaches differed markedly from theirs. Like Webb, Malin spent nearly all of his life in one area. Although born in North Dakota, Malin moved with his family to Kansas when he was ten. Educated in Kansas public schools and later at Baker University and the University of Kansas, Malin was hired by the history department at Kansas in 1921 and remained there until he retired in 1963.

In the 1920s and early 1930s, Malin wrote books and several essays on general topics in American history and also a pioneering study *Indian Policy and Westward Expansion* (1921), but in the mid-1930s he turned to the Kansas grasslands, agricultural history, and historiography, which remained his major emphases for the next generation. In a key essay, "The Turnover of Farm Population in Kansas" (1935), which was later included in what he considered his most significant book, *The Grassland of North America: Prolegomena to Its History* (1947), Malin focused more analytically than any of the other regional historians on the dynamic relationships between land, settlers, and regional cultural identity. In scrutinizing these divergent unities, Malin revised Turner and Webb, disagreed with alarmist interpreters of the Plains, and called for a more optimistic view of a future through a relativistic "possibilism." Malin's careful study of ecology, census patterns, and other scientific and demographic sources that contemporary western historians rarely utilized convinced him that scholars must eschew geographical determinism, lock-stepped theories of human behavior, and pessimistic visions of the future.[15]

Above all, the Kansas curmudgeon strove to infuse his grassland studies with interdisciplinary insights. Trained in ecology and history, and knowledgeable in biology and the social sciences, Malin entirely committed himself to presenting a holistic view of the grasslands. In doing so, he often broke new ground in interdisciplinary research, particularly in his seminal work in environmental and demographic history. Additionally, he challenged the conclusions of Turner and Webb, asserting that "the contriving brain and the skillful hand" of mankind had disproved—and would continue to disprove—their "closed-space doctrines." Malin was totally convinced that pessimists, planners, and alarmists were always mistaken in their predictions of environmental Armageddons, their calls for massive government involvement in environmental design, and their warnings of farming and grazing disaster. For him, reformers and government planners were driven by skewed agendas, so he continuously called for the close study of the total history of regions and subregions. His own studies convinced him that no landscape suffered from environmental deficiencies but instead benefited from rainfall, terrain, and climate suited to the flora and fauna of that locale. If mankind could learn this valuable lesson, Malin concluded, adjustments and accommodations would allow them to live fruitfully on varied physical landscapes.

Unfortunately, Malin's unwillingness to allow editors and copyeditors to refine his turgid prose and his reluctance to revise for publishers who could have circulated his work reduced his influence. Choosing instead to issue privately many of his writings and to avoid historical conferences in his later years, Malin short-circuited the impact his provocative writings could have had on his contemporaries. Still, his lifelong commitment to the in-depth study of Kansas and his illuminating research in local sources continue to illustrate his close ties to regional thinking about the American West.

Another important moment in the history of western regionalism occurred when, in December 1932, Herbert Eugene Bolton, Sather Professor of History at the University of California at Berkeley, presented his presidential address, "The Epic of Greater America," before the American Historical Association's annual meeting in Toronto, Canada. Since the AHA was meeting for the first time in its fifty-year history outside the United States, Bolton's enthusiastic presentation on the need to see the United States in broader perspective was particularly timely. Bolton's call for a larger hemispheric view was likewise an appropriate one, considering the directions his thinking and teaching had moved in his thirty-year career. A regionalist too, Bolton boldly fathered two concepts that broke sharply with the visions of other western regionalists between the wars.

A Wisconsin farm boy who studied history with Turner at Madison at the undergraduate and master's levels and who completed a doctoral dissertation on "The Free Negro in the South before the Civil War" at the University of Pennsylvania in 1899, Bolton a dozen years later was named professor of history at the University of California. By then he was a nationally recognized authority on Spanish influences in the New World. Rising rapidly to the top of his field, Bolton as a teacher, as the author of a mounting number of essays and books, and as the editor of a series of research guides and collections of significant documents urged students and scholars to pay much more attention to Spain's notable rule all along the southern border of the United States from Florida to the Pacific Coast. Bolton synthesized this perspective in his best-known volume, *The Spanish Borderlands: A Chronicle of Old Florida and the Southwest* (1921), which seventy-five years later remains a central narrative of the Borderlands regional school.[16]

Even though the term *Borderlands* was not Bolton's, he represented and spoke for its central theme: students and scholars must pay more attention to the strong Hispanic influence on the southeastern coastal areas from Florida to Louisiana and present-day southwestern borders with Mexico from Texas to California. In his preface to *The Spanish Borderlands,* Bolton reminded readers of the important linguistic, literary, architectural, religious, and other cultural legacies of the Spanish presence in the coastal and border areas. Here was the same regional doctrine he preached to thousands of undergraduates and hundreds of graduate students at the University of California. Over time, he said, evidence of a new kind of Spanish-American society and culture had emerged along the southern portions of what became the United States; those experiences must not be overlooked in interpreting the United States and its West.

In his presidential address to the AHA, Bolton painted an even larger, more complex picture. Severely condensing the outline of his Americas course, which sometimes enrolled a thousand students at Berkeley, Bolton told his audience that they must study the varied European influences on the New World, from northern Canada to the southern cone of South America. Moving far beyond the Anglo-American frontier to which Turner had introduced him at Wisconsin, Bolton had become an intrepid revivalist for his Greater America doctrine. For more than three decades, he sent out his evangelizing disciples by the drove to carry on his work of indoctrinating historians with the importance of the Borderlands and beyond that of Greater America.

Revealingly, the preachments of Bolton and his followers converted far fewer historians than those who chose to follow Turner (and perhaps Webb too) even though Bolton trained a hundred doctoral students and more than three hundred master's students — far more than any other western historian. Perhaps because Bolton's two regional emphases demanded too much work in non-American sources, perhaps because most American historians have not embraced comparative work, or perhaps because Bolton preached his regional doctrines better than he practiced them (he rarely produced systematic, thorough studies of sociocultural trends throughout an extended area), Boltonians have never exerted the influence on western historiography that the students of Turner and Webb have. Ultimately, the Boltonians may become more influential, however. If they can forge links between Bolton's Hispanic-centered emphases and the concerns of Chicano historians, or if the Boltonians can produce more thorough and analytical works like the recent essays and books of David J. Weber, the number of converts to the study of the Borderlands could mushroom. A burgeoning Mexican-American population, increasing interest in the U.S.–Mexican border, and the continuing westward tilt toward the southwestern parts of the United States (as well as toward Florida) promise a growing concern for the regional cultural themes that intrigued Bolton and his disciples earlier in the century.

As notable as their ideas were, Turner, Webb, DeVoto, Malin, and Bolton were not the whole story of western regional historiography. In fact, as the interwar years wore on, regional magazines and government programs also became increasingly important agencies for regionalism. At *The Frontier*, for example, H. G. Merriam instituted an "Open Range" column and a "Historical Section" as two outlets for the publication of reminiscences and manuscript diaries, travel narratives, and collections of pioneer letters. More interested in publishing these nineteenth-century documents and twentieth-century recollections than were other regional editors, Merriam thought pioneer letters were particularly revealing sources for social historians attempting to recapture the everyday life of the past. Toward the end of the 1930s, he also published lists of words, gatherings of regional lore, and interviews that employees of the Federal Writers' Program had collected.

Several other western journals encouraged the study of regional history without emulating Merriam's *Frontier*. Instead, *The Midland, Prairie Schooner,* the *Southwest Review,* and the *New Mexico Quarterly,* eschewing the publication of original nineteenth-century sources or modern western reminiscences, carried dozens of articles discussing the regional literary, artistic, institutional, and folk cultures of the geographical areas they represented. Early on, every issue of *Prairie Schooner* included a brief biographical sketch of a midwestern author such as Willa Cather, Ole Rölvaag, Ruth Suckow, Hamlin Garland, and Bess Streeter Aldrich. Later, western historian John D. Hicks contributed notable essays about the Midwest. Even more numerous were the essays on regional cultural topics in the *Southwest Review* and the *New Mexico Quarterly*. As one overview of regionalism noted, essays in these two journals usually dealt with "the present-day regional issues, or with plans and suggestions for future regional action."[17] In doing so, they paralleled the sociocultural regionalism that Howard W. Odum and Lewis Mumford championed more than the literary regionalism that H. G. Merriam and John T. Frederick espoused in *The Frontier* and *The Midland*.

Federal New Deal programs likewise encouraged western local, state, and regional historical research and writing just as they supported regional efforts in theater, art, and music. As a part of the WPA, the Federal Writers' Project

(FWP) endeavored to support writers and others out of work during the Depression. Under the direction of former journalist and theater director Henry Alsberg, the FWP produced nearly a thousand publications, including a hundred guides to states and territories, cities, and regions. In all these projects, as well as in the FWP's stepchild, the Historical Records Survey, the West participated fully.

Several leading western regionalists played a central role in the FWP. Frederick of *The Midland*, Merriam of *The Frontier*, Lowry C. Wimberly of *Prairie Schooner*, and Botkin of *Folk-Say* either served as state directors, greatly influencing state programs, or in Botkin's case, directed a national segment of the program. As authors of state guides and as supporters of the collecting and publishing missions of the state programs, these regional editors not only served as links between other states and federal programs but also made room in their journals for essays, sketches, and gatherings of folklore that FWP writers produced.

No one better illustrates the close connection between western regional historiography and literature and the direct influence of a government-sponsored project such as the FWP than does Vardis Fisher, who served as the director of the Idaho state FWP from 1935 to 1939. An Idaho native of rural background, Fisher had already earned a Ph.D. in English literature from the University of Chicago and had published several novels before he reluctantly took on the state directorship (H. G. Merriam urged him not to do so). Irascible, headstrong, and impatient but an indefatigable worker, Fisher wrote most of the 400-page state guide in ten months. As he told an interviewer nearly thirty years later, "I worked nearly sixteen hours a day. . . . I was determined to get the *Idaho Guide* out first, and, of course, I did."[18]

But Director Henry Alsberg and his Washington staff labored overtime trying to head off Fisher and to publish the Washington, D.C., guide first. Initially, the FWP administrators attempted to censor Fisher's presentations, forcing him to drop such remarks as saying that Pocatello was "the ugliest of the larger Idaho cities." Next, they tried to ensure that he followed all the mandated guidelines while changing the original requirements and instituting dozens of others. The bureaucrats even sent a trusted assistant to Boise to sabotage Fisher's efforts, but, working on the assistant's thirst for whiskey, Fisher again derailed the Washington efforts.[19]

In the end, the *Idaho Guide* appeared first and received widespread positive notice. Reviewers like Bruce Catton and Bernard DeVoto hailed the volume as a valuable compendium of local history, a guide to national self-understanding, and a well-written example of regional literature. Few of the other state volumes were as vividly written as Fisher's, and no other state director accomplished as much as he on his $200-a-month job, but the other state FWP projects and their publications palpably added to the growing interest in regional history at the end of the 1930s. Here was but one example of government funding and activity that added to the regional tide already sweeping across the country before New Deal policies joined that flood tide. Eventually, similar federal support also influenced regional painters throughout the West.

Chapter 6

REGIONAL ART

M any of the ideas and issues that galvanized regional novelists and historians also sparked painters during the interwar years. Midwestern artists such as Thomas Hart Benton, Grant Wood, John Steuart Curry, as well as others like Alexandre Hogue, the Dallas Nine, and the New Mexican Peter Hurd, became convinced that their paintings must emerge from the physical and cultural environments they knew best rather than from European or eastern American trends such as Impressionism, modernism, and other artistic approaches they considered alien. Although no artistic credo unified these artists and although their diverse training and experience were reflected in their work from the 1920s into the 1950s, these painters nonetheless illustrated many of the ideological and cultural biases that motivated western authors and historians during the same period.

Too often historians and art critics have mistakenly tied the regionalist painters to events and issues of the Depression and the New Deal era when, clearly, the ideas and trends that spawned their earliest regionalist paintings arose before the 1930s. Indeed, as they were for other regionalists, federal policies and agencies, as well as other events of the thirties, encouraged and supported regional ideas and trends already well underway as the decade opened.

When Thomas Hart Benton retreated to his native state of Missouri in 1935, he was returning to the place where his mind and heart had been increasingly moving in the last decade. In fact, Benton is a classic example of Wallace

Stegner's western "square," who goes away to experience his homeland from afar before he can return to a fuller understanding and use of his own region. The theme of returning home is crucial to comprehending the career and ideology of Thomas Hart Benton.

Born in Neosho, Missouri, in 1889, Benton was reared there and in Washington, D.C., while his father served four terms in the U.S. House of Representatives. Gaining a modicum of art training in the nation's capital, in Missouri, and later at the Art Institute of Chicago, he finally decided to go abroad to study at the Académie Julian and elsewhere in Paris. There he introduced himself to the past masters as well as to a full run of the more contemporary Impressionists and modernists in the years from 1908 to 1911. Returning to the United States, he threw himself into the many artistic coteries alive in New York City, experimenting with modernism, including the color and tonal patterns of the Neo-Impressionists and Synchronists. Wrestling with a plethora of forms and styles, he seemed excessively tentative and immature in most of his artistic ventures during the teens.

Meanwhile, other influences impelled Benton in new directions. The French theorist Hippolyte Taine's ideas about the shaping influences on artists of race, time, and place, the resurfacing Populist influences of his family's heritage, his reading of works of social criticism and historiography, and his service in World War I gradually led him away from European and modernist influences and redirected him toward his American and midwestern past. Gradually the heritage of his own country, especially the stories of the common folk, replaced the individualistic, experimental aestheticism of the modernists as his central narrative.

Some of these transformations surfaced in Benton's work in the early and middle 1920s. Between 1919 and 1926 he planned and executed ten panels of his mural *American Historical Epic,* in which he attempted to depict a people's history of the United States. The completed sections, displaying Benton's gradual movement from Europe-trained artist to American scene painter, treat the earliest periods of discovery, settlement, and expansion, revealing a sympathetic attitude toward Indians, religious figures, and explorers, and a mounting discontent, in the words of one critic, with "the embezzlement of the American dream by predatory capitalism."[1] Concurrently, these mural panels and other paintings of his from the 1920s reflect Benton's growing attachment to American themes. Like John Dewey, Lewis Mumford, and Frederick Jackson

Turner, Benton laid increasing stress on the local environment and the artist's need to discover the historical and cultural rhythms of his home region and to incorporate those ideas and experiences into his art. No Ernest Hemingway, Harold Stearns, or H. L. Mencken, Benton felt little betrayal or alienation as a result of World War I, President Wilson's idealism, or the Babbitry of the 1920s. Increasingly Benton wanted to avoid the individualism, art for art's sake, and excessive experimentation he saw in his Parisian and modernistic training. He hoped to exchange those techniques for realistic American paintings in which he treated non-elites as the archetypal common man and with gigantic murals serving as catalogues of grassroots regional experiences. Much of Benton's desire to return west was crystallized in a moment of epiphany when he returned to Missouri in 1924 for his father's dying and death. As he recorded in his autobiography: "I cannot honestly say what happened to me while I watched my father die and listened to the voices of his friends, but I know that when, after his death, I went back East I was moved by a great desire to know more of . . . America. . . . I was moved by a desire to pick up again the threads of my childhood."[2] Eleven years passed before Benton actually returned home, but meanwhile he rapidly loosened his grip on his European and eastern past to come west emotionally and aesthetically.

A clearcut revelation of the transition taking place in Benton's career, *Boomtown* (1928) appeared, as we have seen, in the same year as Curry's painting *Baptism in Kansas,* as Willa Cather's novel *Death Comes for the Archbishop,* and as Walter Prescott Webb was completing his classic history *The Great Plains.* Similar to these works of western art, fiction, and historiography, Benton's *Boomtown* bubbled up as a revealing fountain of the rich western regionalism emerging throughout the region. *Boomtown* is not only one of Benton's finest regionalist paintings, it also resonates with the most revealing ingredients of works illustrating the transition from frontier to region in western cultural history. The compelling significance of Benton's piece is all the more noteworthy considering its modest and unsensational origins.

On the strength of a new commission and desiring to make another jaunt west, Benton struck out on a walking trip through the Ozarks in the spring of 1926. But the journey led farther west. As Benton noted in his second autobiography, he journeyed into "the West Texas oil country, then 'on the boom.'"[3] He made several drawings of the oil country "and the rough life accompanying it. One of these, a street scene in the then wild town of Borger, became the sub-

Thomas Hart Benton, *Boomtown*, 1928. (Memorial Art Gallery of the University of Rochester; Marion Stratton Gould Fund)

ject of one of my best-known 'Regionalist' pictures, 'Boomtown.' "[3] Marrying a Wild West to a nascent oil town Texas, Benton created a cultural oxymoron, a regionalizing Wild West.

All the sections of *Boomtown* display frontier and regional images jostling one another. On the main street, seen from above, Stetsoned cowboys interact with bib-overalled farmers and oil workers. Alongside the frontier cowpunchers are nattily dressed ladies as well as buxom women of the streets. Oil derricks, a railroad, and belching smoke from a nearby carbon mill readily identify the postfrontier status of the town. Hotels trumpet their rooms with bathtubs, and new automobiles dominate the foreground. On the background is pasted an immense sky, and below it a flat Plains landscape stretches from town to sky. Despite the complexity and seeming incoherence of the scene, the tone and mood are those of action and pulsating energy—a setting of newness and change but not dominating violence and chaos. Benton hinted as much in writing that despite the "anarchic carelessness" of Borger, it also exhibited "a breadth," "an expansive grandeur"; it was "a big party—an exploitative whoopee party where capital, its guard down in exultant discovery, joined hands with everybody in a great democratic dance."[4] This celebration of the western scene—of its work patterns, seasons, and harvests—is equally vibrant in several of Benton's other regionalist paintings, such as *Cattle Loading, West Texas* (1930), *Cradling Wheat* (1938), *Threshing Wheat* (1939), *The Hailstorm* (1940), and *July Hay* (1943).

But Benton's work as a muralist gained much more attention and comment than his individual regionalist paintings. So influential were these murals that Benton exerted great influence on government art projects during the New Deal, many of which decorated post offices, city halls, and other public places with murals, even though Benton himself did not participate in any of these federal projects. All of his major murals of the 1930s, however, included important segments on the West. In *America Today* (1930–31), prepared for the New School for Social Research in New York City, Benton included two panels, *Midwest* and *Changing West*, depicting the surging new western influences of oil, airplanes, and industrial workers juxtaposed against background portraits of farmers, cowboys, and Indians. Studies in change and contrast, these paintings, suggesting the trauma of social and economic transformation in the West, were much less idyllic than many of the rural images in the paintings of Grant Wood and John Steuart Curry. No doubt Benton's earlier attachments to Marxism, now waning, made labor conflict more apparent to him than to his two regionalist counterparts. Two years later his *Arts of Life in America* included a section called *Arts of the West*, which, interestingly, consisted of the folk arts of square dancing, fiddling, rifle shooting, card playing, bronco busting, and horseshoe pitching. Another section, called *Indian Arts*, depicted Native Americans hunting buffalo, dancing, making pottery, weaving, and preparing leather goods. Convinced that "the arts" meant the popular arts, Benton indulged his conviction that the regionalist ought to depict the play of ordinary citizens, not that of the elite.

Following a series of murals for the state of Indiana, *A Social History of Indiana* (1933), Benton undertook a similar project for his home state, *A Social History of Missouri* (1935–36). Like the Indiana murals, that in the Jefferson City capitol building endeavored to provide a sociocultural history of Missouri from its Indian origins into the 1930s. More a complex, almost chaotic mosaic of icons, symbolic types, and historical figures than a smoothly flowing, well-modulated sequence, these panels, like Benton's other murals about the West and the South, display the actions, energy, changes, and emotions involved in Missouri's transformation from raw frontier to evolving region. Happy with the result, Benton concluded that " 'the Missouri mural was my best work.' "[5]

Meanwhile, Benton's star as the country's leading regionalist shone even more brilliantly. In its issue of December 24, 1934, *Time* blazoned Benton's self-portrait on its cover—the first time an artist had gained that lordly position—and declared him the leading figure of new American artists in an extended article entitled "The U.S. Scene." Castigating earlier influences of French modernism, the *Time* writer praised Benton as the titular leader of the new Regionalists who were producing notable artwork about the United States free from alien and shackling European traditions. The *Time* story, along with his growing reputation as a muralist in the 1930s and his return to Missouri in 1935, confirmed Benton's status as a major American artist as well as a noteworthy regionalist. Meanwhile, Iowan Grant Wood and Kansan John Steuart Curry were also emerging as significant regional artists.

American artists, Grant Wood wrote in 1935, were gradually turning away from European standards of art and becoming more interested in discovering American guidelines of aesthetic judgment. Further, in realizing the inappropriateness of eastern urban biases, so often linked to French artistic traditions, many Americans were looking to interior America to comprehend there a new truth—"an honest reliance by the artist upon subject matter which he can best interpret because he knows it best." No mere chauvinistic cultism, no mere pandering to the provinces, Wood asserted, this new American spirit boded well for artists, authors, and other custodians of culture. Declaring their cultural independence from European and alien eastern predilections, they were now free to produce an art based "upon certain true and fundamental things which are distinctly ours to use and to exploit."[6]

What Wood asserted in *Revolt against the City* was as much autobiography as cultural criticism. What he said about the new awakenings of other artists was true also about his own rediscoveries. Born in Iowa in 1892, reared in Cedar Falls, and largely self-trained, Wood spent brief periods at several art schools, went abroad in 1920, 1923–24 (where he enrolled in the Académie Julian in Paris), 1926, and 1928. Then, in 1928 in Germany, Wood discovered new glazing techniques and a highly polished, realistic style, owing much to contemporary art he studied in Munich. Returning to Iowa, he utilized these new techniques in a series of midwestern regionalist paintings. *Stone City* (1930), *American Gothic* (1930), *Daughters of Revolution* (1932), and *Death on the Ridge Road* (1934) illustrate these new emphases in Wood's career. Combining them with his new interest in the Renaissance Flemish painters' uses of decorative realism and oil-glazing techniques allowed Wood to give his paintings a permanence and an antique quality that his previous work lacked. In addition, he adopted styles from the Art Deco designers, with their "artificial geometries, clean surfaces, and relentless patterns."[7] Once Wood converted to these realistic and decorative styles, there was but one missing ingredient: local or regional settings. In *Stone City* he completed the picture, depicting a nearly abandoned quarry village three or four miles from his birthplace of Anamosa, following many actual details of buildings, surfaces, and space still visible, even while he omitted, compacted, and spread out other facts to fit his artistic purposes. By marrying techniques from earlier and contemporary artists to his midwestern scenes, Wood launched his career as a regional artist.

He mixed similar ingredients with even more extraordinary results in *American Gothic*, one of the best-known of all American paintings. Here Wood began with a Carpenter Gothic house in tiny Eldon, Iowa, and posed his sister Nan as the spinster daughter and his dentist as the dour father, drawing on the midwestern photographic tradition of stationing a man and woman before an edifice, a sod house, or a clapboard home. To these details, Wood added a series of visual puns and artistic references. The long, narrow faces are reflected in the lines of the house and the tines of the fork, as well as in the bodies of the two subjects. The accompanying plants and plain dress and hairstyle suggest the sturdy traditionalism of the younger woman and the bib overalls and protective masculinity of the older man illustrate his equal adherence to no-nonsense Victorianism.

Did Wood use these details and depictions to harpoon midwestern values and styles, as some critics have argued? Wood assured viewers he had not. Much less ascetic and denunciatory than Benton and more inclined to comment on his material than Curry, Wood nonetheless refrained from attacking Iowa society and culture. The people in *American Gothic* "had bad points," and he had not overlooked these limitations; but, he added, "they were basically good and solid people."[8] Attachment, empathy, wit, and gentle satire infuse Wood's classic painting rather than biting social criticism.

On other occasions, however, Wood could be more sarcastic or gloomy. When the Daughters of the American Revolution criticized Wood, he used his painting *Daughters of Revolution* for revenge, reportedly telling someone: the DAR can " 'ladle it out. I thought I'd see if they could take it.' "[9] Reminding one of the narrow-minded, peevish matrons in John Ford's Law and Order League in his film *Stagecoach* (1939), Wood's women are empty shells of false patriotism, snobbishness, and sterility. Similar reservations about excessive and narrow nationalism inform the artist's *Midnight Ride of Paul Revere* (1931) and *Parson Weems' Fable* (1939). Even if Wood parted company from the debunking criticisms of H. L. Mencken and Sinclair Lewis, he was not a mindless regional or national chauvinist or a naive midwestern bumpkin painting saccharine "pretty pictures," as the general public often sees him.

A few of Wood's other regionalist paintings betrayed his fears about technology and modern trends. Although the meaning of Wood's reported statement that everything significant in his life took place while he was milking a cow can be greatly distorted, he did have large reservations about machines invading midwestern gardens. In *Death on the Ridge Road,* an oncoming truck looms over a sleek, modern automobile attempting to roar past a crawling Ford. This threatened violent confrontation between technological species takes place on a modern paved highway surrounded by verdant countryside. Clearly, the mechanistic invaders threaten to destroy one another in the heart of a rural, agricultural Midwest, with lurking clouds in the background and the crosslike telephone poles reinforcing this threatening atmosphere of modern technology.

In these notable paintings and in others—like *Woman with Plants* (1929), *Dinner for Threshers* (1934), and *Spring in Town* (1941)—Wood labored to catch the people, work patterns, and rhythmic nature in his regional settings. Less interested than Benton in establishing a midwestern regional style and in urging others to break sharply from earlier, nonregional emphases, Wood increasingly wished to paint well what he knew best. Accordingly, he focused on the farm and small-town folk of the Midwest, continuing to depict their lives and activities in the realistic and decorative styles he discovered in the late 1920s and followed for the next decade and half of his career. He urged other artists to find their own styles but also pressed them to make repeated use of their regional background and experiences. Among these was Kansas artist John Steuart Curry.

The third member of the midwestern artistic triumvirate, John Steuart Curry, though less a cheerleader than Benton or Wood, nonetheless furnished dozens

John Steuart Curry, *Baptism in Kansas*, 1928. (Collection of the Whitney Museum of American Art, New York)

of revealing examples of regionalist art. The son of pious Presbyterian parents (his father was a stockman), Curry never shed his close ties to Kansas rural landscapes even though he spent nearly two decades in New York and New England as an illustrator. Returning often to Kansas during summers to take notes for scenes he executed in his Connecticut studio, Curry stormed onto the art scene in 1928 with his *Baptism in Kansas* and his first solo show in 1930. After working as a painter in the WPA's Federal Art Projects, he was named artist in residence at the University of Wisconsin College of Agriculture, where he remained until his death.

If the completion of *Baptism in Kansas* in 1928 obviously threw open the doors of artistic notoriety for Curry, the origins and emphases of this major regional artwork are less well known. Nearly fifteen years after its appearance, he wrote to *Life* magazine, explaining that he "took a month off and painted this picture." It was based on a scene he observed in 1915 at a neighbor's farm. He had tried to set down all the details realistically, hoping to show that the baptism in a farmer's stock tank was no "strange procedure."[10] Indeed, nothing in the painting suggests that Curry treated his fundamentalist scene ironically or satirically. Sympathetic to the religious concerns of the depicted Campbellites, Curry furnishes a remarkably sincere scene emphasizing the piety of his subjects, the spacious Kansas landscape, and the placidness of this natural and populated world. *Baptism in Kansas* not only drew the attention of American art lovers, it also illustrated one of Curry's persistent emphases: the depiction of midwestern folk culture against appealing and sometimes threatening landscapes.

Early on, Curry presented several striking depictions of nature's threats to the Kansas countryside. *Tornado Over Kansas* (1929) depicted a family gathering its pets and fleeing to a storm cellar. The next year *Hogs Killing a Rattlesnake* portrayed a half dozen pigs, one with a writhing snake clamped in its gigantic jaws, and the others closing in on the dramatic scene. Frantic action in the face of threatening nature also dominates the larger *Line Storm* (1934), in which a heavily loaded hay wagon dashes for cover before a blackened sky illuminated by jagged bolts of lightning. Not all these dramatic portrayals of threatening nature pleased Kansas boosters. One custodian of the state's arts, the wife of a former governor, complained that in attempting to catch the Kansas "spirit" Curry had overemphasized cyclones and other "friekish [*sic*] subjects." Why hadn't he "been able to see any of the glories of his home state, of the beauties of the . . . broad, far-reaching landscapes"? Even the distinguished Kansas journalist William Allen White agreed that Curry might have stressed too often the "gloomy . . . unpleasant features of life without taking account of the balancing pleasant features." Like other regionalists, Curry discovered that his perspectives about local scenes or experiences often sandpapered the fragile sensibilities of regional chauvinists. Although these reactions bothered Curry, he never reacted with the vitriol of Benton or the satire of Wood, merely stating laconically that his critics "have Kansas. They hardly need paintings."[11]

These early negative reactions, however, were but a sideshow compared to the main-tent denunciations of Curry when he attempted between 1937 and 1941 to execute a series of murals in the Kansas state capitol in Topeka. Dozens of carpers noted that the tails on Curry's pigs curled the wrong way and that the legs of his cows and bulls were all wrong, but it was his emphasis on tornadoes and a violent John Brown that set off most of the uproar. Critics wanted more conquistadors, covered wagons, and corn, whereas Curry's supporters saluted his truthful treatment of "raw, rough, and true" Kansas history. Eventually Curry refused to sign or complete the murals, because the project was "uncompleted and [did] not represent [his] true idea."[12]

Even though Curry's regionalist visions displeased many faint-hearted Kansans, his work gained major national attention in the 1930s, with a few critics valuing his paintings as more true and less theatrical than those by Benton and Wood. On balance, he will be best remembered for his canvases depicting people against nature—especially in their toil as farmers and in their encounters with tornadoes, floods, and storms. As one critic has noted, "Curry celebrates these struggles because he knows man is not the victim but the triumphant adversary."[13] In these emphases and in this conclusion, John Steuart Curry was a central figure in western regional art during the interwar years.

The rising tide of regionalism that inspired novelists and historians to treat the history and culture of the American West in the 1920s and 1930s and that encouraged Benton, Wood, and Curry likewise influenced artists in other parts of the West. In the Southwest, from Texas to California, individual artists attempted to capture their locales in fresh new ways. In Texas, at the same time that the Southwest Review, Walter Prescott Webb, and J. Frank Dobie were trumpeting the importance of southwestern and plains literature, history, and folklore, Alexandre Hogue was delineating the Southwest in stark, memorable canvases. He persistently argued that he differed greatly from the triumvirate of midwestern artists, but he too insisted that a painter must avoid the deadening hand of foreign influences and fill his work with experiences and scenes he knew firsthand. After intermittent training and study in Minneapolis, New York City, and Texas and an early series of paintings dealing with the peoples and settings of northern New Mexico (where he stayed sporadically in the 1920s), Hogue turned to Texas and Dust Bowl scenes, especially the *Erosion* series for which he is best known.

Unlike most other regionalists, Alexandre Hogue asserted that humans were primarily responsible for the Dust Bowl ravages of the 1930s. As one art historian has argued, Hogue's *Erosion* series was fired by his "deeply-felt sense of tragedy at the wasteful, irreverent attitude that had caused the land's ruin." In such paintings as *Dust Bowl* (1933), *Drouth Stricken Area* (1934), *Drouth Survivors* (1936), and *The Crucified Land* (1939), through an adroit use of tractors, fences, and other agricultural implements and practices, Hogue indicts farmers as villains. Realistic details clearly show the loss, destruction, and death that follow faulty use of the land. Even more explicit is *Mother Earth Laid Bare* (1938), in which, drawing on his mother's teachings about "Mother Earth" and his interest in Native American nature ethics, Hogue portrayed a recumbent nude female, who, he said, symbolized "Mother Earth . . . raped by the plow and laid bare." For all this, Hogue refused to label his paintings as social criticism. "Social comment is negative," he wrote, "my interest in conservatism is positive." Most of all, he wanted his *Erosion* series to depict the " 'terrifying,' compelling beauty" of a devastated landscape and to provide an element of "psychoreality, by which viewers could see and feel what humans and wind and water erosion had done to southwestern rural areas."[14] In these emphases, Hogue had more in common with John Steinbeck, the photographer Dorothea Lange, and the filmmaker Pare Lorentz than he did with Benton, Wood, and Curry. But like the midwesterners, his major concern was for place, for settings he knew firsthand, and for approaches to those scenes arising naturally out of his own experiences. In these thematic and regional emphases, Hogue represented well a cluster of artists who gathered around Dallas, especially its Museum of Fine Arts during the 1930s and early 1940s. Nicknamed the Dallas Nine, they stressed regional art, especially Texas landscapes, and their group included such artists as Dorothy Austin, Jerry Bywaters, Otis Dozier, Florence McClung, and Octavio Medellin. In realistic detail, they endeavored to furnish egalitarian art by drawing on several folk cultures, and they championed a rising cultural regionalism through numerous exhibits in regional art centers, encouraging a new and analytical understanding of the local.[15]

Although New Mexico artist Peter Hurd was well acquainted with some of the Dallas Nine and took part in their activities, he represented another example of western artistic regionalism and illustrated still other trends emerging in another part of the Southwest. Born and reared in Roswell, New Mexico, Hurd attended West Point but withdrew to further his art career. Soon thereafter he met noted illustrator N. C. Wyeth and served a five-year apprenticeship at the artist's home in Chadds Ford, Pennsylvania. Marrying Wyeth's daughter Henriette, Hurd set about diligently and semisuccessfully to make a living as an illustrator and artist, but he yearned to return to New Mexico, which he did for several months each year throughout the 1930s. First in a series of portraits of Hispanic and Anglo farmers and ranch hands and then in varied mural panels, Hurd gradually found his medium in regional works that dealt with the Southwest. In *Ranchería* (1938), *Dry River* (1938), and *Rio Hondo*

Peter Hurd, *The Gate and Beyond,* 1952. (Roswell Museum and Art Center, 1953.7.1)

(1941), he lyrically conveyed the bright light that played on the hill-and-valley landscapes of southern New Mexico. As he wrote to his father-in-law, "This part of New Mexico, so different from the Taos section[,] is utterly untouched by painting." *Dry River,* through its sensitive use of light and color to depict the semi-arid New Mexico terrain, particularly reflected Hurd's regional approach. One commentator saluted the painting for its "undulating rhythms of landscape and sky, strangely interwoven by the atmospheric light breaking through a cloud cover."

When *Life* magazine featured Hurd's life and regional art in July 1939, his career took off, much as earlier stories in *Time* and *Life* had helped launch Thomas Hart Benton and Alexandre Hogue. Continuing to execute murals and portraits, Hurd also did further illustrations for *Life* and *Time.* Although he later denied he was a Regionalist of the midwestern camp, Hurd shared much with those painters, emphasizing the necessity of painting American scenes, particularly ones the artist had experienced firsthand and could depict factually and realistically. Further, his attachment to New Mexico and its environs was as close and emotional as that of other regionalists. He wrote his wife that returning to New Mexico after an absence in the East was "a sort of thing as primordial as birth or death." [16] One of Hurd's later regional works, *The Gate and Beyond* (1952), illustrates his strong attachment to place. A work of huge scale (47" by 90"), but of simple and clear focus, it depicts a southwestern ranch beyond its entry gate. Behind the gate a fence stretches into infinity across the vast terrain. Beyond the facts of fence and farm, Hurd presents a splendid portrait of space and landscape. Indeed, the toned-down colors, the large terrain, and the southwestern aridity combine like a tempting pastry of visual attractiveness and tactile pleasure. The adroit use of poles, posts, and a backgrounded mountain also provide size and depth to the foreground, middle ground, and backdrop of the painting. Fenced out, the viewer becomes an onlooker experiencing a minimalist setting of space and sparseness and yet is drawn in through the work's placid demeanor and muted sublimity. Here was the ultimate depiction of Hurd's major regional theme — the play of human endeavor, light, and color on the eye-stretching landscape of New Mexico.

Like painters in the Midwest and Southwest, artists on the Pacific Coast displayed an interest in regional themes even though no specific ideas or techniques unified them into a coherent school. Indeed, California and Pacific Northwest painters not only differed from one another, they likewise betrayed notable differences among their subregions. As with so many other ingredients of western culture, subregional varieties of art in the interwar years were as significant as regionwide unities.

One of the identifiable groups of California painters during the 1920s and 1930s clustered around the Chouinard School of Art and the California Water Color Society. Drawn to teachers and artists such as E. Tolles Chamberlin, Millard Sheets, Phil Dike, and Rex Brandt, most of these artists, like other regionalists, emphasized the scenes and society that surrounded them. The California watercolorists, however, not only worked in a different medium, they also painted urban scenes like the streets of Los Angeles, drive-ins, palm-lined streets, and sunny southern California. Often working *en plein air,* painting out-of-doors directly on canvas, they completed revealing portraits of California landscapes, displaying large, positive, brightly colored spaces of people working or playing. A few artists, under the influence of the Mexican muralists, executed works of social criticism, but even they were more sunny than satirical. This "California school," as the watercolor regionalists were known in the 1930s, became less and less impressionistic and more and more anecdotal, narrative, and figurative as the Depression decade wore on. Some of the artists, especially Dike and Hardie Gramatky, even maintained their regional emphasis while working as animators in the Disney studios. More than any of the others, however, Sheets as teacher and artist in such works as *Spring Street, Los Angeles* (1929) and *Beer for Prosperity* (1933) and as the organizer of numerous important exhibits, paved the way for the coterie of watercolor regionalists.[17]

Another group of artists congregated in the Bay Area. Known as the Society of Six, these plein-air painters formed an association that dominated the Oakland art scene from World War I to the early 1930s. Unlike many other regionalists, these landscapists adhered to modernist emphases on impressionism, vibrant colors, and bright light. Attuned to and often following European and eastern American artistic trends in the early twentieth century, these "roisterous bohemians," often met for marathon sessions of drinking and then painting in the countryside, loved northern California landscapes, and in the words of one commentator, exhibited " 'a sense of place, an awareness and appreciation of the natural, physical environment.' " The oils of William Clapp, Louis Siegriest, and August Gay, as well as the watercolors of Selden Gile, Bernard von Eichman, and Maurice Logan, include remarkable representations of ocean, farm, and street scenes, notable for their energetic, dramatic, and fresh combinations of color and landscape. Often overlooked in their time, the painters in the Society of Six were important regionalists with a modernist bent, and in linking these often conflicting tendencies, they were significant forerunners of later painterly trends that emerged in California shortly after World War II.[18]

The diversity and shifting nature of artistic trends in California also characterized artistic works in the Pacific Northwest in the quarter-century following World War I. Just as the establishment of the California Palace of the Legion of Honor in 1924 and the persisting importance of the de Young Museum and the California School of Fine Arts were notable for artists in southern and northern California, the Portland Art Association, the Cornish School, and the Seattle Art Museum were similarly important for nurturing art in the Pacific Northwest. Regionalism developed later and in a more fragmented fashion in Oregon and Washington than in the Midwest and Southwest, but it was nonetheless a noticeable trend from the Depression to 1945. If the works of C. S. Price and Mark Tobey began to attract attention in early 1930s, a decade later critics were pointing to the paintings of Tobey, Morris Graves, Kenneth Callahan, and Guy Anderson as sharing enough in common to be termed the

"Northwest School of Art." Tobey and Graves, the two most significant artists, united in their interest in Oriental thought and culture and attempted to work these and other non-Western strains into their paintings. As a convert to the Baha'i World Faith, a visitor in Japan to study calligraphy, and a student of Chinese art, Tobey incessantly traveled, nervously looking for a satisfying synthesis of form and theme. During his stays in Seattle in the 1920s and 1930s, he seemed as much a traveler as a rooted resident of the region. Perhaps Seattle drew him more as a mediating point between Eastern and Western cultures than as the cultural capital of the Pacific Northwest. At any rate, he did utilize the gray skies, the rain, the green landscapes, and the coastline, but more often as shifting ingredients in his varied, complex, and ever-changing career than as the central focus of regional work. Seattle's Public Market is forcefully drawn in *Farmer's Market* (1941), and in a series, *Public Market Type* (1941), but Tobey's better-known "white writing," which combined his interest in calligraphy and his attempts to find oneness in cultures, denotes his desire to be a world citizen rather than denizen of a single place.

Born and reared in the Pacific Northwest, Morris Graves was more closely attached to the region, although he shared Tobey's interest in the Orient, where he traveled to study. The youngest of the major Northwest artists, Graves nevertheless gained national attention earlier than others with his provocative treatment of birds, animals, and trees as revealing indicators of the painter's inward sky. *Bird in the Spirit* (1943), in which a bird seems trapped in a grassy whirligig, suggests the tensions and traumas of humanity. Like Tobey, whose search for transcendence and attachments to Zen much influenced him, Graves searched for a synthesis of ideas and subject matter, an intense journey that often led him away from society and toward a brooding, hermitlike existence in the Northwest woods. If Tobey and Graves were regionalists unlike the Midwest triumvirate — in fact reacted rather negatively toward them — they nonetheless, along with Callahan and Anderson, clearly illustrated the tendency of artists around 1940 to adhere to a "Northwest tradition" linking time and place with a sustained desire to discover a worldview that combined the local and the universal. That urge has been the outstanding characteristic of art in the Pacific Northwest since the 1930s.[19]

In the larger view, Tobey and Graves are important transitional figures in the changing inventions of the American West. On the one hand, they illustrate a regional interest in showing how the interplay between physical settings and people within a specific place spawned unique cultures. On the other, they moved beyond most other regionalists in stressing innovative artistic techniques that Abstract Expressionists and other experimentalists employed after World War II. Similar to contemporaries like John Steinbeck, James C. Malin, and Georgia O'Keeffe, these painters remained among the regionalists even as they anticipated the postregionalism that swept over the West in the following generations.

III

THE WEST AS POSTREGION

INTRODUCTION

For a short time near the end of the 1930s, the American West, like the American South, was awash in a flood of regionalism that united novelists, historians, and painters in their search for regional truths. Then came World War II and a generation later the 1960s. Together these two eras ushered in dramatic changes in western American culture.

What World War I and the Depression were to the transition from frontier to regional interpretations of western culture, World War II and the 1960s were to shifts from regional to postregional interpretations. As historian Gerald D. Nash has written, the war with Germany and Japan transformed the American West. Or, in the words of another scholar, Earl Pomeroy, no event since the Gold Rush had such a dramatic impact on the West as did World War II.[1] If mushrooming urbanization and reoriented transportation and trade grids illustrated the enormous economic and social changes the war unleashed, the cultural transformations were equally pathbreaking.

World War II triggered enormous demographic shifts that have continued to the present. In the decade following 1940, more than 8 million newcomers flooded into the trans-Mississippi West, with more than a third of those invading California, which boomed to a 10.5 million population by 1950. Large proportions of these new immigrants moved into western cities. Many came west to take part in the giant military-industrial complexes rising phoenixlike in the arid spaces of the West; others, who were also looking for new jobs, located near population clusters. All over the West but particularly down the West Coast from Seattle to San Diego and along the southwestern border from California to Texas, military bases and installations sprouted like wild-flowers. Among these new arrivals were many easterners moving west, others were from outside the United States, and still others were westerners relocating in western urban areas for the new jobs and economic benefits that the war-related industries spawned.

Not surprisingly, the newcomers and relocated westerners triggered enormous social and cultural changes throughout the West. Young Indian and Hispanic men who served in the armed forces and then returned to their native villages proved to be dramatic catalysts, especially across the Southwest. Many returning veterans introduced new ways of thinking to their natal areas, and others decided to leave rural hamlets and relocate in towns and cities where their experiences in the service could open job opportunities in booming areas such as Los Angeles, the Bay Area, Texas cities, Denver, and Minneapolis. Concurrently, thousands of African American families moved west to snare war-related jobs. As a result, black populations in Texas and California cities mush-roomed throughout the 1940s. If these shifts transformed the ethnic makeup of several western subregions, they also touched off traumatic changes in western families, with hundreds of thousands of women swarming into war-related industries, moving outside their homes to join the workforce for the first time.

For even larger groups of Americans, including hundreds of thousands of westerners and equal numbers of those becoming new westerners in the 1940s and 1950s, World War II forced them to think internationally. Whether as participants in the war or as custodians of American culture interested in knowing about and perhaps embracing European and Asian intellectual trends, many Americans experienced the war as a break from the past, an open door to a host of new concepts they often examined and sometimes accepted. Additionally, the impact of the war seemed to encourage Americans to scrutinize their own past to see if the truths that seemed so self-evident in the 1920s and 1930s could stand up in the new atmosphere of the postwar world.

As one might expect, all these global transformations had a dramatic impact on the cultural and intellectual life of the American West after 1945. Newcomers spiced and flavored the Far West with their varied cultural backgrounds and also demanded an expansion of existing cultural institutions and outlooks as well as the launching of new ones. Burgeoning communities, sprawling cities, and new suburbs were forced to organize new schools, to establish new churches, and to deal with a welter of diverse cultural experiences. Even if most of these transformations cannot be linked as directly to the expanded federal presence in the West as can defense industries, scientific laboratories, and expanding cities, nonetheless many remarkable cultural changes owed much to the impact of World War II. Novelists, historians, and artists, sometimes even before Pearl Harbor but especially during the 1940s and 1950s, betrayed the unmistakable marks of these wartime influences.

On occasion, the creations of postregional writers and painters after World War II and the 1960s echoed the emphases of the postmodernists. Some western postregionalists discovered, for example, the validity of the postmodernist critique of American culture following the 1960s, that diversity, complexity, disunity, and fragmentation (even messiness) characterized American history more than did consensus, unity, and democratic capitalism. According to this perspective, American society, as well as national social patterns in the American West, had reached new crossroads without being able to locate agreed-upon meeting points. As a result, westerners like California novelist Joan Didion, and many other Americans as well, concurred with postmodernists that Americans lacked a culture with a recognizable center.

Yet western postregionalism, even while reflecting facets of postmodernism, was more than a ripple in that larger current. For one, the preponderance of the country's Native Americans, Hispanics, and Asians made a difference in the West, where their voices were even more evident than elsewhere in American fiction and art. Dozens of novelists, historians, and artists, reordering previous images of the West, placed additional stress on the central roles of these racial and ethnic groups. For other postregionalists, the hegemonic Wild West myth had to be challenged, even destroyed, if women's experiences in the American West were to be understood. Novelist Marilynne Robinson, historians Joan Jensen and Glenda Riley, and artist Judith Baca were among many reconfiguring traditional masculine narratives about the frontier and regional Wests. Concurrently, still other postregionalists like novelist Edward Abbey and historians Richard White and Donald Worster called for new, more realistic interpretations of the environment.

These revisionings are evident as well in other areas of modern western culture, including poetry, nonfiction, music, and architecture. Even clearer are parallel changes in Western films during the past two generations. Moving from the celebrated frontier emphases of *High Noon* and *Shane* in the early 1950s to the notable counterclassics of *Butch Cassidy and the Sundance Kid, The Wild Bunch,* and *Little Big Man* in 1969 and 1970, and on to the Grey West in the Oscar-winning film *Unforgiven* in 1992, Western movies since World War II are another revealing palimpsest of the recent postregional invention of the American West.

Among postregional novelists, some writers advanced new visions of the West resulting from their experiences during the 1930s and the war years. Others whose careers were already launched began to see the West in a new light. Both groups, however, broke from the predominant perspectives of the literary regionalists of the 1920s and 1930s.

Chapter 7

POSTREGIONAL NOVELS

Even before Pearl Harbor, novelists in the West broke from fictional patterns popular among frontier and regional authors. During the 1930s, newcomers such as the detective novelist James M. Cain, the Englishman Aldous Huxley, and the New Yorker Nathanael West depicted Hollywood and southern California not as an Eldorado nourishing immigrants but as a flawed Eden beset with the treacherous serpents of materialism, greed, and ostentation. In his memorable surrealistic treatment of Hollywood, *The Day of the Locust* (1939), West repudiated southern California as a nightmarish riot of absurd dress styles, architecture, food, and behavior. Victims of the area's cultural chaos and lacking their own cultural moorings, his fictional characters search for identity through an endless series of quests and journeys. West's holocaustic view of southern California gradually disintegrating—because it bought and sold itself in fadistic fleshmarts and because it reflected Americans' dreamlike attachments to super salesmen—was but the most Hollywoodesque enactment of the materialism, phoneyness, and bizarre fantasies that sent Americans in general toward destructive ends. Nathanael West's novel reflects a nascent worried attitude about the momentous changes that invaded the Far West in the 1930s and especially the 1940s. As will become evident, his fiction is but an early example of a straight line of anti-California literature leading through the Beats to Joan Didion and on to the most recent novelistic bashing of the Golden State.[1]

Yet one must not overlook *The Grapes of Wrath* as another example of this critical strain increasingly apparent in western postregional literature. It, too, adumbrates the emerging fretful mood—and later nearly nihilistic despair—that invaded dozens of postregional novels. Steinbeck's Okies, convinced that California is their Last Best Hope for jobs, homes, and eventual retirement, act out a modern-day exodus only to find that the Far West lacks a pot of gold at the end of its fabled rainbow of opportunity. Instead, the Joads discover a California rife with greedy entrepreneurs, selfish growers, and thousands of other migrants willing to trade their souls for daily milk and bread, even though they may destroy other needy folk in the process. If most regional fiction published between the wars put on an optimistic face about the West as a place and portrayed it primarily as a helpful and beneficial location for residents, Steinbeck moved in another direction. The California of *The Grapes of Wrath* is a tragic setting, a place of debt and doubt. No longer the frontier of dreamed-of opportunity, no longer the site of shared community, it has become a stage on which excessive competition, insensitivity, and violence dominate. Unlike his contemporaries Cain, Huxley, and West, Steinbeck was a native Californian; but, like them, by the end of the 1930s he had begun to see his home state as more a nightmare than a dream.

The growing importance of California as a target for criticism, as well as a host for critics was, again, symbolized as the Beat writers roared into view on the West Coast in the 1950s. As much impetus for this controversial literary outburst came from San Francisco and other areas of California as from New York City. Eastern writers such as Jack Kerouac and Allen Ginsberg found the Bay Area an inviting setting for their coffee-house readings that criticized a conforming Eisenhower era. Kerouac's frenetic novel *On the Road* (1957), as well as Ginsberg's lengthy poem *Howl* (1956), helped announce a third Bay Area renaissance of the 1950s and 1960s, following the early halcyon years of Bret Harte and the *Overland Monthly* in 1860s and 1870s and those of Jack London and his contemporaries early in the twentieth century. Symbolic of renewed literary activity in San Francisco was poet Lawrence Ferlinghetti's all-night City Lights Bookstore, a new rendezvous for innovative literary types such as the Beats. If the Beats, as opponents argued, created little heat and less light, they nonetheless furnished an important hint of California's emerging importance as a cultural core, an illustration of national trends in popular culture, as well as supplying cultural cues for many westerners.

A half-dozen years later native Californian Joan Didion exhibited similar somber moods in her postregional fiction. Slicing through what she considered misleading myths that encouraged far westerners to think of California as an endless utopia of opportunity and progress, Didion in her first two novels, *Run River* (1963) and *Play It as It Lays* (1970), excoriates her home state as being without a moral compass, bereft of sympathy, and driven by false expectations. Her major characters—lacking a sense of family, community, or individual identity—fail to win in the daily games of chance in which they are forced to participate and wander across blighted landscapes of depression, despair, and frequent failure.

Published before the cultural reorientation of the 1960s had fully arrived, Didion's major western novels occupy a central position in the new postregional fiction. What *The Virginian* was to frontier literature, what Cather's novels were to regional writing, Didion's western fiction is to postregionalism. Reared on a frontier ethic but now caught in a booming, urban-industrial California, her protagonists flounder between the nationalistic, heroic myths of their pioneer forebears and the contemporary traumatic changes thrust upon them in a post–World War II West. In *Run River*, the heroes and heroines tumble into the yawning chasm between these myths and realities. Although the hop ranchers and their families along the Sacramento River in the late 1950s try to abide by their inherited frontier idealizations, searing tranformations invade and discomfit their worlds. In this regard, Didion writes about a college-bound son who comprehends sociocultural changes his mother and father can neither recognize nor understand:

> She and his father would never seem to get it through their heads that things were changing in Sacramento, that Aerojet General and Douglas Aircraft and even the State College were bringing in a whole new class of people, people who had lived back East, people who read things. She and his father were going to be pretty surprised if and when they ever woke up to the fact that nobody in Sacramento anymore had even heard of the McClellans. Or the Knights. Not that he thought they would ever wake up. They'd just go right along dedicating their grubby goddamn camellia trees in Capitol Park to the memory of their grubby goddamn pioneers.[2]

A similar despairing mood arising from conflicting dreams and realities, another failed Eden, and still other flawed families characterizes *Play It as It Lays*. The heroine, Maria, instructed by her father that, like a pioneer woman, she must maintain a stiff upper lip and must play only the cards she holds, tries to live by these guidelines even when they prove to be inappropriate in a phony dreamland world driven by meaningless sexual encounters, false and destructive "families," and a deadening materialism that destroys love, empathy, and feeling. Unable to find or construct a vital center, Maria spends hours and days aimlessly driving the Los Angeles freeways. Also adding to her directionless existence are a traumatic abortion, her inability to nurture a much-loved but institutionalized daughter, and her loveless affairs with crass and ambitious partners. Even though these events transpire in a suburban and Hollywoodish Los Angeles and in the deserts of Nevada, place is much less significant than the depressing mood and tone that dominate the novel. Breaking from the regionalists of the 1920s and 1930s, Didion chooses to emphasize mood rather than setting in a defective West. And, as we shall see, like several other postregional novelists, she also raises important feminist concerns — subjects that a few regionalists addressed but that became increasingly important to postregional writers after the 1960s.

Although the doubters of the 1930s, the Beats, and John Steinbeck and Joan Didion foreshadowed central themes of postregional literature, theirs were not the only images of the American West emerging in its post–World War II literature. Chief among those responsible for moving beyond the concerns of western regionalists and introducing other themes important to western postregionalism were the three novelists Walter Van Tilburg Clark, A. B. Guthrie, Jr., and especially Wallace Stegner.

Clark wrote a handful of polished novels and shorter fictional works, but he is rightly remembered most for his pathbreaking novel *The Ox-Bow Incident* (1940). A blistering depiction of the tragic outcome of misguided prejudices and violence, Clark's novel is in part a trenchant answer to Wister's dangerous acceptance of vigilantism in *The Virginian,* as well as an explicit statement of what European totalitarianism under Hitler and Mussolini might lead to. But most of all it is a warning about "a kind of American Nazism" that might destroy democratic freedoms in the United States. Ideology aside, the author also wanted to prove, as he wrote to Walter Prescott Webb, that he could utilize "all the ingredients of the standard western" "with a theme that concerned me," and "bring both the people and the situations alive again." Obviously Clark had produced a notable meta-Western, one that employed well-known stereotypes of the popular Western genre even as it commented on and undercut those stereotypes.[3] As he revealed in a later novel, *The Track of the Cat* (1949), and in such stories as "The Indian Well," "The Wind and the Snow of Winter," "The Watchful Gods," and "The Portable Phonograph," Clark moved beyond the regionalists in adumbrating concerns of postregionalists, particularly their emphasis on a dark, brooding West, their pronounced stress on ecological topics, and their interest in remythologizing the West. Although not as well known as Guthrie and Stegner, Clark too provides a bridge between western regionalism and postregionalism.

Even though A. B. Guthrie did not publish his first major novel until he was in his mid-forties, he completed his six-volume fictional history of the West, several other novels and works of nonfiction, and dozens of stories, essays, and sketches before his death in 1991. Beginning with *The Big Sky* (1947) and *The Way West* (1949), for which Guthrie won a Pulitzer Prize, through *These Thousand Hills* (1956) and *Arfive* (1970), and on to the final segments in the series, *The Last Valley* (1975) and *Fair Land, Fair Land* (1982), Guthrie was an increasingly outspoken environmental advocate. Indeed, in the last decade of his life, his fictional heroes often spoke the same environmental language as their creator. Foreshadowing the criticisms by wilderness advocates, ecologically minded postregionalists, and the New Western historians, Guthrie lambasted the extractive practices of mountain men, pioneers, and ranchers, as well as the greed and selfishness of farmers, townsmen, and reclamationists. Like Bernard DeVoto and Wallace Stegner, Guthrie defended policies that set aside wilderness areas, embraced new efforts at conservation, and ripped bureaucrats and government policies and agencies more interested in "progress" and profits than preservation. His fictional villains "sp'ile" the mountains, overgraze their pastures, rip up unfarmable land, and dam every stream wider than a broad jump. By the 1980s, Guthrie had become a nationally known spokesman for environmental efforts, using his fiction much as postregionalists would, as a vehicle for expressing his views on ecology.[4]

The career of Wallace Stegner, historian, biographer, novelist, and spokesman on environmental issues, is the most crucial link between the western regional and postregional literatures. Reared and schooled on the tail end of the Canadian and American frontiers, Stegner began his career with a series of essays and books that drew on his own western experiences. With the publication of *The Big Rock Candy Mountain* in 1943, his return to the West and his teaching and writing at Stanford, and his mounting reputation as a leading man of western letters, Stegner catapulted to the forefront of western novelists.

Early on, particularly in *The Big Rock Candy Mountain*, Stegner demonstrated (at least a generation before other writers) an understanding of the mythologies that were damaging to many westerners. In depicting the differences between husband and wife Bo and Elsa Mason, Stegner creates the masculine boomer, the "strong, dominant kind of man, and in a way a dangerous one . . . deluded, socially deluded, the product of frontiers which now all of a sudden have closed." He dreams eternally of the "big candy rock mountain" just over the horizon, while his domestic, nurturing wife hopes to build a protective, safe nest for her family. In some ways "exorcising" his own father and "making some kind of recompense" to his mother, in treating gender relations in the West, and in demonstrating the dangerous tendencies of the acquisitive, selfish westerner turned loose on his region, Stegner was treating topics that few other western authors of the time addressed.[5]

Even more noteworthy in this regard is Stegner's novel *Angle of Repose* (1971), which garnered a Pulitzer Prize. On one level the story of an eastern woman artist (Susan Burling) who marries an eastern engineer (Lyman Ward) and follows him west to live in a series of mining camps and other western towns, and on another the story of Susan's grandson, Lyman Ward, a retired historian, amputee, and profoundly disillusioned man, the novel undertakes the huge task of treating a full century of western history. Stegner succeeds by focusing on two major questions about western history: (1) What are the key relationships between the East and West, and should their differences or similarities be emphasized more? and (2) What comparisons and contrasts can be made between the pioneer West and the New West? In dramatizing these central historiographical themes, Stegner the novelist joined the scholars Earl Pomeroy and Gerald Nash in raising notable interpretations that continue to intrigue recent novelists and historians. Further, Stegner's narrator urges readers to avoid distorted, romanticized views of the past. Too many want the drama and color of the stylized Wild West, but that kind of history, the narrator continues, is worthless: "Every fourth-rate antiquarian in the West has panned Lola's [Montez] poor little gravel. My grandparents are in a deep vein that has never been dug. They were *people*." [6]

Drawing much from the life and writings of Mary Hallock Foote and chronicling the difficulties of several families attempting to reach their "angles of repose," the story line focuses on conflicts between husbands and wives or unmarried lovers. Stegner's memorable novel, as well as much of his other premier fiction, signaled that families, particularly women's experiences, were about to receive attention in postregional fiction. Few male writers have emphasized western women as thoroughly and appealingly as did Stegner, but numerous women writers have.

Even most women writers dealing with the West before the 1920s, however, rarely dealt extensively with women's experiences. Early on, Mary Hallock Foote, B. M. Bower, and Eva Emery Dye had focused on families, including numerous female characters, but they treated the West primarily as a masculine frontier, not as a stage for fictional heroines. In the next generation, Mary Austin, Willa Cather, and Mari Sandoz showed increasing concern for western women, including immigrant and ethnic women, in a regional West. But not until the post-1960s West did feminist perspectives come to the forefront of western literature. At the same time that scholars began to examine extensively the histories of women and families in the trans-Mississippi West, women especially began to produce a series of extraordinary novels with gender as a main thematic concern. Some women, like Marilynne Robinson and Barbara Kingsolver, reinterpret the modern American West through the eyes of their heroines; others, such as Leslie Marmon Silko and Louise Erdrich, do so as part of their ethnic heritage. The yeasty 1960s raised the consciousness of these writers, as they did for all Americans, inspiring them to turn to women's experiences in the West as the central subjects for their novels.

Marilynne Robinson's *Housekeeping* (1981) immediately struck readers as a remarkably fresh novel about the northern West. Obviously the forest- and lake-filled setting attracted readers, but the novel's extraordinary cast of female characters is even more attention-catching. Ruth Stone, the adolescent narrator, spins a yarn about her mother's suicide, her sister's relentless competition, and her aunts' eccentricities. Living among characters straight out of one of Charles Dickens's macabre novels, Ruth tries to discover her place, to set up "housekeeping" with another female; but ultimately she and her Aunt Sylvie destroy their house, leave town, and set out on years of wandering. Through a long line of female relatives and acquaintances—no major male character inhabits the novel—Ruth looks for stability and meaning. Stumbling about in a world nearly as chaotic as those in Didion's novels, Ruth fails to find that stasis for which she longs. Although the natural backdrop plays an integral role in Ruth's story, her unsuccessful quest for a stable anchor against the flux and disorder that threaten her overshadow the novel's setting, illustrating its postregional character.

In the Southwest, Kentucky immigrant Barbara Kingsolver's three novels treat women's journeys toward self-understanding. In *The Bean Trees* (1988) and in *Pigs in Heaven* (1993), but particularly in *Animal Dreams* (1990), she produces not so much regional novels as feminist fictions. Place is significant in the latter novel, for instance, but women as persons, their ideas and their

moods, are even more central. Even though the heroine's small Arizona hometown of Grace reflects the Native American/Hispanic/Anglo cultural mixing
of its environs, more important is the search of Cosina (Codi) Noline for connections, community, and hope. Codi, who is in her early thirties, has been
unable to discover who she is, instead—by turns—pretending, abandoning,
lying, running away, and retreating to escapist dreams and desires. Gradually,
after slouching back to Grace, she stumbles toward attachment and commitment but only after trying to erect new barriers to protect her vulnerability.
Bit by bit she discovers her father's full identity, her Hispanic heritage, and her
rekindled attachment to her Indian lover. Even more reawakening results from
the catalytic actions of Codi's sister Halimeda (Hallie), who dares to travel
to Nicaragua to fight the Contras and in so doing exhibits courage, connection, and a give-a-damn attitude that Codi lacks. Hallie's gesture—and later
death—seems to galvanize Codi, or at least to impel her down the path of self-
understanding.

Animal Dreams is another testament of the postregional desire to break free
from an excessive reliance on regional settings. Indeed, some of Kingsolver's
attempts to drag in the cultures of Native Americans and Hispanics seem a bit
contrived, not well integrated into the plot. This novel is, most of all, an appealing account of a young woman's reluctant but nonetheless gradual steps
toward self-knowledge and action. Acceptance and healing follow the heroine's
willingness to act and move on her own. True, Indian and Hispanic cultures
are checkpoints on the highway toward self-comprehension, but they are less
central than the feminine concerns the author blends into her fiction. Perhaps
Kingsolver best defined her approach when she pointed out that her fiction is
primarily " 'western–contemporary–hard times–struggle novels.' . . . 'the way
life goes today.' "[7]

If the late 1960s and 1970s reoriented the thinking of many Americans
toward the roles of women and families, those years also shocked Americans into reconsidering their views about racial and ethnic groups. As a result of gaining these new perspectives, western novelists, like other writers
throughout the country, began focusing their fiction increasingly on ethnic
subjects. Ethnic writers like Charles Eastman, Black Elk (through John Neihardt), John M. Oskison, D'Arcy McNickle, and José Antonio Villarreal had
published nonfiction and fiction about their ethnic groups before the 1960s,
and Oliver La Farge, Frank Waters, Harvey Fergusson, and John Steinbeck
wrote memorable books about Indians and Hispanics; but most of the premier

western fiction produced about racial and ethnic groups has appeared in the last twenty-five years. No one should argue that the fiction of Indian authors like N. Scott Momaday, Leslie Marmon Silko, James Welch, and Louise Erdrich; Hispanics like Rudolfo Anaya, Tomás Rivera, and Denise Chávez; Asians like Maxine Hong Kingston and Amy Tan; or African-Americans like Terry McMillan overlooks the central regional dictum that setting shapes character. But few critics would cite these writings as primarily works about the Southwest, the Far West, or the northern West. Instead, they are, first of all, novels about Indians, Hispanics, Asians, and blacks. It is as *ethnic* rather than *regional* literature that they have entered the canon. A clutch of Native American novelists illustrates the central importance of an enlarged sense of ethnic identity in western postregional literature.

N. Scott Momaday's *House Made of Dawn* (1968) did more than any other novel by an Indian author to signal that Native American voices would be heard in increasing numbers and volume in the next quarter of a century. Written in a complex Faulknerian style with a full run of experimental fictional techniques and incorporating dozens of samples of Indian history, lore, and literature, Momaday's novel is a revealing if somber and even pessimistic cultural document. Set primarily in New Mexico and making use of that state's terrain and multicultural tensions and accommodations, *House Made of Dawn* is most of all concerned with a young Indian man's pilgrimage toward personal and cultural understanding. Readers remember the *Indianness* of the work (and perhaps its experimental form and content) more than its setting.

Pessimism and bleakness likewise exude from Silko's *Ceremony* (1977) and Welch's *Winter in the Blood* (1974) even though both novels end on cautious affirmative notes. In *Ceremony,* a returning World War II veteran, Tayo, fails to overcome his boyhood and war-induced traumas until he undergoes Indian rituals to exorcise the evil and confining legacies of the past. Silko is particularly adept at embedding Tayo's passage within the beliefs and values of his southwestern Indian culture and especially emphasizes his renewed sense of land as he works his way tortuously back to balance and self-acceptance. Furthermore, she notes how much female figures play central roles in Tayo's troubles, as well as in his reformation. Concurrently, *Winter in the Blood* also depicts the pilgrimage of a young Indian male toward self-respect. The nameless narrator of this novel of the northern Rockies must sort out his past, reject the baleful influences of tragedies and self-pity, and gain new appreciations of his family and ethnic heritage before he faces himself. In the novel's final scene, reminiscent of the ending of the western film *Heartland* (1979), a work by Welch's colleagues at Missoula, the author allows the hero the courageous act of rescuing a bogged cow, and through this deed he discovers a renewed sense of self-worth. Throughout *Winter in the Blood*, Welch is more upbeat, more inclined to treat his characters warmly, and to see a less bleak future for them than have most other Native American writers.

Of all the Indian novelists, none has been more prolific and has gained national—even international—attention more rapidly than Louise Erdrich. Of Chippewa and German heritage, Erdrich situates her novels *Love Medicine* (1984), *The Beet Queen* (1986), and *Tracks* (1988) on the northern Plains, treating reservation and small-town life through the experiences of a series of dysfunctional and conflictive families. Her portraits of Native lives blighted from ethnocentric prejudices and driven by sexual obsessions and irrational fears are particularly perceptive and imaginative.

Tracks is a palpable example of several ingredients of postregional fiction. Here the ethnic author centers on Indian traditions and government and non-Indian religious policies that threaten those customs. In emphasizing the detrimental impact of these alien influences, Erdrich uses the alternating voices of elderly Nanapush and mixed-blood Pauline Puyat to dramatize Old Ways of ritual and belief shoved aside by the New Ways of lumber companies, Catholic churches, government schools, nearby white towns, the Agent, motorized vehicles, traps and oxen, and World War I and the diseases it spawns. Yet intratribal struggles, controversial native religious practices, and vain and jealous urgings also undermine the Indians. Although set in the early twentieth century, *Tracks* clearly exhibits the discontents of more recent revisionists. In addition to its social criticism, Erdrich's work also reflects strong environmental concerns. In the final scene, in which Indian culture is disintegrating and the natives are decimated by disease, they are symbolically compared to the nearby forests, which greedy lumbering companies are loudly and viciously destroying. Erdrich's explicit environmental comments reflect another increasingly popular theme in postregional western literature.

Sometimes a pronounced emphasis on ethnicity simultaneously illuminates and strengthens a writer's work, as well as undercutting and limiting it. Such is the case with Rudolfo Anaya. His first work, *Bless Me, Ultima* (1972), remains one of the premier Chicano novels, rich in ethnic detail, inviting in tone, and memorable in characterization. The coming-of-age story of Antonio Márez— caught between his mother's Luna people (folk of the moon, of the soil) and his father's Márez traditions (people of the plains and sea) — Anaya's novel appealingly depicts Antonio's bittersweet negotiations with family, church, peers, sexuality, and ethnic and cultural traditions as he stumbles toward adulthood. Something of a Chicano Huck Finn, Antonio believably acts out his dilemmas. Authorial intrusions and pulpiteering are kept to a minimum, allowing readers to experience Anaya's novels without his looking over their shoulders.

Unfortunately, that is not the case with Anaya's more recent novel *Alburquerque* (1992). As one reviewer noted, the author tries to bait too many hooks: mystery, romance, sex and violence, local color, and an ethnic manifesto.[8] Abrán González's search for his physical father leads him through a labyrinthine quest for personal and ethnic identity, but the author's intrusions through the omniscient narrator wall-in Abrán's freedoms and turn him into a young man who loves his Hispanic mother figures, who scores too easily with young, willing Chicanas, and who nearly always finds his opponents in villainous Anglos. The author tries to do too much, squandering his rich ethnic materials in the marts of popular fiction and producing more a tract than a nuanced work of fiction.

For a full century, western writers have paid close and continuing attention to setting, with regionalists like Mary Austin and Willa Cather early in the 1900s stressing the shaping power of place on character. But environmentalism and ecological themes became increasingly popular after Americans were bombarded with Earth Days, environmental impact studies, and pessimistic reports of overgrazing, natural resource mismanagement, and oil spills during the 1960s and 1970s. Well before that, however, Bernard DeVoto, Wallace Stegner, and A. B. Guthrie had surfaced as notable spokesmen for wilderness preservation. Indeed, for more than forty years Stegner was an outspoken but balanced advocate of thoughtful conservation policies and wise uses of western outbacks and public lands. The essays gathered in *The Sound of Mountain Water* (1969) and *Where the Bluebird Sings to the Lemonade Springs* (1992) testify to his wisdom and evenhandedness.

Several nonfiction writers of the northern West echo Stegner's perspectives. Montanan Ivan Doig illustrates, initially in his autobiographical memoir *This House of Sky* (1978) and later in a series of superbly written novels about the Pacific Northwest, an enlarged postregional understanding of the clashes between nature and culture in the northern interior West. His memoir movingly depicts the forces — big ranches, corporations, and nonwestern powers — that redefine rural Montana, making it a "plundered province." Here and in *English*

Creek (1984) Doig's sparkling descriptions of one-telephone and two-saloon towns and small ranches and farms dumped along the eastern flanks of the Rockies are extraordinary portraits of a twentieth-century West, nourished on frontier myths of progress and abundance but now dyspeptic from upsetting environmental, economic, and bureaucratic transformations. *English Creek* also illustrates Doig's abundant talent for understanding and capturing the cultural and economic forces that whiplashed Montana in the 1930s through the eyes of an adolescent aware of the bittersweet out-of-doors, floundering to right himself and webbed in by an environment experiencing the profound, undulating rhythms that perplex much of the modern West.

More stridently environmentalist are the later writings of Edward Abbey. Especially in *The Monkey Wrench Gang* (1975) but also in *Desert Solitaire* (1968), *Black Sun* (1971), *Good News* (1980), and other collections of stories, essays, and sketches, Abbey climbed into his ecological pulpit to denounce politicians, real estate developers, government programs, and many other malefactors with which he disagreed. Delighting in controversy and polemics, Abbey dispatches his eco-raiders in *The Monkey Wrench Gang,* and they sabotage dams, trains, construction sites, and equipment and machines of all sorts. His bands of ecological terrorists attack all semblances of development and federal entry. Less angry and more humorous than several of Abbey's other books, this novel epitomizes a new environmental consciousness and an advocacy drum beat that many postregionalists have increasingly marched to since 1970.

A host of other writers, in their fiction and nonfiction, participate in this new emphasis on environmentalism. In fact, more postregionalists deal with this subject than any other theme of the past two decades, although their perspectives vary a good deal. Much less bombastic than Abbey but sharing many of his views, Gretel Ehrlich and William Kittredge furnish prime examples of postregional rereadings of northern Rockies landscapes. Born and reared in California but more recently a ranch woman in Wyoming, Ehrlich gradually moves from an "I" to a "we" perspective as she pleasantly sketches her assimilation into the small-town sheep-ranching life of Wyoming in *The Solace of Open Spaces* (1985). Gently reminding readers of her feminine biases, she is no raucous ecological revivalist of the Abbey persuasion. One senses her year-by-year accommodation to the chilling winds, hot summers, and open skies of her adoptive state. The imposing environment—physical, human, and cultural—

is alive here in the author's stretched spaces, humorously and genuinely depicted. Gretel Ehrlich well represents other new western women writers like Ann Zwinger, Linda Hasselstrom, Mary Clearman Blew, Kathleen Norris, and Terry Tempest Williams who have furnished in the last decade compelling feminine perspectives on several subregional natural settings in the West.

Situated between Abbey and Ehrlich in his environmentalism, William Kittredge is the new pivot of a notable literary colony in western Montana. In a series of earlier stories and essays but especially in his recent autobiography, *Hole in the Sky: A Memoir* (1992), Kittredge supplies—in the tradition of Stegner, Guthrie, and Doig—a moving memoir, part confession, part cautionary tale. Limning in broad detail his family's winning and losing a sprawling ranch in south central Oregon, Kittredge, in the pose of a repentant sinner, also testifies to his own greed and ego—his desire to "own it all"—which helped destroy two marriages and shattered friendships. In one revealing passage, the author encapsulates the materialist, expansionist drives that he concludes have ruined the West: "We must define a story," he writes, "which encourages us to make use of the place where we live without killing it, and we must understand that the living world cannot be replicated. There will never be another setup like the one in which we have thrived. Ruin it and we have lost ourselves, and that *is* craziness."[9]

If some regionalists have remythologized the West and others have emphasized gender, ethnic, or environmental themes, still others have revealed a new interest in focusing on specific subregions or borders of the American West. Indeed, even before westerners have been able to fashion a sense of shared community with their neighbors, a new subregionalism has invaded the West, reorienting and redefining several parts of the region's cultural life. Oregonians rail against the Californication of their state, New Mexicans war against a phalanx of swaggering big-bucks Texans, and Minnesotans cast North Dakotans as the thick-headed dumbbells of the northern plains. Others attack Mormon influences spilling out of the central West, organize against Indians moving off their reservations or Hispanics mushrooming into suburbs, or harpoon Yuppie newcomers, whose presence drives up home prices in Dallas, San Diego, and Seattle. If these intraregional clashes threaten to undercut or destroy regional coherence, other rumored regional alignments, geographical or cultural, that would tie the West to a Sunbelt South, a seceding western Canada, or to new allies across the Pacific or along the Mexican border reveal a heightened subregionalism infecting most of the West. Historians, journalists, artists, architects, and other custodians of western culture employ these symbols of difference and fragmentation in their works. So have a few novelists.

In their recent, penetrating studies of local cultures in California's interior valleys and in Montana, historian James Gregory and literary scholar Bill Bevis describe how these locales have spawned important examples of subregional literature and culture.[10] The Okie subculture, particularly its religious ideas, music, and politics, supplied important subjects and character types for John Steinbeck and for the later western writer Gerald Haslam. Meanwhile, building on the earlier literary leadership of H. G. Merriam and Richard Hugo, William Kittredge is captaining a new subregional literary ship, keeping on board native Montanans such as Ivan Doig, James Welch, and Mary Clearman Blew and shanghaiing immigrants like Norman Maclean, Annick Smith, David Quammen, David Long, and Deidre McNamer. In another subregion, Richard Bradford, John Nichols, and Tony Hillerman generally set their fiction in Taos, Santa Fe, and other parts of the interior Southwest. And a host of writers, including Tom Robbins, Ursula LeGuin, and Craig Lesley, find the Pacific Northwest fertile ground for a new crop of fiction. Perhaps *Newsweek* reporters spoke more revealingly than they knew when they listed Portland, Albuquerque, and "all of Montana" as the new hotspots of western writing.

The uses to which these authors have put their subregions are as varied and swiftly changing as the writers and their Wests. Bradford and Nichols, for example, use gentle satire to treat a seriocomic, multicultural New Mexico in *Red Sky at Morning* (1968) and *The Milagro Beanfield War* (1974), whereas the Montana school seems more interested in dealing with rural and environmental topics of the Big Sky, especially those focusing on land issues, federal abuses of the landscape, the area's dilemmas following the collapse of mining and energy booms, and Montanans trying to ride out or accommodate to these sharp changes. Nearby, centering on the coastal areas of Washington, Oregon, and northern California, Ernest Callenbach's *Ecotopia* (1975), a hybrid tract and "politics fiction," sounds shrill ecological notes while it treats a fermenting subregion of the early twenty-first century.

Those authors zeroing in on another subregion—the U.S.–Mexican border —have frequently emphasized cultural conflicts and controversial legacies between the two countries. Earlier, José Antonio Villarreal, in *Pocho* (1959), used to good effect Mexican and American competition within one family attempting to retain its Mexican heritage but gradually losing its children to the new host society in the United States. Later, the leading Chicano novelist Rudolfo Anaya capitalized on Mexican and border transitions in *Bless Me, Ultima*. Other authors such as J.P.S. Brown and particularly Cormac McCarthy in his much-praised *All the Pretty Horses* (1992) trace cowboy, cattleman, vaquero, and ranch traditions across the border, spicing their fiction with memorable characters and events illustrating these important cross-national influences and legacies.

Other borders have also gained new attention. As Henry Nash Smith pointed out two generations ago in his brilliant study *Virgin Land,* many Americans in the late eighteenth and nineteenth centuries viewed their West as a Passage to India. Later, from Walt Whitman through the Beats and up to writers such as Gary Snyder and painters Morris Graves and Mark Tobey, westerners have persisted in looking across the Pacific to trace their sociocultural heritage or to gain new artistic inspiration. Since World War II, this glance to the west/Far East has continued, even broadened. If Carlos Bulosan and John Okada depicted Filipino and Japanese influences in the United States in their pioneering works *America Is in the Heart* (1946) and *No-No Boy* (1957), Maxine Hong Kingston and Amy Tan deal with conflicts and convergences between Old World and New World Chinese cultures. In such books as Kingston's *The Woman Warrior* (1976) and Tan's *The Joy Luck Club* (1989), these Chinese-American women writers suggest how rich "border" materials are for postregional writers. Tan's engrossing novel in particular illustrates the recent strong emphases of western writers on ethnic and gender matters more than on place. Locations in mainland China and the San Francisco Bay area matter less than powerful Chinese legacies of family, religion, and popular culture in shaping the lives of Tan's mothers and daughters.

Surprisingly few authors, however, have utilized borders stretching between the American and Canadian Wests and between the West and the American South. Of those treating the northern border, Wallace Stegner's *Big Rock Candy Mountain* and *Wolf Willow* (1962) contain particularly provocative comparisons between the histories of the two Wests and suggest how these differences and similarities might be treated in transnational, national, and regional literatures. Among other recent western writers, Guthrie, Robert Lewis Taylor, Richard Bradford, and Barbara Kingsolver trace briefly but suggestively southern influences on the West. Few other western novelists have undertaken even abbreviated comparisons of the West and the South, even though trends in race relations, music, folklore, politics, and foodways suggest subjects rich in comparative possibilities. Like western historians, novelists of the West seem reluctant to embark on such daunting comparative tasks.

One other notable ingredient of postregional western literature begs for comment. When college audiences burst into enthusiastic applause as General George Custer and his soldiers blue were decimated in the film *Little Big Man* (1970) and when the same viewers booed and hissed Custer's earlier massacre of Indians at the Battle of Washita, and when the bare buttocks of a five-foot seven-inch Jewish hero romped from bed to bed in an Indian lodge, and when an Indian chief fully and humorously praised the sexual prowess of his men, even blindly loyal aficionados of an earlier Wild West frontier mythology knew their West was achanging. Dozens of screenwriters, historians, artists, and novelists were remythologizing the West, some by pointing out the inanity of earlier accounts; some by satirizing a sacrosanct Old West; some by viciously undercutting western heroes and heroines like Billy the Kid, Calamity Jane, and General Custer; and nearly all by suggesting that previous western images and myths were more useful for cultural reorientations than as true guides to the western history. Many of the same subjects became favorite targets for such revisionist films as *The Wild Bunch* (1969), the spaghetti Westerns, and *Blazing Saddles* (1974), the evocative writings of several New Western historians, and the parodic paintings of Fritz Scholder. All were illustrating the new kinds of western history appearing in a postregional western culture.

Although the more cautious of the literary revisionists seemed to aim merely at appealing and entertaining fiction, others moved on to much more probing—and sometimes sarcastic and biting—interpretations of the West. For example, Max Evans's *The Rounders* (1960), a hilarious novel about cowboys whose work patterns, sexual miscalculations, and incessant drinking remind one more of the genial, tongue-in-cheek mood of the film *Cat Ballou* (1965) than of the tone or point of view displayed in the fictional and cinematic versions of *Little Big Man* (1964, 1970). The comic tone Evans adopts is also present in Robert Flynn's *North to Yesterday* (1967) and Robert Day's *The Last Cattle Drive* (1977), both of which treat cowboys attempting heroic, coming-of-age cattle drives long after the trail drives disappeared. But Ken Kesey's *One Flew Over the Cuckoo's Nest* (1962), though set in an Oregon mental institution, is neither a regional novel (as defined here) nor a gentle satire or pleasant parody of the Evans, Flynn, or Day stripe. Employing his cowboy–logger–Lone Ranger hero, Randle Patrick McMurphy, as something of a frontier individualist attempting to defeat an increasingly bureaucratic, institutionalizing, and numbing world, Kesey implies that self-assertiveness, no matter how heroic and admirable, is no longer possible in modern America. Even though his well-conceived companion, Chief Bromden, escapes to return to his reservation, McMurphy is eventually lobotomized, leaving him a mindless vegetable. Even more nihilistic are the western worlds depicted in E. L. Doctorow's *Welcome to Hard Times* (1960) and John Seelye's *The Kid* (1972). Extreme violence, racism, and empty sex dominate these depressing novels, implying that the frontier West was rarely if ever the land of the free and the home of the brave.

No one has done more than Texas author Larry McMurtry to popularize this new remythologized West. From his first novel, *Horseman, Pass By* (1961), through *The Last Picture Show* (1966) and *Lonesome Dove* (1985), and on to *Anything for Billy* (1988) and *Buffalo Girls* (1990), McMurtry has depicted a complex, unheroic, gray West devoid of the Zane Grey–Louis L'Amour popular images. Picturing a modern West, as well as a pioneer west, rife with conflict and conflicting values represented in cowboy, Cadillac, and oil-tainted mythologies, McMurtry re-imagines a West foreign to earlier frontier and regional writers. All these novels reveal that, in remythologizing the West, postregional literature has dramatically broken away from major trends in western fiction before 1950. Several parallel transformations are clear in recent historical writings about the West.

Chapter 8

POSTREGIONAL HISTORIES

The impact of World War II was more immediate and clear on novelists and painters than on historians. If postregional fiction and art bore the unmistakable marks of war-wrought changes in the West, historians were slower to exhibit those influences. Indeed, frontier and regional historical narratives persisted well into the 1960s. Most historians in the generation following the war depicted the West as a frontier, as *the* influence in shaping American history and culture. At the same time, a few historians, including Walter Prescott Webb and James C. Malin, continued to conceive of the West — or parts of it — as an evolving region whose cultural identity, which so strongly resulted from its unique environment, clearly differed from the cultures of other American regions.[1]

More than any other cultural or intellectual force, the staying power of Turner's frontier interpretation of the West undoubtedly forestalled fresh readings of western history. Although historians in the 1930s, 1940s, and 1950s such as Charles A. Beard, George W. Pierson, and Richard Hofstadter, along with several others, questioned the major conclusions of Turner and his disciples, the frontier hypothesis survived. For example, when westerner John Caughey polled American historians about their favorite books in their field, they ranked Turner's *The Frontier in American History* second behind Vernon L. Parrington's *Main Currents in American History* and ahead of Charles and Mary Beard's *The Rise of American Civilization*. A dozen years later, a revealing survey of western historiography concluded that "the ideas of Turner

and the pro-Turnerians [were] still dominant," although the writer also predicted that it was "only a matter of time" until the non-Turnerians attained
"majority status."[2] Well into the 1960s and 1970s, many authorities on the
American West, including the authors of major textbooks in the field, followed
the frontier thesis, convinced that it furnished the most defensible way of interpreting the American West.

Even though Turnerians and regionalists predominated for at least two decades after the war's end, other historians advanced alternative views that, a
generation or so later, increasingly influenced western historiography. Major
books and essays by Henry Nash Smith, Earl Pomeroy, and Wallace Stegner
first appeared in the 1950s, urging writers to reconsider their view of the West
solely as an advancing frontier. In so doing, they served as forerunners of postregional interpretations of the West.

Among these pathbreaking works none has been more influential than
Smith's brilliant *Virgin Land: The American West as Symbol and Myth* (1950).
In two specific ways *Virgin Land* broke from previous historiographical trends.
Not only did Smith utilize research materials that most western historians had
overlooked, he also taught them to understand that *beliefs* (he used the words
"myths" and "symbols") about the West, whether true or not, were often as
important as facts in understanding western history. Immediately hailed as an
important new interpretation of the West in American thought and culture,
Smith's book remains the most provocative work ever written on the mythic
West, immensely influential among all specialists on western history and culture. Indeed, two generations after its publication, specialists place it at the
top of the list of books that have shaped their thinking and writing.[3]

Drafted in part as one of the first dissertations in the field of American
Civilization at Harvard in the late 1930s, Smith's book imaginatively employs
a wide variety of research materials. Not unexpectedly, he analyzes the western writings of James Fenimore Cooper, Walt Whitman, and Hamlin Garland.
But unlike earlier students of western history, he also furnishes careful, probing readings of such "subliterary" works as reports of explorers, surveyors,
and geologists, travel accounts, and dime novels. The two chapters devoted
to heroes and heroines of the dime novel, as well as those that trace popular beliefs about agrarianism, illustrate the author's commitment to studying
all types of writing about the West. Through a close study of the characters,
plots, and themes of dime novels and popular treatises on the West as desert
or garden, Smith demonstrates how popular literature reflected many of the

controlling assumptions of the day about the nature of the American West. Smith's provocative use of historiography, literature, sociology, and cultural anthropology reveals his strong attachment to the interdisciplinary approaches that characterized the early American Studies movement.[4]

Virgin Land also influenced western historiography in still another, more significant way. Smith taught historians that they frequently misused the term *myths,* speaking of myths as opposite of truths, when in fact, he asserted, they were important belief systems that shaped as well as reflected a complex, interrelated set of historical, emotional, and psychological experiences. Since a symbol or a myth, which Smith defined as "an intellectual construction that fuses concept and emotion into an image,"[5] was often as important as an observable fact or event in shaping what actually took place in the West, historians must scrutinize their use of all kinds of historical sources. Practicing what he preached, Smith opens his book with a discussion of the views of Benjamin Franklin and Thomas Jefferson and then proceeds to show how other ideas about the West clustered around three central myths: the West as "Passage to India," as home of "The Sons of Leatherstocking," and as "The Garden of the World." Through this holistic approach of showing myths and symbols as central to understanding American thinking about the West in the nineteenth century, Smith is able to demonstrate that Turner's famous essay of 1893 was part fact and part of the mythology that had grown up in the previous century.

The final chapter of *Virgin Land,* in discussing Turner, clearly illustrates Smith's use of symbolic analysis. The idea of the West as Garden of the World captured Turner's imagination, Smith argues, and encouraged him, unconsciously, to utilize the richly connoted words *nature* and *civilization* in so many of his writings. The author shows that Turner's use of *nature* often moved beyond social analysis into poetry, a transition that reflected Turner's ties to "the agrarian myth." Employing the close-reading techniques of literary criticism, Smith demonstrates that Turner's use of *nature* was frequently more metaphorical than factual.

A decade or so transpired before western historians applied Smith's innovative research techniques and utilized his conclusions. Once discovered, however, *Virgin Land* has strongly influenced western historiography during the last three decades. In fact, no other recent trend in western historical writing seems so tied to one book as does the study of the West as myth. One group of historians, heeding Smith's admonition to take seriously the widely held and emotionally charged convictions of nineteenth-century Americans about the frontier West, has produced a notable collection of western cultural histories. The best of these are Kevin Starr's magnificent multivolume cultural study of California, four volumes of which have been published: *Americans and the California Dream* (1973), *Inventing the Dream: California through the Progressive Era* (1985), *Material Dreams: Southern California through the 1920s* (1990), and *Endangered Dreams: The Great Depression in California* (1996). Another coterie of scholars, especially those trained in American Studies and less interested in studying literary and cultural history than with understanding the ideologies that have influenced the West, follow nonwesterner Richard Slotkin in stressing destructive ideas that misshaped the frontier and the American West. Slotkin's massive, influential trilogy—*Regeneration through Violence* (1973), *The Fatal Environment* (1985), and *Gunfighter Nation* (1992)—exhaustively utilizes histories, novels, and numerous sources of popular culture, much as Smith had in *Virgin Land*. Still another group of scholars, less inclined to follow Slotkin's revisionist bent and moving beyond Smith's major emphasis on the nineteenth century, use his chapters on the dime novel as a model for their examinations of popular Westerns in the twentieth century. For example, John G. Cawelti's influential books on popular Western novels and films, *The Six-Gun Mystique* (1971, 1984) and *Adventure, Mystery, and Romance* (1976)— which analyze the structural and thematic formulae in the fiction of Owen Wister and Zane Grey and the films of William S. Hart and John Ford—clearly betray his strong ties to Smith's pioneering work on the West as myth. These scholars and a host of others illustrate the central influence of *Virgin Land* on western historiography since the 1960s.

The historian Earl Pomeroy also advanced an interpretation of the West that broke sharply from preponderant views of the pre–World War II period. A challenge to the West simply as a unique and innovating frontier surfaced earlier in the twentieth century, but that challenge received its most forceful statement in 1955 in Pomeroy's pathbreaking essay "Toward a Reorientation of Western History: Continuity and Environment."[6] In the 1920s and 1930s such writers as Benjamin F. Wright, Dixon Ryan Fox, and John D. Hicks either questioned that the frontier radically redirected incoming cultural forces or argued that eastern and frontier streams were equally blended in shaping midwestern culture. Then, for a decade or two, discussions of change versus continuity disappeared from the scene, no doubt forgotten during the traumatic times of the Depression, New Deal, World War II, and the Cold War.

Before Pomeroy in the 1950s, no western historian so pointedly addressed this central question: Was the West the product of a radically innovative western environment, or did it owe more to the replication of ideas from the American East and Europe? From the beginning of his career in the late 1930s, Pomeroy, influenced by his extensive reading about relationships between the colonies and the mother country in early American history and his research on national political and western territorial configurations, set out to examine the lines of political, constitutional, economic, and sociocultural influences linking the East and the West. Contrary to what some critics argued, Pomeroy did not assert that the East dominated the West, and thus he did not "exchange new narrowness for old" (596). Instead, in a key phrase he summarized his position that "conservativism, inheritance, and continuity bulked at least as large in the history of the West as radicalism and environment" (581). Granted, in trying to persuade readers of the validity of his argument, he devoted most of his essay to demonstrating continuities and gave less attention to western innovations, but he clarified his own approach by saying of Turner: "he had . . . errors to combat in his time, by overemphasis if necessary" (599). Nor did Pomeroy attack Turner, as some argued. Rather, he hoped that subsequent historical writing about the West would avoid the shortcomings and narrowness of those "romanticists and antiquarians, who borrowed Turner's phrases rather than his methods and the range of his imagination." Or, as Pomeroy added: "the trouble with western history may be that we are not enough like Turner in his larger qualities: his concern for both analysis and synthesis, his effective English style, and the keenness of his mind" (599).

Pomeroy's challenge to historians gained little headway in the 1950s and 1960s; western historians were still enamored with the frontier West. Yet a few historians agreed with Pomeroy, some following his lead and others coming independently to similar conclusions. Published in the same year as Pomeroy's "Reorientation" essay, Louis B. Wright's *Culture on the Moving Frontier* (1955) concluded that Anglo-Saxon traditions, primarily those emanating from England, did more than the physical frontier to shape cultural life in these succeeding frontier areas. That is, churches, schools, and other cultural institutions owed more to English custodians of culture who moved to the frontier than to frontiersmen (the "powers of darkness"), who showed much less interest in bringing cultural institutions to the new pioneer areas. In the next decade, William Goetzmann also traced the powerful influences of European and eastern American ideas on explorers, scientists, army men, and artists who traveled west as representatives of the federal government or at their own expense. These newcomers were more than intrepid men marching to the frontier; they too were culture carriers, whose ideas did much to influence frontier and postfrontier settlements in the West. Nowhere are these conclusions clearer than in Goetzmann's discussions of the "emulative West" in his magnificent Pulitzer Prize-winning study *Exploration and Empire* (1966).

Later, in the 1970s and 1980s, growing numbers of western historians found Pomeroy's thesis to their liking. In a provocative study of western women, Julie Roy Jeffrey concluded that frontier women carried eastern attitudes and expectations to the frontier more often than they established innovative socio-cultural patterns unique to the demanding new country. Similarly, legal historian John Phillip Reid discovered parallel ideas and acts of cultural persistence in his studies of legal and constitutional issues among western pioneers. Geographer Terry G. Jordan and historian John D. W. Guice located analogous chains of continuity between colonial coastal cattle-raising and the cattle industry that sprang up in southern Texas. And several urban historians follow Pomeroy in tracing precedents in eastern urban areas transplanted to frontier and western cities.[7]

Pomeroy also suggested another kind of continuity in his classic essay of 1955. Asking writers to rethink the tendency of historians to "cut . . . off western history in the 1890's," he urged them instead to exercise "the breadth and flexibility of mind that will disregard arbitrary borders in time and space" (581, 599). And Pomeroy followed his own preachments in *The Pacific Slope* (1965), where he employed trends in urbanization, economic development, and political activity to determine his periodization rather than following, lock step, the traditional division of western history at the closing of the frontier in the 1890s. Although Pomeroy's blueprint for tracing continuities between the nineteenth and twentieth centuries seemed to go at first unheeded, recent publications indicate that ties between the two centuries are now being traced. As we shall see later, such writers as Howard Lamar, Patricia Nelson Limerick, Donald Worster, Kevin Starr, and Richard White, among many others, are now calling attention to clear lines of influence between the pioneer and modern Wests.[8]

By the mid-1990s, many western historians influenced by Earl Pomeroy were less inclined to emphasize the frontier as *the* source from which most elements of frontier and western society and culture sprang. They now placed increased stress on the frontier and the West as imitators rather than as innovators. At the same time, other writers discovered important legacies that connected the nineteenth and twentieth centuries and gradually abandoned the traditional idea that the 1890s profoundly separated an older frontier from the twentieth-century West.

The third of the triumvirate of works that signaled new approaches in western historiography soon after World War II was Wallace Stegner's sparkling biography, *Beyond the Hundredth Meridian: John Wesley Powell and the Second Opening of the West* (1954). Perhaps less well known among western specialists than Smith's *Virgin Land* and Pomeroy's "Reorientation" essay, Stegner's biography nonetheless advances interpretations of Powell and western history that have been increasingly influential in the past generation, especially among social, economic, and environmental historians.

Stegner's thesis may be stated succinctly: Had Americans, especially westerners, followed the rational scientific arguments of John Wesley Powell rather than the romantic idealism of William Gilpin and other tub-thumpers, the American West could have avoided many of its economic busts, environmental disasters, and even cultural tragedies. In his compelling and smoothly written life story of Powell, Stegner repeatedly demonstrates the foresight, wisdom, and practical insights of Powell, which he learned, accumulated, and preached after his extensive explorations of the varied terrain of the interior West. Seeing far beyond the boosters and manifest destinarians of his age, Powell urged government agencies, planners, and settlers to adapt a "blueprint for a dry-land democracy" based on realistic estimates of the number of newcomers that arid regions could sustain. For the most part, as Stegner convincingly shows, Powell was an unheeded voice crying in the wilderness.[9]

Although no holy dictum derived from a burning bush, Stegner's message has gained an increasing number of listeners. In *Virgin Land*, Henry Nash Smith championed Powell's hardheaded insights over against the muddled enthusiasm of unthinking expansionists, but Stegner advances beyond Smith in calling attention to Powell's larger, more expansive design for government control and administration of the West. Political gridlock, Gilded Age materialism, and Powell's competitors blocked or stalled several of his plans and generally derailed his engine of reform, which would have linked government power and public needs; but as Stegner wondered forty years ago, perhaps Powell remained on a prominence overlooking the West, "with some confidence wait[ing] for the future to catch up with him" (367).

Some westerners have begun to do just that. A host of environmentally minded historians, often through Stegner's provocative account of Powell, or by way of his other notable books and essays on the West, have come to see western physical and cultural landscapes in a far different way. As we shall see, historians of the 1980s and 1990s, such as Donald Worster, William Cronon, and Richard White, echo the ideas of Powell as Stegner outlines them in his remarkable book. Granted, Powell's *Report on the Lands of the Arid Region of the United States* (1878) received notable attention in the histories of Walter Prescott Webb and James C. Malin and treatment in Nash's *Virgin Land,* but it was Wallace Stegner who demonstrated for the next two generations of western historians how much Powell and his understanding of the arid West had to contribute to a larger comprehension of the American West. As such, Stegner's *Beyond the Hundredth Meridian* moved beyond emphases in many earlier frontier and regional interpretations and pointed the way to themes that postregional historians took up after 1970.

The cycles of change that seemed to cut across the West each generation in the twentieth century erupted again in the late 1960s. Just as the late twenties and late forties hosted earlier discontinuities, so the late sixties and early seventies saw the emergence of several new trends in western historiography. For the first time, western historians examined the main contours of the twentieth-century West. Paralleling shifts among western novelists and moviemakers and following trends among American historians, they quickly moved to deal with new interests in ethnic, family, and environmental history. Many of these new studies came from the pens of younger historians, but well-known veterans such as Ray Allen Billington, Francis Paul Prucha, and Robert Utley likewise reflected these historiographical shifts. Together, these scholars introduced a New Western historiography that focused on many of the topics that intrigued postregional novelists. Later, in the late 1980s and early 1990s, a small group of younger scholars, building on the new trends in western historiography that emerged in the 1970s and 1980s, launched what they termed a New Western history. As we shall see, this lively new school was a logical outcome of historiographical currents of the previous generation.[10]

The current that first pulsated through western historical writing in the 1970s was the newly discovered and rapidly expanding subfield of the twentieth-century West. Although Frederick Jackson Turner, Walter Prescott Webb, and other writers supplied brief pioneering studies of the modern West in the first half of the century, not until Earl Pomeroy and Gerald D. Nash published their pathbreaking volumes in the 1960s and 1970s did the field seem a viable one for research and publication. In recent decades, several western historians have urged their colleagues to explore the modern West, and following this urging, many have begun to take up the challenge.

That historians waited so long to treat the modern West reveals much about western historiography. For a variety of reasons, but especially because of their ties to the frontier thesis and their stress on the westward movement (to-the-West historiography), academics seemed reluctant to deal with the post-1900 West. Thus, nearly three quarters of the twentieth century passed before the publication of the first overview synthesis of the modern West. The gradual discovery of the contemporary West and its treatment in a growing number of popular accounts and monographs are a revealing part of postregional western culture.

If earlier historians and journalists published partial portraits and later impressionistic overviews, Pomeroy and Nash provided benchmark interpretations that influenced much of what is currently being written about the twentieth-century West. Practicing what he had preached in his earlier essay on the reorientation of western historical writing, Pomeroy, in *The Pacific Slope* (1965), skips over much of the romantic and narrative frontier history that filled previous accounts of the Far West and emphasizes instead eastern and international influences on the Pacific Slope, continuities between the nineteenth and twentieth centuries, and the expanding hegemony of western urban areas. In his arresting opening paragraph, Pomeroy signals the provocative quality of his thinking about the West: "The Pacific Slope is the most Western and, after the East itself, the most Eastern part of America. No other section is more like the Atlantic seaboard and Western Europe; no part is more different; and no part has wished to be both."[11]

In emphasizing the twentieth century, Pomeroy draws no fault line across the 1890s, separating the pioneer era and the later urbanizing and industrializing Far West. For Pomeroy, the Pacific Slope was surprisingly urban from its English-speaking beginnings, and the region owes as much or more to eastern legacies as to unique western circumstances. Indeed, in his longest and pivotal chapter, "The Power of the Metropolis," Pomeroy demonstrates that the urban development of the Far West made little sense if divided at the normal breaking point of the 1890s. Instead, one must see the continuities between the years of origin and the dramatic rise of urban power well into the twentieth century. In two ways, then, Pomeroy broke fellowship with the close-knit fraternity of earlier frontier historians: he downplayed the molding power of a new, unique frontier environment, and he stressed the recent rather than the pioneer West.

Whereas Pomeroy limited his notably interpretive volume to the Pacific Slope territories and states, Gerald Nash treated the full range of states west of the ninety-fifth meridian in his *American West in the Twentieth Century* (1973), the first full-scale history of the modern West. Nash points out that the recent West is best understood when divided into colonial (1898–1941) and pacesetting (1941–1971) eras. Although westerners viewed themselves as victims of a colonial economy and culture until the outbreak of World War II, that event did more than any other occurrence to move the West in a new direction. Largely as a result of spiraling government expenditures, mushrooming urban-industrial complexes (particularly in California), and burgeoning populations in many areas of the West, the region shrugged off much of its earlier colonialism and, in some ways, became an economic and sociocultural pacesetter for the rest of the nation. Like Pomeroy, Nash devotes lengthy sections to economic and political developments and demonstrates how these regional developments are often closely tied to national and global happenings.[12]

Since the pioneering work of Pomeroy and Nash, increasing numbers of historians have focused on the twentieth-century West. Notable among their writings were two additional volumes by Nash treating the sociocultural and economic impact of World War II on the West. In the most recent overview of the post-1900 West, Michael P. Malone and Richard W. Etulain's *The American West: A Twentieth-Century History* (1989), although clearly indebted to the earlier writings of Webb, Pomeroy, and Nash, add emphases missing from earlier studies. Stressing more than previous writers the roles of women and family, historiography, and religion, for example, Malone and Etulain also emphasize the plains and interior West, in addition to pointing out the burgeoning power of the West's two behemoths — California and Texas.

These pioneering and more recent works on the twentieth-century West illustrate central themes of postregional western culture. Not only do these authors abandon the frontier tyranny that held sway in western historiography well into the 1960s, but by and large they also avoid the chauvinism that marked the regional writings of DeVoto and Webb in the 1930s and 1940s. Concurrently, historians treating the modern West frequently trace continuities from the pioneer era into the twentieth century, thereby bridging the Rubicon of the 1890s at the same time that they gradually view the modern West in national and international circumstances rather than limiting their accounts solely to regional stories. Long in coming and mostly of recent origin, these discussions of the modern West signal sharp breaks with the major emphases of earlier frontier and regional historiography.

In the past generation, many western historians have also stressed other subjects that are popular in postregional western literature and in recent western films, and influential among American historians in general. Beginning in the 1970s and during the next two decades a New Western historiography (as distinct from the more recent New Western history) gradually emerged, in which historians of the West paid increasing attention to racial and ethnic groups, women, families, and gender, and environmental topics. Opting likewise to place less stress on Turner's frontier, these western historians turned increasingly toward viewing the West as a region of America and as a subregion of the world. This New Western historiography parted company with historiographical concepts prior to the 1960s and demonstrated how much social and cultural currents of that yeasty decade and the years immediately following have spawned new trends in western historical writing and have naturally led to the rise of a New Western history at the end of the 1980s. Although the frontier and regional concepts of Turner, Bolton, Webb, and Malin were by no means dead, they have been put to use for different purposes since the 1970s.

In the mid-1980s two prominent scholars, Rodman W. Paul and Michael P. Malone, argued that western historians had "ventured only cautiously and partially into the ferment of new thinking that [had] characterized the profession nationally" and that they had been "noticeably slow in taking up the newer methodologies that became popular during the 1970s."[13] With additional perspective, one can conclude that revolution in western historiography was clearly underway by the 1980s and, at century's close, is even more apparent. Nowhere are those dramatic historiographical shifts more apparent than in the innovative treatments of racial and ethnic groups in the American West.

Previous to 1970, the most probing treatments of Indians in the trans-Mississippi West resulted from the work of ethnologists or from historians studying Indian policy or military history. The trickle of their publications turned to a stream and then to a flood in the 1970s and 1980s as numerous western historians turned to studying Native Americans and helped to produce what has been called the "New Indian history."[14] Gradually, these new histories moved beyond the study of contact or policy and began to stress an "Indian-Indian" history, or accounts of the internal affairs of tribal history. In employing the insights of ethnologists, psychologists, and other students of human cultures, western historians began to see Indian societies with different eyes.

The works of Richard White, especially his *Roots of Dependency* (1983) and *The Middle Ground* (1991), are superb examples of this recent pathbreaking research on Indians. In the first of these memorable studies, White invokes theories of dependency and hegemony to demonstrate how often the history of American Indians has been a conflict between outside influences and tribal desires for independence. More daring conceptually and much lauded for its pathbreaking research and interpretation, *The Middle Ground* moves far beyond stories of invasion, clash-and-conflict, and assimilation and accommodation to fashion a new kind of narrative, a narrative of how Europeans and Native Americans met, mingled, and structured—in the Great Lakes region from 1650 to 1815—a new cultural *patois* that incorporated elements from both groups and that was understandable and usable for natives and newcomers alike. White's perceptive analysis of this intermingling of cultures sets his work dramatically apart from earlier frontier accounts that treated Indians as savages or primitive, childlike peoples who were barriers to civilization. It also separates his publications from those popular revisionist accounts of the 1960s and 1970s that nearly always portrayed Indians as virtuous, Edenic peoples invariably wronged by invading, rapacious Europeans. In his complex, finely textured books, Richard White illustrates how far postregional western historiography has moved beyond earlier accounts in probing the meaning of Indian experiences on the frontier and in the West.

Similar innovative work characterizes recent interpretations of Chicanos in the American West. But this new historiography builds on a different tradition. If Indians have always been central figures in frontier-western histories, Spanish-speaking peoples have not. Frontier historians like Turner and Paxson, and the regionalists (with the notable exception of Bolton and the extremely slanted chapters in Webb's volumes) scarcely noted the important roles of Hispanics in the Southwest and California. That oversight and these initial historiographical views had changed dramatically by the late 1970s.

Indeed, few areas of historical writing have been more alive with activity and controversy than the recent interpretations of Chicanos. These interpretations have largely followed two routes. In the late 1970s and early 1980s, one group of writers—such as Albert Camarillo, Mario T. García, Ricardo Romo, and Richard Griswold del Castillo—produced admirable monographs on Chicano communities in California and the Southwest. All these authors, clearly displaying their links to recent methodological trends in the New Social History, make abundant use of statistics, demography, and other social science methods to plot changes and continuities over time within these ethnic communities. All point to the profoundly negative impact of American racism on Chicanos, and all assert that Hispanics, rather than passively accepting the bureaucratic dominance of the larger American society, strove to structure a barrio life that protected residents from outside prejudice and domination.[15]

Those historians following another route, such as Rodolfo Acuña, Juan Gómez-Quiñones, Oscar Martínez, and Robert J. Rosenbaum, frequently building on this spate of new monographs and interpretive essays but sometimes working through primary sources, have furnished overviews of Hispanic experiences in the nineteenth and twentieth centuries, have examined general themes in Chicano historiography, and have treated specific questions of race, class, and gender. Much more so than recent writings about Native Americans, nearly all these studies of Chicanos are by members of the group being studied and employ explicitly theoretical frameworks foreign to earlier frontier or regional western historians. More outspoken and assertive—sometimes even shrill—these accounts differ markedly in tone, argument, and conclusions from most recent studies of western ethnic groups. At the same time, they are suggestive of the broader and richer possibilities for studying ethnicity in the West.[16]

Even work in the more traditional field of Borderlands studies reflects changes typical of western postregional historiography. No one has done more to broaden this Boltonian field than has David J. Weber. First in a series of monographic and bibliographical essays, next in his *Mexican Frontier, 1821–1846* (1982), and then in his memorable book *The Spanish Frontier in North America* (1992), Weber produces Borderlands history updated through exhaustive research in manuscript and other primary documents but particularly enlarged through the perspectives of revisionist secondary works dealing with environmental, racial, and class issues. Critiquing the earlier Black Legend, moving beyond Bolton's Hispanic-centered views, and embracing new insights on the environment and Indians, Weber supplies fresh views of the Spanish presence in North America not by utilizing a bold, innovative approach to his huge supply of research materials but by furnishing a synthetic view that builds on Bolton and is enriched by the New Western historiography of the past generation. His *Spanish Frontier in North America* supplies, in effect, a richer, more complex design for a familiar tapestry.

Recent works on Asian and black experiences in the West have been less numerous and pathbreaking than those on Indians and Chicanos, but other historians have been remarkably prolific and innovative in treating European ethnic groups in the American West. The most significant of these are the essays and books of Frederick C. Luebke, whose major research focuses on Germans in the West, but who has laid out interpretive frameworks drawing upon the research of geographers, folklorists, linguists, anthropologists, and demographers. Sensitive to how new immigrant groups used their western lands, how they congregated in varying communities, and how they attempted to retain their culture, Luebke furnishes more probing and sophisticated models for the study of European ethnicity in the West than did frontier and regional historians.[17] Concurrently, other scholars, reflecting the quickly expanding interest in ethnic groups following the 1960s, supplied new overviews of Basques, Greeks, and Jews, model monographs on the Irish and Italians, and useful collections on several ethnic groups. This burgeoning scholarship illustrates anew the fresh topics in the West's cultural legacies that have intrigued postregional historians.

These historians also exhibit a mounting interest in the roles of gender and family in the West. Clearly an extraordinary fascination with a distorted Wild West, which emphasized a masculine frontier, blocked earlier studies of western women and families. Yet recent historians of the West were no more reluctant than writers in other regions to address these topics. At much the same time that American scholars began to deal with the subjects of gender and family, western historians initiated work on these new subjects.

More than a decade ago in their superb historiographical overview, Joan M. Jensen and Darlis A. Miller called for more attention to cross-cultural topics, the twentieth century, and new approaches to women's history.[18] Even as Jensen and Miller published their pathbreaking essay, other scholars were examining subjects they listed as meriting more research. Sandra Myres and Glenda Riley completed synthetic studies of nineteenth-century western women, and in doing so they opened up an important new field even while following traditional perspectives owing more to frontier historiography than to the innovative approaches of the New Social History emerging in the 1960s and 1970s. Julie Roy Jeffrey, beginning with feminist assumptions of female assertiveness on the frontier, discovered instead that western women replicated eastern experiences more often than they lived novel, pathbreaking lives in the West. More revisionist, the books and essays of Lillian Schlissel and John Mack

Faragher, emphasizing women's reluctance to move west and females' unwillingness to be passive pawns of patriarchal fathers, husbands, and brothers, reflected the methods and conclusions of American social historians of the post-1960s era.[19]

In still another area, environmental history, western historians have had more impact on American historical writing than they have in other historiographical subfields. One might ask why. Why has environmental history become almost *de rigueur* among frontier and western historians but not among other regional historians? Does this interest stem from earlier emphases on new environments among Turner and the frontier historians, from the urban oases themes of Webb and the regionalists, or from the emerging regional consciousness that swept across the country and through historiographical circles in the 1970s and 1980s? Undoubtedly all these impulses influence recent frontier and western historians to emphasize environmental topics. One suspects, too, the centuries-long view of the West as a tabula rasa, an endless mythic space, so present in the fictional, cinematic, and other popular cultural images of the West, has encouraged scholars to think of the region as a place to be saved for the future. If frontier novelists, historians, artists, and film directors such as Wister, Turner, Russell, and John Ford singled out the frontier or the West as the place for progress and future prosperity or regionalists like Webb and Stegner pointed to the Great Plains and the Rockies as the locus of a redeemed West or an ecological sanctuary, it is more understandable that postregional historians again cite the frontier and the West as locations for new understandings of land, landscapes, and cultures. Whatever the major reasons for this burst of interest, westerners have surfaced as the leading environmental historians in the United States. Indeed, when the prestigious *Journal of American History* lined up a special issue on the new field of environmental history, three of the essays — half of the special issue — came from frontier and western historians.[20]

In those essays, in many others, and in notable books, writers such as Donald Worster, Patricia Nelson Limerick, Richard White, and William Cronon have rushed to the forefront of pathbreaking interpretations of the environment that illustrate postregional thinking about the American West. In less than a decade, these western writers have done more than any other authors to establish a new field in American historiography.

The book-length studies are of two types. Worster, in his intellectual history, *Nature's Economy: The Roots of Ecology* (1977), which includes a major section on ecological thinking about the Great Plains, represents western historians who often viewed the environment through the history of ideas. Trained in American Studies at Yale, Worster utilized intellectual history in his provocative first book, as well as in his later *Dust Bowl* (1979) and *Rivers of Empire* (1985). Another Yale American Studies dissertation became Patricia Nelson Limerick's initial volume, *Desert Passages* (1985), which, like Worster's volumes, is as much cultural and intellectual as environmental history. Worster and Limerick became particularly well known for these provocative overviews, as did Limerick for her *Legacy of Conquest* (1987) and her lively prose urging Americans to rethink their stereotypes of deserts and earlier mistreatments of western lands and landscapes; for Worster's stern warnings against ecological disaster that moved well beyond the earlier views of Webb, DeVoto, and Stegner.

Meanwhile, White and Cronon, agreeing with much of what Worster and Limerick had written, were producing other kinds of environment studies. White's first book, *Land Use, Environment, and Social Change* (1980), a model monograph, supplied a case study of human rearrangement of the environment in Island County, Washington, from Indian times to the 1960s. Showing how people transformed the land as a result of their shifting social needs and desires, White turned Turner and the frontier historians on their heads in emphasizing the shaping power of culture rather than the molding forces of a powerful new environment. Remarkably similar in many of its emphases was William Cronon's pathbreaking *Changes in the Land* (1983), a Yale seminar paper expanded into the young author's first book. He too reminded readers that Indians made dramatic changes in the environment before the first Europeans arrived, but once those newcomers invaded New England, Native Americans were forced to make changes in order to survive under the capitalist market economies of the invaders. Monographic, like White's case study, Cronon's volume was also interdisciplinary and broad in its research. Even though narrowly focused, both books illustrated how skilled conceptualists and talented writers might attack a novel subject.

Most of these new studies had appeared by the mid-1980s. In the years since, Worster, White, and Cronon have pioneered in still other areas of environmental history. Illustrating the postregional desire to see the American West in a global perspective, Worster attempts in *Rivers of Empire* to show how the limitations of earlier hydraulic water kingdoms in Egypt and China resurfaced in several subregions of the American West. In other edited volumes and essays, he demonstrates his knowledge of worldwide environmental experiences and their parallels in the trans-Mississippi West. Meanwhile, White, reflecting the postregional interest in multiculturalism, compares and contrasts the ecological designs and experiences of Native Americans, Europeans, and white North Americans in *The Roots of Dependency* and *The Middle Ground*. In both volumes, but especially in the latter book, White furnishes a new paradigm for studying the cultural contacts, conflicts, and accommodations, including their differing treatments of the environment, of two or more societies. The same sophistication of thinking and thoroughness of research mark Cronon's second book *Nature's Metropolis: Chicago and the Great West* (1991), a brilliant treatment of the environmental, economic, and rural-urban complexities that defined Chicago and its Great Western hinterlands.

Most intriguing is how soon this quartet of frontier and western scholars assumed leadership among the country's environmental historians. Revealingly, when William Cronon listed those of his contemporaries who had influenced him most, the names of Worster, White, and Limerick were especially prominent.[21] And, as we shall see, these frontier and western historians were exactly those named most often as the leaders in the New Western history movement that flashed across the West in the late 1980s.

But the New Western historiography—again as something larger and less recent than the New Western history—included more than these significant new studies of racial, ethnic, gender, and environmental topics. If one had pages enough and time, innovative discussions of urban history, fresh treatments of water and land, and new comparative works on social change would also merit discussion. Nor would one want to overlook the large impact that social scientists, including geographers, political scientists, sociologists and anthropologists have had on recent western historiography.

In another subfield—cultural studies—historical writing in the American West follows national historiographical trends, builds on previous western writings, and thus parallels recent currents in western fiction and art. Yet the outstanding intellectual influence in this area is still Smith's *Virgin Land*, which nearly a half century after its publication continues to overshadow much of what is written about culture in the American West. On the one hand, the three previously mentioned books by Richard Slotkin bear the identifiable marks of Smith's myth and symbol emphasis in Slotkin's nearly exhaustive treatment of the Myth of the Frontier from 1600 to the 1980s. Slotkin relentlessly traces what he conceives as the central mythology from the Puritans through the latest Westerns of the Reagan years. Much less inclined to ride myths as hard as Slotkin, Kevin Starr nonetheless betrays his ties to the American Civilization (or American Studies) background he shares with Smith and Slotkin. In his four-volume study of the California Dream, Starr serves up a thorough, thick description of the dreams—the visions, the designs, and the myths—that shaped and sometimes misshaped the patterns of California from 1850 through the 1920s. Published at the same time as Slotkin's trilogy and equally expansive, Starr's volumes owe more to earlier cultural historians, like westerners Franklin Walker and Carey McWilliams, than to the revisionist theorists that power Slotkin's perspectives.[22] Together they epitomize the rich diversity of recent cultural studies of the West.

Moving in another direction but owing much to Smith and in some ways paralleling the routes Slotkin and Starr have followed, are the increasing numbers of books about popular representations of the West. If Smith seemed inclined to dismiss popular fiction about the West after the gradual demise of the dime novel Western, others have not. Several scholars have furnished valuable studies that take seriously such writers as Zane Grey, Ernest Haycox, and Louis L'Amour and their popular Westerns as important embodiments of twentieth-century myths about the West.[23] An equally large number of books and essays in the last two decades focus on Western films as illustrations of cultural myths, Western and national. Illustrative of this new trend is William H. Goetzmann and William N. Goetzmann, *The West of the Imagination* (1986), the companion volume to a six-part PBS series that examined nineteenth- and twentieth-century ideas and images about the West. These authors, and several others, not only traced the form and importance of these popular notions, they also demonstrated how western novelists, artists, and filmmakers, as part of postregional culture, remythologized such figures as Indians, cowboys, and General Custer, using traditional western heroes and villains for new, revisionist purposes.

Still another trend in western cultural studies owed less to *Virgin Land* than to new emphases in the social sciences and in community and case studies that emerged in American historiography after the mid-1960s. For instance, geographer D. W. Meinig and social scientist Raymond D. Gastil demonstrated in their examinations of western regions that the West was more complex culturally than previous studies had suggested. David Montejano, in his prize-winning monograph focusing on Tejano-Anglo conflicts along the Rio Grande border in south Texas and James Gregory's equally illuminating examination of Okie culture in interior California dramatically illustrate how cultural studies have sharply shifted away from work in that field by previous generations.[24] It is as if these historians were following a newly outlined agenda that called for the study of "the significance of cultural subregions in the modern American West." They clearly point toward the necessity of understanding what Richard White terms a "relational West" — a recognition that persisting shifts and changes continually redefine the West and its subregional cultures.[25] What was true culturally of California, Texas, or the Mormon core region a generation ago, for example, is not likely to remain true for the present or a decade or two hence.

For nearly three decades the New Western historiography has been a vital force in gradually reshaping historical interpretations of the American West. The new emphases on race and ethnicity, women and families, the environment, and cultural complexities, as well as parallel stress on the twentieth century and urbanization, have helped to re-vision the West since the 1960s.

At this point, several questions seem paramount: Will these new visions of the West remain separate from those that conceptualize the West as a frontier or region? Are syntheses that combine the older frontier and regional perspectives with the postregional ones possible, or is a new synthesis, based primarily on the fresh emphases of the New Western historiography, now probable? The answers to these questions not only help to explain historical writing about the West published since 1970, they also suggest agendas for western historians through the first years of the new century.

A handful of examples indicates that several types of syntheses are now possible. The most recent editions of widely adopted texts by Ray Allen Billington, Martin Ridge, and Robert Hine in the 1980s illustrate one phase of this synthesis. These writers incorporate new research on ethnic groups and women into their bibliographies, and Hine has added a closing chapter on the twentieth century. Recent books by Rodman Paul, Gerald D. Nash, and Michael P. Malone and Richard W. Etulain exemplify the next stage of the synthesis. Paul's volume in the New American Nation series, in treating the West from the Civil War to 1900, builds primarily on the author's solid work on frontier economic developments, but it also draws extensively on new studies of mining, social and economic mobility, urbanization, and ethnicity. This middle stage of the synthesis is also apparent in Gerald Nash's *The American West Transformed* (1985), another example of that author's pioneering work on the recent West and a volume strengthened by Nash's judicious emphases on urbanization and minority groups. Meanwhile, Malone and Etulain, while using the frontier and regional ideas of Turner and Webb, also heed Pomeroy's call for attention to continuities between East and West even as they discuss western cities, ethnic groups, families, and cultural currents more extensively than earlier overview syntheses.[26]

If these historians represent two stages of synthesis that juxtapose traditional narratives with new topical or innovative methodological emphases, other interpreters have pushed on to a third stage. The boldest and most controversial of these provocative volumes illustrate the rousing new movement called the New Western history. Although the new movement was officially born in Santa Fe in September 1989, its parentage, moment of conception, and gestation are less clear. As part of a larger NEH-funded project, "Trails through Time," the roundup in New Mexico boldly titled itself "Trails: Toward a New Western History." Endeavoring to "draw upon recent scholarship" that challenged "conventional views and stereotypes of Western history," the symposium opened with Donald Worster's provocative paper "Beyond the Agrarian Myth," featured Richard White's "Trashing the Trails," and included other presentations by Albert Camarillo, Richard Maxwell Brown, Peggy Pascoe, and Alfonso Ortiz. Meanwhile, Patricia Nelson Limerick served variously as conference trail boss, indefatigable chair of sessions, and general designated hitter throughout the conference.[27]

When pressed for a definition of the New Western history shortly before the gathering in Santa Fe, Professor Limerick supplied a useful one-page outline of the movement's major themes. New Western historians, she wrote, emphasized the West as place or region rather than as process or frontier because the latter was frequently too "nationalistic and often racist." In addition, the 1890s were no longer an "end to the frontier"; instead continuities from the earliest invasion, conquest, and colonization "to the present would be emphasized." And narratives of the New Western history would be more balanced: while dealing with heroism, virtue, and nobility, they would also reveal villainy, vice, and shoddiness in "roughly the same proportions." Finally, the new historians would cast off "the conventional, never-very-convincing claim of an omniscient, neutral objectivity," and instead take upon themselves the demanding roles of public intellectuals and "to put [their] concern[s] on record."[28]

This one-page manifesto summarized previous important contributions to the New Western history and adumbrated others. The most significant of the overview studies were Limerick's *The Legacy of Conquest: The Unbroken Past of the American West* (1987) and Richard White's *"It's Your Misfortune and None of My Own": A New History of the American West* (1991). Both volumes clearly represented fusions of the old and new but particularly illustrated novel approaches and tones in historical writing about the West.

Similar to several postregional novelists and artists, Limerick emphasized ethnic, gender, and environmental themes in *Legacy of Conquest*. She was convinced that too much western historiography had been a white man's view, suffused with themes of frontier progress and triumph. Historians ought to abandon Turner's misleading views about the frontier, she said, and strike out on new paths emphasizing continuity, environmental difficulties, racialism, the destructive power of capitalism, and the excessive materialism of too many pioneers—in short, "the Burdens of Western American History." If we can "deemphasize the frontier and its supposed end," if "the corral built to contain Western history" can be "knocked apart," we can replace them with a pluralistic western history, more complex, more realistic, and more helpful to all interested in the West. No one has done more than Patricia Limerick to champion these ideas in western circles. Her perspectives have both entertained and challenged general audiences even while they have provoked specialists in the field.[29]

More conceptual, more inclined to draw on the theoretical work of social scientists, Richard White nonetheless shares many of Limerick's conclusions in his textual synthesis *"It's Your Misfortune and None of My Own."* His mammoth overview of nearly 650 oversized pages reiterates many of the concerns of the New Western historians. Employing clash-and-conflict themes, emphasizing ethnic and class diversity, and stressing both numerous changes over time and continuities between the nineteenth and twentieth centuries, White avoids what like-minded historians consider the excessively romantic and triumphalist tone of many frontier and regional narratives and employs the realistic and critical—if not dark and somber—tones of the New Western history. Particularly probing are his examinations of the centers and peripheries of power that defined the West from the 1880s into the 1920s and his illuminating discussions of environmental, racial, and bureaucratic topics. Altogether, his large volume serves as a palpable summary of the New Western history and its differences from previous interpretations of the American West.[30]

Not all western specialists, of course, agree with these stuttering steps toward synthesis. Some point to what they consider an anti-Turner bias and an excessive emphasis on the negative, dark aspects of western history among the New Western historians. Others accuse them of close-mindedness, of an unwillingness to accept the validity of any opposing viewpoints. But defenders of the New Western history admire its sense of wholeness, its attempts to utilize the new findings and research of the past generation to move beyond frontier interpretations that overlook the twentieth century, discount cultural diversity, and underemphasize the conflicts and darker sides of western history. They argue that writers like Limerick, White, and Worster provide new accounts of the webs of association that entangle as well as direct the West: legacies from the pioneer past, ties to other regions and the nation, and links between the region and the larger world.[31]

Whatever one concludes about the New Western history—the conflicting viewpoints have been fractious, persisting, and invigorating—one must admit that postregional western historiography is throbbing with activity. If scarcely a decade ago specialists were lamenting the backward-looking, provincial, and static nature of western history, the same commentators agree that the field is now as lively as any regional historiography in the country. Perhaps the earlier visions of Turner, Webb, Bolton, Billington, and Pomeroy, among others, and revisionist accounts of the last two decades can pollinate one another. If so, from this union will spring an even newer postregional western historiography, the fruits of both a New Western historiography and a New Western history.

Chapter 9

POSTREGIONAL ART

When the eastern artist Georgia O'Keeffe arrived in New Mexico for her first extended stay in 1929, and to which she returned for several summers before moving there permanently in 1949, she enthusiastically embraced the new scenes and materials that soon infused her artwork. Already introduced to the southwestern plains while serving as a public school and college teacher in west Texas, O'Keeffe viewed the terrain and cultures of the Southwest as dramatically different from those of Wisconsin, Virginia, and New York that spawned her first paintings. O'Keeffe arrived with a thorough background in several of the avant garde artistic trends of her day. An early student of William Merritt Chase and Arthur Wesley Dow and later the protégé, lover, and wife of noted modernist critic and photographer Alfred Stieglitz, O'Keeffe quickly applied her training and interests to the arid scenes and southwestern artifacts she discovered in New Mexico. By the 1940s and 1950s her midwestern and eastern artistic background had already become linked to her new experiences in the Southwest.

As O'Keeffe began her summer jaunts to New Mexico, Wyoming-born Jackson Pollock turned eastward from his Rocky Mountain and southwestern origins for what became a spectacular career as a major figure in the Abstract Expressionist movement. Drawing upon, as well as reacting to, his western backgrounds, his interest in Navajo sandpainting, and his earlier training with noted regionalist and American Scene artist Thomas Hart Benton, Pollock burst upon the New York scene in the early 1940s and by the end of the decade may have been America's best-known artist, particularly through his controversial drip paintings.

O'Keeffe's movement from the East to the West and Pollock's from the West to the East symbolize the notable cross-fertilization that characterized postregional art in the American West after Pearl Harbor and that epitomized the major differences between western regionalist artists of the interwar years and the diverse, complex groups of artists who painted in the West after 1940. Postregionalist western art clearly illustrates Richard White's apt observation that "the boundaries of the American West are a series of doors pretending to be walls," and that the cultural West is "open to the outside and divided within."[1] The careers and major artworks of numerous painters of the recent American West illustrate, as have those of increasing numbers of novelists and historians, that postregionalism dominates cultural trends in the West. Dozens of Abstract Expressionists, Figurative artists, proponents of Pop Art, Photo Realism, Earthworks art, and hosts of other experimentalists, as well as dozens of new ethnic painters, represent the counter-regional and yeasty postregional trends that distinguish art in the American West during the last half century.

World War II flashed across the American cultural and intellectual scene like an unexpected flood, eroding away traditions, redirecting other tendencies, and introducing still other trends. If the war demonstrated the military might of the United States, it likewise served as a midwife for its new cultural eminence. For example, in the decade following the peace, New York City emerged to replace Paris as the art capital of the world. Soon thereafter, American artistic influence radiated out to Europe, as well as throughout the remainder of the United States. Up and down the Pacific Coast and across the Southwest to Texas, but particularly in California, painters found the American West hospitable to their artistic endeavors. Some incoming artists executed paintings in the West similar to those they had produced in the East or in Europe. Others attempted to link their previous work with new western experiences. Still others were sufficiently influential as western painters to shape national artistic trends.

One reason for New York City's rapid rise as an international art center was its emergence as the citadel of Abstract Expressionism. Never a well-organized, coherent movement, Abstract Expressionism nonetheless reflected several intellectual and cultural currents that circulated during the Depression and World War II. Convinced that the decade and a half after 1930 illustrated the often irrational actions of institutions and people, intrigued with the prospect of depicting the primitive and unconscious images that Jungians had discovered, and hungry to test novel compositional techniques, Abstract Expressionists arrived as the controversial newcomers to the international art scene in the 1940s and 1950s. Although Abstract Expressionism is frequently discussed as solely an East Coast phenomenon, its ideas and painterly methods spread throughout the country. In the case of the Bay Area, the movement sometimes took on a regional face different from its most recognizable characteristics in New York City.

In the generation following Pearl Harbor, the Bay Area gathered unto itself a coterie of Abstract Expressionists and Figurative painters much as the "New York School" provided a convenient label for a host of diverse artists who clustered around New York City from the 1940s to the 1960s. If Far West artists were perhaps less cosmopolitan and possibly less cohesive, they simultaneously experienced more rapid cultural change and participated in more artistic experimentation than their eastern counterparts. The fermentative literary and cultural forces that spawned the Beats and North Beach and helped launch San Francisco and Berkeley as innovative cultural centers before 1970 paralleled impulses that helped establish the Bay Area as *the* western artistic center immediately following the war.

The artistic explosion on the West Coast detonated soon after the war's end. Indeed, as one critic has written, "Abstract Expressionism swept through the ranks of Bay Area painters in the late 1940s with the intensity of a religious revival."[2] When Clyfford Still and Mark Rothko accepted short-term or summer teaching positions at the California School of Fine Arts (later the San Francisco Art Institute), the fireworks soon began among instructors and students alike. So impressed were students with the teaching and artwork of Still and Rothko, for example, that the disciples found themselves faced with the ironic dilemma of sensing complete artistic freedom but only achieving it in slavishly following their mentors.

Clyfford Still was by far the most important figure among the Bay Area Abstract Expressionists in the late 1940s. Born in North Dakota, reared on the prairies of Alberta, and educated and gaining his first teaching in Washington state, Still spent a few sporadic and uncertain years in the East before arriving in California, launching his first major exhibits, and beginning a four-year teaching stint at the School of Fine Arts in 1946. Always something of an outsider, a "cantankerous nonjoiner," " 'a maverick who didn't play the art game,'" Still thumbed his nose at academic modernism, deciding to "begin again" in the mid-1930s by turning increasingly to abstract painting in the following decades.[3] Often aloof, sometimes so demanding that no one could speak to him without an appointment, Still was nonetheless a magnetic presence, particularly through his innovative and daring artwork. Acquainted with and yet separate from several leading New York experimentalists, he offered his West Coast colleagues and students a tangible link with the Abstract Expressionism then taking artists by storm. Simultaneously, however, the movement frequently alienated general audiences, who, fired by their Cold War ideologies, sometimes denounced abstract painters as absurd know-nothings, if not dangerous liberals or even Communists.

As independently spirited in his painterly techniques as in his criticism of artistic traditions, Still embodied courageous artistic innovation. Filled with jagged, brightly colored shapes spread over flat canvases, his art seemed to suggest, like contemporary Existentialism, that existence preceded meaning. His large, rectangular canvases resembled jigsaw pieces of black, white, yellow, and red splotches. When pressed to interpret his paintings, Still demurred, commenting instead on the artist's need for total freedom to fill his works with his own ideas.

Still's experimental and daring canvases, usually untitled and carrying only identifying numbers, startled viewers and critics. Some thought Still's paintings resembled the large, open landscapes of his western homeland. Searching for the cultural-intellectual origins of Still's "freer, more open and electrifying" works, one commentator linked his ideas to the American West. "His paintings evoke the West," Katharine Kuh wrote, "not . . . in appearance, but in feeling. . . . It is the overwhelming sense of freedom and the lack of any constraining barrier or finite limitation that give these paintings their extramundane quality."[4]

Still was immensely influential in the Bay Area in the late 1940s, and when Mark Rothko taught summer sessions at the California School of Fine Arts and executed paintings similar to those for which Still was gaining national attention, journalists and critics began to speak of the important coterie of experimental artists gathering in San Francisco. Was there a West Coast "school" of Abstract Expressionism? Some observers, then and now, thought so, noting how these artists had broken more clearly than had their eastern counterparts from European and academic traditions, emphasizing their separation from the New York School, and stressing their avoidance of the "dry and intellec-

Clyfford Still, *1957-D No. 1*, 1957. (Albright-Knox Art Gallery, Buffalo, New York; gift of Seymour H. Knox, 1959)

tual" influences of the East Coast.[5] Other commentators pointed out that Bay Area painters were less inclined to "action painting," what Still contemptuously harpooned as the "drip and drool school." True, San Francisco abstractionists lacked numerous museums and found few buyers for their new works. They also rarely attracted much attention among leading critics—unless they maintained connections with the New York art scene. Yet other critics maintained that the sensual, emotional, intuitive, and naturalistic qualities of the Bay Area painters set their works apart from those of the more well-known nucleus of Abstract Expressionists gathered in and around New York City.[6]

Perhaps more than a school of painters adhering to a well-defined, ordered, and coherent core of ideas and techniques, the Bay Area artists were a loosely organized group of artists committed to abstractionism and to individualistic interpretations of a variety of complex topics. They clearly agreed with many of their contemporaries about the chaos of the botched postwar world in which they lived. Unanimously, they asserted as well that artists must free themselves from the outmoded, detrimental artistic traditions of Europe and the American past if they were to make important new contributions in their generation. In a blistering attack on architects but one meant as well for other custodians of culture, Still wrote to Mark Rothko: "I stand in opposition to nearly everything I have heard and seen by these men who would take me in and integrate or obliterate me. I refuse to be seduced by their social blarney, their measured cities, their repetitious devices, or their invitation to compromise."[7]

Although Still and the other Abstract Expressionists dominated West Coast art from the mid-1940s into the 1950s, the scene quickly changed. Still left for New York, the abstractionists lost much of their dominance, and a new trend soon emerged. By the mid-1950s a Figurative School arose in San Francisco, with artists such as David Park and Richard Diebenkorn becoming the leaders of the new movement.

A story, perhaps apocryphal, suggests the rapid, decisive transformation that took place in western art at midcentury. Soon after exhibiting a collection of his early work—primarily abstract expressionist paintings—in San Francisco in 1949, David Park gathered up those canvases, deposited them at the city dump, and embarked on a bold new path.[8] When Park's figurative painting *Kids on Bikes* (1950) shortly appeared, his good friend, Richard Diebenkorn, then in New Mexico, declared, "My God, what's happened to David?" Others wondered if Park meant to launch a new career or if he had "chickened out" in retreating from his earlier abstractionist stage.

The transition from abstraction to figuration by the mid-1950s was, of course, more complex than either this story or these reactions suggest. National, regional, and personal forces were at work in the transition. Just as World War II and the dilemmas of the postconflict years motivated the Abstract Expressionists to break with previous artistic traditions, so too did the less charged atmosphere of the Eisenhower 1950s encourage other painters to return to more representational and figurative techniques even as they continued to utilize facets of the new abstractionism. Personal and professional jealousies and competition among the leading Bay Area painters complicated the scene as well.

The life and artwork of David Park exemplified some of these changes. Originally from Boston, Park moved to Los Angeles as a teenager and soon thereafter to San Francisco, where he lived for the remainder of his life. After brief stints of art training, Park taught at the California School of Fine Arts from 1943 to 1952, and at Berkeley from 1955 to his death from cancer in 1960. Gradually growing discontented with what he considered the hegemonic control of the Abstract Expressionists and Clyfford Still in the late 1940s, he decided to move in his own directions, to return to the figures of his earliest work.

Kids on Bikes, often considered the first major work of the California Figurative School, illustrates Park's continuing links to Abstract Expressionism even as it reveals his movement toward figuration. Featuring the bright Fauvistic coloration and the jagged designs popular with his colleagues Still and Rothko, the painting also breaks from those emphases in its focus on figures, in this case two boys on bikes. One rider dominates the foreground on the left side of the work, the other biker, his back turned, pedals off. The painting's bland background exemplifies the abstractionist fondness for flat canvases, but here the plane is disrupted by the foregrounded rider on the left as well as the fence on the right. *Nudes by a River* (1954) also represents Park's juxtaposition of bright coloration and bold figures. More revealing, the focus on a nude interracial couple, their backs to one another, was exceptional for western as well as for American artists in the mid-1950s.

Two of Park's later paintings, *Four Men* (1958) and *Cellist* (1959), represent still other facets of his figurative work. The earlier of the two demonstrates how much Park differed from the regionalists. His four figures, three standing on shore and a fourth rowing a boat, fill much of the painting's 57" by 92" space, but they do not tell a people-landscape story, *the* narration that so intrigued the regionalists. The second work, Park's final oil, utilizes light and dark and brilliantly contrasted colors to depict a self-engrossed musician. Like so many of Park's figures, she seems more interested in her own thoughts and actions than in communicating with an audience.[9]

A decade younger than Park and both his student and colleague, Richard Diebenkorn moved during his adolescent years to California from his natal Oregon. He studied art at Stanford and Berkeley and briefly at the California School of Fine Arts before beginning his long teaching career at the latter institution. After gaining an MFA at the University of New Mexico in 1951 and after short stops in Illinois and New York City, Diebenkorn returned to California, his residence for the remainder of his career. He was first exposed to Abstract Expressionism as a student of Still and Rothko, but by the mid-1950s his dissatisfaction with that movement impelled him in new directions. "I came to mistrust my desire to explode the picture and supercharge it," he wrote; "what is more important is a feeling of strength in reserve—tension beneath the calm. I don't want to be less violent or discordant or less shocking than before, but I think I can make my paintings more powerful this way."[10]

Woman on Porch (1958) typifies the new figured approach to which Diebenkorn turned. A six-foot by six-foot oil, this painting, suffused with bright colors, depicts a skirted female seated in an armchair in the left foreground, partially shaded from an intense Pacific sun. The layered colors of orange, red, blue, and yellow remind one of his *Berkeley #32* (1955), which betrays even closer ties to his early Abstract Expressionist work. As they do in nearly all of his figurative paintings, humans (or other figures) and brilliant colors dominate the canvas.

On occasion, for instance in *Interior with a Book* (1959), *Interior with Doorway* (1962), and *Window* (1967), judiciously placed chairs and their relationships with windows function like people-space juxtapositions in Diebenkorn's other paintings. In fact, in the earliest of these works, an adroitly positioned outdoor shrub and a book neatly placed on a nearby table resemble the head and lap of a seated figure. Here, too, laminated or banded colors dramatize the figure-space unities so important to figurative artists.

A lone human figure, situated near a chair and set off by bright splotches of yellow, green, and blue, also dominates *Figure on Porch* (1959). This painting illustrates the strong influences of American artist Edward Hopper's work on Diebenkorn, as well as his tendency to place figures in a landscape or setting without implying the shaping power of backdrop on character. This relationship lies at the center of western regionalist art. Critics of Diebenkorn and his California figurative works attacked such paintings as too celebratory of "the domestic and mundane values of the Western way of living." As one reviewer argued, "[There] is no harsh or jarring disturbance; life is very beautiful and the only pit is for barbecues. [The paintings] have the beauty of a ripe California navel orange. . . . But like the orange, they are often bland; they look delicious but there isn't much juice."[11] This was a minority view, however; most commentators found more substance and vivacity, some even profundity, in Diebenkorn's mature work.

These lively, increasingly varied artistic moods rising out of California illustrate what historian Gerald Nash has labeled the "pacesetting" culture of the Far West. If western regional artists of the interwar years focused primarily on close-at-hand scenes and experiences within the West or if other artists in the next generations emulated nonwestern artists in their canvases, western artistic trends in the 1960s and thereafter frequently demonstrated a novelty and individualism of technique, subject matter, and approach that influenced artists throughout the West and in areas outside the West as well. Rather than following outsiders and continuing their roles as cautious colonials and provincials, far westerners often exchanged roles, with increasing numbers of artists pioneering in paintings that influenced outsiders instead of merely reiterating nonwestern artworks.[12]

This new cultural realignment gradually came into focus. If New York City saw itself as the artistic core of the United States in the generation following World War II, its cultural hegemony over the regional outlands began to shift in the 1960s. In the field of experimental art, as in filmmaking, television, and literature, the West Coast began to challenge East Coast dominance, refusing to be considered a distant and rustic artistic colony. Revealingly, painters in California, and later in other western subregions, pioneered artistic developments paralleling the literary and cultural challenges Beats, Hippies, and other countercultural groups were mounting at the same time. Among painters these innovative efforts appeared in Pop, Photo Realistic, and Earthwork art.

Within a decade after the Abstract Expressionists moved to center stage in the American art scene in the 1950s, dissatisfaction with the approaches and emphases of the abstractionists surfaced. A new generation of painters came to maturity after 1945. These artists were shaped more by the affluence and anxieties of the late 1950s and 1960s than the traumas of the Depression and World War II that helped spawn the Abstract Expressionists. For the newcomers, painters should not only utilize the artifacts of popular culture, they should also utilize the recognizable mediums from that mass culture. As a result, the techniques and subject matter of commercial art — advertisements, billboards, comic books and strips, movies, and (above all) photographs — became important ingredients of a new wave of artistic interpretation, termed Pop Art.[13]

Pop Art conjures images of Andy Warhol's Campbell's Soup and Marilyn Monroe paintings, the comic strip–like work of Roy Lichtenstein, and the gigantic hamburgers of Claes Oldenburg. Early in the 1960s those artists were attracting most of the attention paid to Pop Art, but in that same decade West Coast painters also turned to Pop. As one survey of Western European and American art points out, "California, with its Hollywood glamour mills, its big-sign, freeway, and surf-board culture, its hot-rodders driving 'customized' cars, very quickly transformed itself from a source of Pop imagery into a breeding ground for an indigenous brand of Pop Art."[14]

A series of illuminative events in the early 1960s proved that the West Coast was already a pioneer in Pop. In September 1962 the Pasadena Art Museum mounted what may have been the first national show devoted entirely to the movement, "The New Painting of Common Objects"; and earlier that summer the Ferus Gallery in Los Angeles sponsored the premier exhibit of Warhol's Campbell's Soup paintings. In November the Dwan Gallery, also in Los Angeles, hosted another Pop-influenced show, "My Country 'Tis of Thee.'" Within the next year in California, other exhibits featured notable examples of Pop Art. In all these shows, Pop artists in California and other parts of the West played large roles. At the same time publication of the journal *Artforum* in California for nearly a decade, with its full commentary on West Coast and national art (including Pop artists), revealed the new strength of western postregional art.[15] In the same decade that novelist Joan Didion, the Berkeley Free Speech Movement, and the counterculture invaded San Francisco, as well as the first works of the New Western historiography began to appear, West Coast artists mounted a large challenge against New York City as the sole sponsor of the nation's art scene.

In the Bay Area, Wayne Thiebaud and Mel Ramos, and in Los Angeles Ed Ruscha, were soon recognized as important new names among Pop artists. The oldest of the trio, Thiebaud, Arizona-born and California-trained, flirted with Abstract Expressionism before turning to Pop Art in the late 1950s and early 1960s. Experimenting with mundane subjects like pastries, gumball and pinball machines, and lipstick cases and compacts, Thiebaud painted from memory, infusing his works with an "anonymous tone of mass production." In *Desserts* (1961) and *Window Cakes* (1963), two oils depicting "cafeteria goodies and . . . neon-lit bakeshop specials," Thiebaud illustrated the Pop (and postmodern) dictum that assembly-line and mass-culture artifacts were acceptable subjects for artists, that no large barriers should divide "high" (or elite) from "popular" art. As the artist explained, in his work he played "with reality— making an illusion which grows out of an exploration of the properties of materials." Thiebaud tried, for example, to unite medium and message by employing a "white, gooey, shiny, sticky oil paint spread out on top of a painted cake to 'become' frosting." [16]

Mel Ramos, a one-time student of Thiebaud and also trained in northern California, began a Batman series in the early 1960s as part of his celebrations of comic book heroes and heroines. More inclined than Thiebaud to utilize popular culture symbols, Ramos treated these subjects in a straightforward manner. Later he produced a series of "nameless, clothesless heroines of the girlie circuit and garage calendars." [17] His *Chiquita* (1964) depicts an attractive blonde nude standing within an empty banana peel, whereas his even more erotic *Kar Kween* (1964) shows another blond, curvaceous nude embracing a phallic, human-sized spark plug. Ironically juxtaposing cheesecake and mass-produced or processed emblems, Ramos illustrated the Pop artists' goal of utilizing as well as commenting on symbols created by an increasingly standardized urban-industrial society.

More widely known nationally, Ed Ruscha, born in Nebraska and trained at the influential Chouinard Art Institute in Los Angeles, launched his career with a series of word, billboard, and service station paintings. His word paintings, such as *Ace, Radio, Honk,* and *Noise,* all of which are illuminated through his adroit use of varied colors, represent (in the words of one critic) "a kind of willed muteness." Fascinated with letters, Ruscha also created the much-reproduced *20th Century Fox with Spotlights* (1961), a gigantic oil on canvas in which words and dark and light colors suggest much about Hollywood, popular culture, and a society that creates and embraces the movie industry. The artist's deadpan look at service stations, particularly in *Standard Station* (1963) as part of his book on twenty-six gas stations, again comments paradoxically on the "standardization" of the American highway, car, and transportation cultures. These service station paintings, drawn from Ruscha's nighttime commutes along Route 66, illustrate—along with his treatments of southern California franchise restaurants—how much Pop Art used "verbal/visual equations" to depict and comment on American mass culture.[18]

Emerging a few years later but also part of the artistic realism that surfaced in the 1960s, as well as being directly influenced by Pop Art, Photo Realists reacted to what they considered the excesses of the expressionists, urging painters instead to refocus their attention on the reality of objects and their representation rather than on the clouded emotions of artists. Gestural or action painters, realists asserted, distorted reality through excessive emphasis on abstraction and "brushy painting." The "observed object," for the new realists, must have central focus; "its unique *thingness*" must be "represent[ed] . . . accurately—rigorously." From the 1960s through the 1980s, these opinions circulated widely among artists on both coasts, suggesting that discontent with modernism and Abstract Expressionism, barely a generation old, was driving artists in new directions. The Photo Realists differed from other realists, however, in their use of photographs, their willingness to depict the most mundane of American scenes and subjects, and their employment of airbrushes rather than hand-held brushes. If Pop artists turned to billboards, comics, and advertisements as prime sources for their art, Photo Realists made equal use of photographs.[19]

Photo Realism quickly took root on the West Coast. Mushrooming western cities (the West is the country's most urban area) provided numerous examples of the drab, bland, monotonous, and suburban-dominated life the Photo Realists revealed. In fact, one recent study of the Photo Realists cites several westerners as major figures in the movement. Chuck Close and Richard McLean, born, reared, and educated in Washington state, and the Californians Robert Bechtle and Ralph Goings are among notable examples of Photo Realism.

Chuck Close's ties to Photo Realism resemble Wayne Thiebaud's to Pop Art. Even though critics often note the differences between these two artists and the movements with which they are associated, they are forced to admit that parallels outweigh dissimilarities. Reared in western Washington and educated in Seattle and at Yale, Close early on employed the camera and photographs for his paintings, but unlike other Photo Realists, he frequently changed the ways he utilized these photographs. Indeed, most of his best-known paintings are of people, not of the street scenes, stores, and automobiles that fascinated the "Sharp Focus" or Photo Realists. Increasingly dissatisfied with abstract art by the mid-1960s, Close began to employ photographs, including numerous closeups, for the gigantic, blown-up faces on his canvases. At first limiting himself to black-and-white scenes and just a few tablespoons of pigment for his expansive paintings, he also abandoned brushes and knives for the airbrush. Working with a grid method unpopular with other Photo Realists, Close produced dozens of heads and faces, utilizing acrylic on canvas for works that stretched into nine-foot paintings, such as *Keith* (1970) and *Self-Portrait* (1976–77). By devoting so much time and attention to an eyebrow, a nostril, or even a reflection in eyeglasses, Close seemed to be transplanting total reality (the "real") onto his canvases.

Even though Richard McLean, like Close, was born in Washington state, his Photo Realism moved in other directions. He drew particularly on his rodeoing and cow-milking experiences to produce numerous scenes of horses and ranches. In *Rustler Charger* (1971), he situated a girl presenting a trophy to a seated horseman against a background billboard advertising an Appaloosa Horse Show in Huron, South Dakota. To the uninitiated, the painting might seem merely a large photograph of a western horse show. But McLean moved beyond photography. In fact, unusual for "Sharp Focus" painters, McLean used brushes to achieve the verisimilitude of his works, which, he admitted, were his effort to capture "the private experience of the guy holding a wrench."[20]

If Close and McLean favored faces and horses, the Californians Bechtle and Goings filled their artwork with a welter of cars and pickups, an automotive menagerie. Placing ordinary individuals and families in front of or alongside ordinary cars in such paintings as *'56 Chrysler* (1964), *'61 Pontiac* (1969), and *Alameda Gran Torino* (1974), Bechtle pursued his claim that he could paint anything the eye could see. He vowed to paint the average middle class, noting that Pop Art had led him "to an awareness of commercial art techniques." Although he argued that his paintings were "dumb," devoid of "satire or social comment," he nonetheless admitted that his works forced him to "confront [the] values" of his culture. In the end, this confrontation led to paintings "different from the photograph and certainly different from the 'real thing.'"[21]

Goings, a fellow student with Bechtle and McLean at the California College of Arts and Crafts in Oakland, betrayed the influences of Pop Artists Thiebaud and Ramos in his early works, but by the late 1960s and early 1970s he had embarked on a series of pickup trucks. Trying to avoid what he considered the sloppiness of Pop Art, he attempted to "render" the photographs he utilized, to practice "the craft of copying with exacting care." In painting every con-

ceivable kind and color of pickup, Goings aimed at "believable authenticity."
For him, "Realist paintings provide[d] an occasion to visually savor reality."[22]
Later, in a series of canvases depicting Safeway stores, diners, and fast-food
outlets like Kentucky Fried Chicken and Burger Chef that included *Dairy
Queen Interior* (1972), McLean continued to produce paintings that achieved
as much literal realism as he could muster.

For another group of artists, sometimes viewed as part of the Conceptual
Art movement of the 1970s and 1980s and often labeled Earthworks or Land
Artists, the American West was an ideal setting for their large-scale recon-
ceptualizations of land and the environment. Driven by the notion that art
must free itself from the confines of museums, galleries, and public places, artists such as Robert Smithson, Michael Heizer, and Walter de Maria found the
large spaces, the broad landscapes, and the open terrains of the West appealing stages on which to enact their daring experiments. As one art historian
has noted, for their sites Earthworks artists "favored . . . what was left of the
American wilderness, continuing the romance of the American frontier that
harks back to the nineteenth-century painters of the West, such as Albert Bierstadt and Thomas Moran."[23]

Robert Smithson's *Spiral Jetty* (1969–70), a gigantic, spiraled roadbed of
compacted rock stretching out into the Great Salt Lake (more than 6,650 tons
of rock were used to build the jetty) is perhaps the best-known example of the
Earthworks. To some, this site suggested a meditation on geology and time,
resembling the Indian Serpent Mounds of the Midwest and calling to mind
disjunctions between prehistoric Utah and later invasions of a modern technological society. Smithson was especially attracted to the Utah site, he wrote, because the old piers, rusted junk, and collected waste cluttering the shore "gave
evidence of a succession of man-made systems mired in abandoned hopes."[24]
Eventually, the site also vividly illustrates the powers of entropy because, now
covered with water and virtually inaccessible, it is visible only through photographs and video. By displacing nature and yet allowing the site to revert to
something less intrusive, Smithson implied, as postregional novelists and environmental historians have, that Americans needed a new, more comprehensive understanding of ecology and the impact of time and humankind on the
environment.

In *Double Negative* (1969–70), native westerner Michael Heizer utilized
a bulldozer to move more than 240,000 tons of dirt and rocks on a remote Nevada site. Attempting through displacement (in contrast to Smithson's

augmentation) to create a new site, Heizer and his team gouged out two channels fifty feet deep and thirty feet wide that paralleled one another across a canyon. The isolated desert site was ideal because, for the artist, it represented "that kind of unraped peaceful religious space artists have always tried to put in their work."[25] Minimalist in design, monumental in setting, *Double Negative* seemed to symbolize Heizer's acceptance of an open, balanced marriage between nature and man-made forms.

Like Smithson and Heizer, Walter de Maria urged observers to take a more comprehensive and realistic view of the environment. His first Earthwork, *Mile Long Drawing* (1968), consisted of two chalk lines twelve feet apart stretching across the Mojave Desert to depict the impermanence and fragility of nature. Later, in *Lightning Field* (1971–77), he planted 400 stainless steel poles in a grid formation crisscrossing an isolated New Mexico desert landscape. When discharged flashes of lightning from passing storms struck the strategically placed poles, nature (with the artist's help) created a sensational, if momentary, "happening," electrifying earth and sky. Similar to other Earthwork artists, de Maria depicted an environment in which even the unseen carried dramatic meaning for the artist, the audience, and, especially, for the ecologically inspired.[26]

If Frederic Remington and Charles Russell and the later midwestern trio Thomas Hart Benton, Grant Wood, and John Steuart Curry deserve recognition as the most notable frontier and regional artists, Georgia O'Keeffe obviously merits similar attention among postregional painters. As a link to modernistic trends from the East Coast, as a notable interpreter of the desert Southwest, and as a superbly talented woman artist, O'Keeffe did more than any other painter after the 1930s to draw the nation's attention to the artistic possibilities of the American West. Yet she cannot be pigeonholed in one or two artistic movements. Although her memorable works illustrate several trends in modern American art, she remains independent of—perhaps beyond—the restrictions and clichés of such traditions. Like architect Frank Lloyd Wright, whom she knew and much admired, Georgia O'Keeffe supplied a new ingredient in western cultural history by combining her earlier modernistic methods and her later southwestern scenes featuring western landscapes, crosses, bones, and brightly colored plateaus and hills.

Although O'Keeffe grew up in rural Wisconsin and knew other nonurban areas as well, she seemed unprepared for the dramatic impact the West ini tially had on her. First while an art supervisor in the schools of Amarillo, Texas (1912–1914), and then as an art instructor at West Texas State Normal College in Canyon (1916–1918), she reacted emotionally to the spaces, colors, and canyons of West Texas. "It is absurd the way I love this country," she wrote to a close friend. "I am loving the plains more than ever it seems—and the SKY—... you've never seen such SKY—it is wonderful."[27] The eye-stretching distances, the freedom, the loneliness, the wind—all appealed to her emotions and aesthetic senses.

The similarities between O'Keeffe's and the frontier artists' reactions to the new landscapes they encountered could not have been more different. In the same years that Charlie Russell was limning his romantic, nostalgic depictions of the cowboys and Indians of pioneer days, O'Keeffe was producing a notable run of experimental oils, watercolors, and charcoal drawings. Whether her abstract *Blue Lines No. 10* (1916) is a representation of male/female sexual identities or other dualities, or is primarily an illustration of O'Keeffe's artistic individualism, it startlingly reveals her abundant early talents. Intense and varied coloration, impressive figurative control with nudes, appealing uses of charcoal were other notable features of these initial paintings. The artworks O'Keeffe executed during these four years in Texas were clear indicators that her paintings would differ remarkably from those of artistic contemporaries in the West.

For nearly a decade after returning to New York City in 1918 and after coming under the dominance of Stieglitz, O'Keeffe remained away from the West, steadily painting and gaining an expanding reputation. A profusion of flowers—especially lilies (canna and calla), poppies, and irises, all in brilliant colors—and often in blown-up sizes—dominated her work in the 1920s. A series of exhibits, Stieglitz's enthusiastic cheerleading for her art, and increasing critical attention indicated that O'Keeffe had arrived as a major American artist.[28]

Then she made a career-shaping trip to New Mexico in 1929 at the invitation of the redoubtable Mabel Dodge Luhan. Nearly every summer until she moved permanently to the Southwest in 1949 after the death of Stieglitz freed her from her major tie to New York City, O'Keeffe visited New Mexico. The pull was immediate and persistent. "After a few days there," she told Anita Pollitzer, "in my mind, I was always on my way back to New Mexico."[29] O'Keeffe delighted in the unique physical and human landscapes, flora and fauna, and color combinations of the state.

She quickly translated this new fascination into a series of remarkable paintings. It should be remembered, too, that in the same years that O'Keeffe was executing her paintings of New Mexico hills, crosses, and bones, Benton, Wood, and Curry were producing their earliest well-known regionalist canvases. Although completed roughly between 1928 and the mid-1930s, O'Keeffe's paintings, with their extraordinary combinations of colors, spaces, and expressive suggestiveness, adumbrated later artistic work about the West whereas the more historical, realistic, and place-based work of the Regionalists seemed much less innovative and experimental. Like so many facets of her personal life and other art, O'Keeffe's paintings of the Southwest seemed independent of tradition and contemporary expectations.

Even though O'Keeffe painted first what fascinated most newcomers to New Mexico—the Taos pueblo, the church at Ranchos de Taos, Penitente crosses, and the area's arid landscapes—her efforts bore the stamp of her pronounced individualism. For example, *Taos Pueblo* (1929), through the artist's careful balance of realism and expressionism, photographic detail and artistic license, becomes a work of "near abstraction." As art historian Sharyn Rohlfsen Udall points out, this work provides "an example of a realistic motif serving as genesis for plastic invention."[30] A similar marriage of realism and invention characterizes O'Keeffe's depictions of the famous pueblo-style church at Ranchos de Taos. Her *Rancho Church* (1930), part of a series on the edifice, exhibits the artist's use of exaggerated angles and curves to furnish her vision and version of perhaps the most frequently painted building in the United States. In omitting nearby buildings to give larger focus to the church, in utilizing a synecdochic approach of using a part to illustrate a whole, the artist implies a balance, rhythm, and quietude between the built landscape and its natural surroundings. Another of O'Keeffe's early southwestern oils, *Black Cross with Red Sky* (1929), also epitomizes her career-long desire to fill large spaces with eye-catching manipulations of objects and colors within those spaces. Here, a black cross is silhouetted against blue-black hills and a scarlet red sky. Other painters of the Southwest frequently keyed on the religious and cultural suggestiveness of these symbols—the Catholic Church and New Mexico Penitentes—but in this painting and several others containing similar objects, O'Keeffe seems more intrigued with the interrelationships among spaces, colors, and objects than with cultural symbolism.

These emphases dominate other O'Keeffe canvases of the 1930s. In the much-reprinted *Cow's Skull—Red, White and Blue* (1931), the artist, illustrating her intense interest in skulls, fills a 40" by 36" oil by framing it with red, white, and blue edges. Intrigued at the time with widespread comment about "American scene" art and literature, particularly as part of the regionalist movement in the late 1920s and the 1930s, she decided her painting would be the Great American Painting, her "joke on the American scene." Although some viewers asserted that O'Keeffe's use of the skull clearly indicated a commentary on death, art historian Charles C. Eldredge persuasively argues that, instead, O'Keeffe avoided the Dust Bowl and moribund symbols of the 1930s by "treating her bones as still-life objects isolated from their natural surroundings. By severing the skull from its setting, the artist at once simplified her form and image, yet complicated its symbolic resonance."[31]

After 1940, O'Keeffe continued earlier emphases and began new ones. Two counterimpulses likewise ruled her personal life. Once settled in rural New Mexico at Abiquiu in the 1950s, she relished her isolation and independence, but she also participated in several exhibitions of her work and embarked on worldwide trips, all of which conflicted with her desire to be alone to do her work. Meanwhile, she continued to fill her canvases with southwestern objects, places, and scenes. In the 1940s, pelvic bones replaced the earlier skulls, with *Pelvis with Pedernal* (1943) and *Pelvis with Shadows and the Moon* (1943) allowing the viewer to see large stretches of dark and light blue landscapes over and through the huge, foregrounded pelvic bones. These compositions illustrated again O'Keeffe's desire to fill large spaces with intriguing relationships between near-at-hand objects and distant, brightly colored backgrounds.

Other paintings in the 1950s and 1960s demonstrated that even into her late seventies O'Keeffe continued to be an artist of extraordinary power and diversity. *Patio Door with Green Leaf* (1956) and *White Patio with Red Door* (1960) were minimalist evocations of the spaces, designs, and adobe buildings of New Mexico that so intrigued her. On the other hand, *Sky above White Clouds I* (1962) and *Sky above Clouds IV* (1965) — "cloudscapes" based on O'Keeffe's recent airplane flights — astonished critics with their ambitiousness and their break from her previous work. Gradual loss of eyesight, her declining hearing, and the precariousness of her health during the 1970s reduced O'Keeffe's output even as her reputation continued to expand.

In one painting, *From the Faraway Nearby* (1937), O'Keeffe provocatively illustrated her large, probing understanding of the possibilities for western art. Juxtaposing a gigantic set of bleached antlers in the foreground ("nearby") against a broad-canvas background of desert, mountains, and sky ("faraway"), the painting suggests an image of the West much beyond frontier or regional

Georgia O'Keeffe, *From the Faraway Nearby*, 1937. (The Metropolitan Museum of Art, Alfred Stieglitz Collection, 1959 [59.204.2])

visions. As a subregion of the world, the West could encompass the "faraway" (global or national cultural traditions) even as it nourished its "nearby" (novel local happenings). Well before other contemporary artists in the West—and much more analytically and successfully—O'Keeffe fused modernistic techniques with western objects, scenes, and colors to produce a series of premier paintings illustrating postregional trends in western culture.

The 1960s and the 1970s also markedly influenced Chicano and Native American artists. In these and subsequent decades, dozens of Chicano novelists and poets, dramatists, and historians joined the contemporary Chicano activists Reies López Tijerina, Corky Gonzales, and José Angel Gutiérrez in furnishing pathbreaking commentaries about Hispanic experiences in the United States. The same was true for painters. The Chicano Movement, which raised up César

Chávez as a major spokesman, also encouraged muralists and other Chicano artists to deal more concretely and vocally with their past and present.[32]

The lid flew off in the late 1960s and early 1970s. The surging Chicano Movimiento quickly led to an outburst of new artistic forms and subjects. The most conspicuous of these emerging forms were the Chicano wall murals that suddenly appeared across the Southwest from California to Texas. Drawing upon the rich Mexican mural tradition—especially as embodied in the work of Diego Rivera, José Clemente Orozco, and David A. Siqueiros—these new murals functioned as expressive outlets for Chicano recontextualizations of their history, their frustrations, and their search for cultural identity. The largest and best-known of the murals, *The Great Wall of Los Angeles* (1967–), under the direction of Judith Baca, stretches for more than a half-mile along the San Fernando Valley. The colorful, revealing segments of this and hundreds of other murals, as well as thousands of wall posters and *placas* (graffiti inscriptions) that appeared throughout the 1970s, addressed problems of racism, exclusion, cultural conflict, and identity squabbles that Chicanos faced throughout the Southwest. Attempting to "reclaim 'lost history' " and to construct "walls with tongues," muralists presented combined portraits of early Indian figures, Mexican revolutionary characters, and Chicano heroes of the past and present like Joaquín Murieta and César Chávez. Complex images of "resistance and affirmation" jostled one another in these huge, engaging murals, celebrations of identity as well as commentaries on injustices and prejudice.[33]

The artwork of Judith Baca illustrates a Chicana perspective that also surfaced in the 1970s. In addition to providing able leadership in the multiracial, multicultural efforts sustaining the Great Wall and other mural projects, Baca furnished revealing annotations on the shifting roles of Chicanas as *pachucas* and *cholas* in her painting *Las Tres Marias* (1976) and on the repositioning of Mexican-American women in *Uprising of the Mujeres* (1979). In these "socially charged" works, Baca, along with members of the Las Mujeres Muralists and other feminists, painted the conflictive roles Chicanas faced in a host culture that discriminated against them and within their own subculture, which they considered patriarchically dominated. Subverting and reinterpreting earlier traditions, these feminist artists (including Santa Barraza and Carmen Lomas Garza of Texas and Patssi Valdez, Yolanda M. López, and Ester Hernandez of California) celebrated the nurturing roles of their *abuelas* and *madres*, as well as enlarging the religio-cultural meaning of La Virgen de Guadalupe. López's *Portrait of the Artist as the Virgin of Guadalupe* (1978) and Hernandez's *Sun*

Judith Baca, *The Pickers,* from her mural *Guadalupe,* 1990. (Social and Public Art Resource Center, Venice, California)

Mad (1982) are particularly telling illustrations of the cultural reinventing that characterizes recent Chicano and postregional art.[34]

On other occasions, Chicano artists betrayed a spirit of *"rasquachismo"* rather than one of biting social criticism. Assuming an outrageous or comic pose, something akin to the nose-thumbing iconoclasm animating the Beats, advocates of rasquacha adopted a "funky, irreverent stance" to satirize through humor and irony. Like Luis Valdez's well-known drama group El Teatro Campesino, rasquacha artists used lowriders, cholos, punkers, and *con safos* (C/S— the "voice of the downtrodden safeguarding its presence and point of view") to reconceptualize what they thought American culture should be.[35]

By the 1990s Chicano art had clearly become even more explicit, more socially engaged, experimental, and yet diverse in its presentations. For example, increasing numbers of Chicano artists followed the outspoken socio-critical agenda Mel Casas pioneered with his *Humanscope 62* (1970), an artistic montage commenting on the "Brownies of the Southwest." Asco and other urban art-performing groups challenged social inequities through their unannounced appearances and staged exhibitions. Still other Chicano artists organized regional art groups to encourage a fuller understanding of La Raza and to broaden the public's comprehension of Anglo and Mexican cultures.

Will this explosion of ethnic art congeal into one or two recognizable trends of "Chicano art"? Perhaps not. Obviously, however, Chicano artists, along with Chicano novelists and historians, are creating a new cultural perspective in the West. All across the Southwest, but particularly in the urban areas of California and Texas, Mexican-American muralists and other artists are producing eye-catching scenes on aqueducts, freeway supports, and walls of buildings, as well as on canvases and through experimental assemblages and happenings. Sometimes inspirational, often critical, but always revealing cultural commentaries, these artworks serve as expressive histories and reinterpretations of Chicano experiences in the United States. Frequently ironic and satirical marriages of history, myth, and artistic statement, these ethnic documents are notable examples of the growing diversity of postregional western culture.

Of all the burgeoning ethnic groups in the modern West, Native Americans have been the most active as postregional artists. Their early artistic endeavors in rock art, sandpaintings, ledger book and hide paintings, and teepee decorations gained a modicum of notoriety before 1900, but in the twentieth century, especially since World War II, Indian artistic achievements have gained national—even international—recognition. In their clear emergence in the last fifty years and with the increasing attention their work has gained, Indian painters have become an important segment of recent developments in western art.

Several pivotal occurrences helped lead to this expanding recognition. In the early decades of the twentieth century, several colleges and universities, along with other organizations, began to offer formal and informal training for aspiring Indian artists. Notable programs in New Mexico and Oklahoma encouraged Native Americans to enroll in courses designed to introduce them to the history of European art and to foster additional use of their own cultural traditions in a variety of artistic forms. New Deal arts programs in the

1930s especially attempted to enroll Native Americans, but the most famous of the training schools was The Studio, which Dorothy Dunn established in 1932 at the Santa Fe Indian School. Directing The Studio until 1937, she urged her students to capitalize on traditional Native American reactions to the natural world, including their animistic attitudes toward flora, fauna, and the climate in colorful two-dimensional forms. Her predispositions about the content and organization of Indian art, carried on under the loyal leadership of her student Gerónima Cruz Montoya (a San Juan Pueblo), who directed The Studio until 1962, meant that Dunn's program had a large and lasting impact on hundreds of young Indian artists well into the 1960s.[36]

Still, some graduates of The Studio, after beginning their careers influenced by Dunn's prescriptions, rebelled and moved in new directions. Oscar Howe was such a student. In paintings like *Dakota Eagle Dancer* (1962), *Sioux Medicine Man* (1962), and especially *Medicine Man* (n.d.), this Sioux artist borrowed from the modernistic techniques of the Cubists and Surrealists to reinterpret the complexities of the Native American past. Much more than many of his contemporaries, Howe was convinced that Indian artists had to avoid the excessively stylized Native American art of the first half of the twentieth century and to employ instead the most recent European painterly methods to depict Native American cultures. As an artist himself and as a teacher of others who became well-known Indian artists, he clearly influenced Native American painters to abandon the narrower, more confining Dunn tradition of "Indian art."

Another former student at the Santa Fe Studio, R. C. Gorman, has attracted more attention than any other Indian modernist. Born the son of a Code Talker and artist on the Navajo Reservation, Gorman took formal art training at a mission school, later enrolled in college art classes, and then studied in Mexico before launching his own career in the 1960s. At first working as an abstract artist, he soon tired of that style and turned to representational approaches. His numerous depictions of Indian women, including controversial paintings of nudes, demonstrate the influence of Mexican muralists as well as Gorman's attempts to bridge the gap between Indian cultural traditions and recent European artistic trends. Profiting enormously from popular interest in things Indian in the 1960s and 1970s, he became probably the country's best-known Native American artist. The serenity and beauty of his smoothly wrought figures, such as those in *Old Navajo* (1971) and *Happy Old Navajo*

Couple (n.d.), are typical of the peaceful and powerful continuities evident in most of Gorman's thousands of highly sought after canvases.[37]

Later, under the direction of Lloyd Kiva New, first at a Southwest Indian Project in the summers of 1961 and 1962 at the University of Arizona and subsequently at the Institute of American Indian Arts in Santa Fe in the 1960s and 1970s, hundreds of young artists were encouraged to be even more daring and more in touch with contemporary American culture. New not only urged his classes to "recognize the importance of a thorough knowledge of the tribal heritage, [he also] taught them to use contemporary materials and [to] understand current aesthetic theories, and trained them to work and live in contemporary America."[38] Some observers criticized New for what they considered his abandonment of the more traditional subjects and methods of Dunn's studio and his superimposing of a political agenda on Indian art.

Undoubtedly these critics were overreacting, but the career of Fritz Scholder, the most notorious of the Indian revisionists, seemed to represent much of what the detractors disliked about the new Indian art. Scholder startled Native Americans and non-Indians alike with his powerful paintings in the 1960s and 1970s. Part Luiseño on his father's side, Scholder grew up with limited recognition of his Indian heritage, but that changed radically under the tutelage of Oscar Howe in South Dakota and Pop Artist Wayne Thiebaud in California, and particularly after he took a graduate degree in Arizona and began teaching in New Mexico. "It was time," he asserted, "for a new idiom in Indian painting."[39]

Scholder's *Indian Series,* begun in 1967 and completed in 1980, and including such paintings as *Indian with Beer Can* (1969) and *Super Indian No. 2* (1972), clearly illustrated his break with traditional Indian art of the earlier twentieth century. Drawing upon his knowledge of Abstract Expressionism and Pop Art, endeavoring to utilize conflictive images of humor and irony, and convinced that Indians faced a bewilderingly complex set of social and cultural issues, Scholder employed Coors beer cans, ice cream cones, and even a reinvented General Custer to remythologize contemporary American Indians. Largely avoiding the past except to comment on the present, Scholder utilized a bittersweet iconography to depict "paradoxical Indians," Native Americans caught in the tensions of alienation and assimilation, tradition and modernity. Dubbed "native American postmodernism," Scholder's artwork attempted to deconstruct the cultural clichés and stereotypes that he thought had engulfed

Indians and to undermine the Studio traditions of earlier decades. Revealingly, even though Scholder labeled himself "a non-Indian Indian painter" and on one occasion pointed out that he "didn't consider [himself] an Indian painter," his best-known works are all provocative reinterpretations of Native American culture.[40]

Many other contemporary Indian painters have followed a similar revisionist agenda. Scholder's widely acclaimed student, T. C. Cannon (Caddo/Kiowa), likewise employed abstractionist and popular mediums to treat the agonizing complexities Indians faced in such paintings as *Two Guns Arikara* (n.d.) and *Village with Bomb* (1972). The latter work depicts an Indian woman and her cradled child against a threatening backdrop of a fiendish, blood-red bomb explosion. The same blending of abstract and Pop Art characterizes the canvases of activist Billy Soza War Soldier (Cahuilla-Apache) and those of Alfred Youngman (Cree). All three artists, alumni of the Institute of American Indian Arts, dramatize the disparities between stereotyped images of Indians and the dilemmas and tragedies of their daily lives.

More individualistic, more conceptual, and less prone to follow the dictates of Pop Art, Jaune Quick-to-See Smith (Flathead/Cree/Shoshone) employs ledger art for her reconstructed images of contemporary Indian life. Widely traveled and well versed in art history and criticism, Smith combines, on the one hand, Indian pictographic painting and the theories and methods of Joseph Albers and Paul Klee on the other. "These and other parallels," she comments, "seem as fresh and spontaneous to me as the most contemporary art."[41] Smith seems less inclined than many other Indian artists to focus solely on Indian cultural traditions or on the contemporary problems of Native Americans.

If one compares the paintings of most Indian artists at the time of World War II with those produced in the 1990s, clear differences become evident. By the mid-1940s, still under the thrall of traditional Indian art taught in Dorothy Dunn's Studio since the 1930s, Indian artists emphasized the flat, two-dimensional style presented in their classrooms, an approach particularly devoid of explicit social commentary. Gradually in the next two generations, first in the work of artists like Oscar Howe and Joe Herrera and then in the paintings of R. C. Gorman, painters broke from the Studio tradition to produce "Pueblo modernism," which exhibited a "double-cross pollination" combining age-old Indian material culture and history with modernistic or abstractionist designs. For other recent Indian artists like Scholder, Cannon, and Soza War Soldier, painting became an outlet for social criticism, allowing them to comment on the alienation and anger Indians felt and on the dislocating dilemmas they experienced. In their strong emphasis on ethnic culture and in their willingness to satirize and condemn the sociocultural inequities they saw in modern America, these Native American artists are revealing examples of similar postregionalist attitudes marking the fiction of the Indian novelists Leslie Marmon Silko and James Welch, writings of New Western historians treating Native Americans, and revisionist Western films like *Dances with Wolves* (1990) and *Geronimo* (1993).

Artists who painted the West after World War II, so diverse in their subjects and techniques, clearly illustrate the complexities of postregionalism. Some artists, dissatisfied with the stress regionalists placed on setting, followed the lead of the Abstract Expressionists and other experimentalists. Others, like Georgia O'Keeffe, found the West a fertile staging area for paintings that fuse modernistic training with western scenes and experiences. Still other artists utilized their artwork to provide social commentaries about their ethnic cultures. Like postregional novelists and historians, these varied artists invented an American West that owed more to social and economic change, ethnic experiences, and cultural reorientation in the post-1960s West than to the previous regional emphasis on place and core-periphery relations with the American East.

EPILOGUE:
TOWARD A RE-IMAGINED
AMERICAN WEST

I magine an all-discerning cultural historian perched on an elevated, fully
illuminated location in the central American West, able to see and understand the panoramas of space and time. Undoubtedly he or she would be
struck with two hallmarks of modern western culture: diversity and change.
The diverse western subregions would especially catch his attention. From the
flat wheat fields of North Dakota to the burgeoning cities and gigantic farms
of California, from the sprawling ranches and mushrooming urban centers of
Texas to the green and brown expanses of the Pacific Northwest, the West en-
compasses a remarkable variety of physical and cultural landscapes. The wet
and fertile areas bounding the eastern and western rims of the West contrast
sharply with the high and dry terrains of its interior heartland. And, paradoxically, California, the most populous state in the West and in the nation, is
also the richest agriculturally.

Our imagined seer would also understand that the rhythms of agricultural
life that shape the society and culture of the Great Plains states are far less central to New Mexico, Arizona, and Nevada. Nor is the dominating urbanization
of California and the Sunbelt characteristic of the sparsely populated interior
West, except for the Rocky Mountain front range flanking Denver and Salt
Lake City. Generally speaking, the most notable cultural achievements have
occurred in the larger cities, but no one should ignore the literary and artistic
colonies in northern New Mexico, Carmel, California, and central and western

Montana. In cultural oases such as these, spectacular surrounding landscapes truly symbolize the environmental barriers to a unified western culture.

Our onlooker would realize that these differences are evident beyond page and palette. In western architectural forms, for example, an eclecticism and subregional diversity emerged in the nineteenth century that continues to the present day. Ranch style homes, so popular in many western suburbs, have not gained much favor in the Southwest, where Pueblo styles are widespread. Nor has the sprawling, unplanned growth of the Sunbelt West, so characteristic of Los Angeles, Phoenix, and Houston, received equal play in Boise, Billings, and Fargo. And the silo and grain-elevator-built landscapes of midwestern farm states are foreign to much of the Great Basin and the Pacific Coast. Similarly, the International Style, so much a product of California and the coastal Pacific Northwest, is alien to most Rocky Mountain and Mormon areas.

Equally significant differences mark other aspects of modern western culture. California's influential higher education system, with its master plan of university and college organization, and the notable bilingual programs in numerous southwestern schools and colleges represent but two major differences. Another is the diversity of religious experience in the American West. Evangelicals west of the Mississippi now outnumber those in any other region, and the panoply of Far Eastern religions, varied cults, and a full run of fundamentalist preachers, schools, and organizations in California make it the most active religious arena in contemporary America. At the same time, Roman Catholic parishes continue to expand as a result of floods of newcomers along our southwestern borders, Mainline Protestants remain dominant in scattered areas of the Midwest and northern Plains, and the Mormons continue to overflow from the central West into other parts of the country, and even overseas.

Rapid, persistent change has been equally at work in shaping other facets of contemporary western culture. At times these ever-present displacements seem to redirect the modern West like a rolling, bobbing tumbleweed continually blown in new directions by rapid bursts of wind-driven change. Rarely has any perspective on the West gone unchallenged for more than two generations, although Turner's frontier thesis, the frontier paintings of Remington and Russell, and the regionalism of Cather and Steinbeck all exhibit remarkable staying power. The mushrooming populations of the West, the traumatic impact of two world wars and the Depression and New Deal, and the sociocultural upheavals of the 1960s have again and again broken the cultural cake of custom during the last century. Indeed, once our observer begins to ponder the power and preponderance of these innovations in the American West, he will not be surprised to find that change has usually sideswiped continuity through the decades. He might well argue that the West has experienced *more* persisting cultural change than any other American region during the twentieth century.

But those changes have not influenced all parts of the West equally, whether in their relation to other American regions or to other subregions within the West. California and other urban areas have undergone the most accelerated and complex cultural changes, whereas several of the section's rural interior regions have yet to experience many of the trends of postregionalism. If California and Texas have flashed into view as new cultural cores, perhaps even as new subregions of the world, interior sections of the West now owe added provincial allegiance to these *western* powers, even while suffering from domination from *eastern* concentrations of power. Our observer might agree with others that California and the southwestern Sunbelt have become as culturally alive as any area of the United States since the 1960s, at the same time that more secluded stretches of the West clearly remain under the lion's paw of outside cultural influence.

Cultural subregionalism in the West is now even more apparent than earlier in the century. Residents of the less populous West complain about the other westerners as nuisances even as they continue to berate easterners of old. Oregonians, Coloradans, and Utahns grumble about "Californication," the invading swarms of Californians and their suburban ways. Arizonans grouse that living next to California is like trying to sleep next to a restless elephant. And Oklahomans and New Mexicans joke about an imperial Texas buying up their states. Put another way, cultural currents rising within the region now flow as strongly as those coursing in from outside.

Probably our omniscient cultural historian would share the misguided human tendency to simplify and clarify these differences and changes by concluding that the entire West is one coherent unit and by seeing one time period smoothly replacing another — the West as region supplanting the West as frontier, and West as postregion replacing the two earlier periods. But careful scrutiny would remind him of leakages and overlappings.

If our cultural historian could be enticed away from his elevated perch and into any large bookstore in the West, he would experience firsthand the numerous overlapping visions of the West as frontier, region, and postregion. In the regional section of any bookstore, he would find juxtaposed Owen Wister's frontier *Virginian,* Walter Prescott Webb's regional *Great Plains,* and Native American James Welch's postregional *Winter in the Blood.* A step or two away he would discover the frontier Westerns of Luke Short, the regional fiction of John Steinbeck and Wallace Stegner, and the postregional novels of Indian novelist Leslie Marmon Silko. Nearby would be the frontier fiction of Louis L'Amour, the regional works of Oliver La Farge and Sinclair Lewis, and the postregional historical writings of Patricia Nelson Limerick. The same kind of cultural bundling would characterize the western art section. The frontier artworks of Remington and Russell would likely stand close to those of Benton, Wood, and Curry, and not too far from volumes on Clyfford Still, Georgia O'Keeffe, and Fritz Scholder.

These juxtapositions reveal more than proximity in a neighborhood bookstore. Even though historians of the twentieth-century West may endeavor to separate and examine the frontier, regional, and postregional inventions of the region's cultural life, those interpretations remain, like a tightly entwined Gordian knot, virtually inseparable. No western writer challenges the popularity of frontier author Louis L'Amour even though he launched his immensely successful career only after World War II. Mary Austin and Willa Cather prefigured western regionalism well before that view became popular between the wars, and Nathanael West, several detective writers, and the historians Henry Nash Smith and Earl Pomeroy challenged major themes of frontier and regional historiography nearly a generation before other postregional historians tried to reorient major emphases of the field.

Our all-knowing observer would encounter similar trends and overlappings if he sauntered a few steps to the superstore's collection of video Westerns. Next to recent releases of silent films starring Broncho Billy, William S. Hart, and Tom Mix stand Westerns like *Stagecoach* (1939), *The Ox-Bow Incident* (1943), *Broken Arrow* (1950), and *The Searchers* (1956), whose complex characterizations and skillful use of settings and ethnic subjects challenge the more traditional inventions of pre-1930 films. Even though the concentrated plot lines of most films preclude treating change over time within place (the subject that intrigued so many contemporary regionalists) Westerns from World War II through the 1950s nonetheless often focused on the traumas of settlement and community-building in the generation or two following the pioneers' movement west. Beginning in the 1960s, however, films like *Cat Ballou* (1965), the spaghetti Westerns of Sergio Leone and Clint Eastwood, the counterclassics such as *The Wild Bunch* (1969) and *Little Big Man* (1970), and even later films like Oscar winners *Dances with Wolves* (1990) and *The Unforgiven* (1992) paralleled the cultural shifts from frontier to postregionalism so apparent in fiction, history, and art. In their nearly a century of development, Western films revealingly parallel the changing inventions of the West that authors and artists provided.

In the end, our commentator would be hard-pressed to discover a single, simple metaphor to characterize the cultural history of the modern American West. Overly simplistic dichotomies of then and now, there and here, they and we, he and she all shortchange understanding and obscure the region's dynamic culture. Instead, our imagined seer would be forced to adopt a more complicated symbol. *Complexity* and *change* must be given central focus. Even though societal pressures and academic trends often stress single-subject interpretations such as race, ethnicity, gender, and place, students of western culture must embrace a much broader view if they are to understand the full significance of the fragmented unity of the contemporary West. Only when all these notable subjects are viewed as spokes intersecting at the hub of western experience will one discover the large and lasting significance of modern western culture.

NOTES

PROLOGUE

1. Portions of this prologue appeared earlier in Richard W. Etulain, "Introduction: The Rise of Western Historiography," *Writing Western History: Essays on Major Western Historians* (Albuquerque: University of New Mexico Press, 1991), 2–7; and Etulain, "Art and Architecture in the West," *Montana: The Magazine of Western History* 40 (Autumn 1990): 2–11.

2. Stephen Crane, *Stephen Crane in the West and Mexico*, ed. Joseph Katz (Kent, Ohio: Kent State University Press, 1970), 31; Richard Harding Davis, *The West from a Car-Window* (New York: Harper & Brothers, 1892), 6.

3. Owen Wister, *Owen Wister Out West: His Journals and Letters*, ed. Fanny Kemble Wister (Chicago: University of Chicago Press, 1958); Rudyard Kipling, *American Notes: Rudyard Kipling's West*, ed. Arrell Morgan Gibson (Norman: University of Oklahoma Press, 1981).

4. Loren Baritz, "The Idea of the West," *American Historical Review* 66 (April 1961): 618–40; Henry Nash Smith, *Virgin Land: The American West as Symbol and Myth* (Cambridge, Mass.: Harvard University Press, 1950).

5. Richard Slotkin, *Regeneration through Violence: The Myth of the American Frontier, 1600–1860* (Middletown, Conn.: Wesleyan University Press, 1973).

6. Kent L. Steckmesser, *The Western Hero in History and Legend* (Norman: University of Oklahoma Press, 1965).

7. Richard M. Dorson, *American Folklore* (Chicago: University of Chicago Press, 1959), 214, 219, 221.

8. Daryl Jones, *The Dime Novel Western* (Bowling Green, Ohio: Bowling Green Uni-

versity Popular Press, 1978); Christine Bold, *Selling the Wild West: Popular Western Fiction, 1860–1960* (Bloomington: Indiana University Press, 1987).

9. For useful comments on the Wild West tradition, see William H. Goetzmann and William N. Goetzmann, *The West of the Imagination* (New York: W. W. Norton, 1986); and Ray Allen Billington, *Land of Savagery/Land of Promise: The European Image of the American Frontier in the Nineteenth Century* (New York: W. W. Norton, 1981).

10. A provocative interpretation of the dominating eastern influences on western American literature appears in Robert Edson Lee, *From East to West: Studies in the Literature of the American West* (Urbana: University of Illinois Press, 1966).

11. The most extensive source on western literature is J. Golden Taylor and Thomas J. Lyon et al., eds., *A Literary History of the American West* (Fort Worth: Texas Christian University Press, 1982). For an illuminating discussion of eastern influences on evolving views of the West, see G. Edward White, *The Eastern Establishment and the Western Experience: The West of Frederic Remington, Theodore Roosevelt, and Owen Wister* (New Haven, Conn.: Yale University Press, 1968). The Parkman quote is on p. 43.

12. Susan Shelby Magoffin, *Down the Santa Fe Trail and Into Mexico: The Diary of Susan Shelby Magoffin, 1846–1847,* ed. Stella M. Drumm (New Haven, Conn.: Yale University Press, 1926), 95.

13. In addition to pertinent chapters in Goetzmann and Goetzmann, *The West of the Imagination,* consult Patricia Trenton and Peter H. Hassrick, *The Rocky Mountains: A Vision for Artists in the Nineteenth Century* (Norman: University of Oklahoma Press, 1983), and John C. Ewers, *Artists of the Old West* (Garden City, N.Y.: Doubleday, 1965), for useful overviews of nineteenth-century artists.

PART I. THE WEST AS FRONTIER

INTRODUCTION

1. James Bryce, *The American Commonwealth,* new ed., 2 vols. (New York: Macmillan, 1912), 2: 892, 891n.

CHAPTER 1. FRONTIER NOVELS

1. Sections of this discussion of Owen Wister appeared earlier in Richard W. Etulain, *Owen Wister* (Boise, Idaho: Boise State College, 1973); and "From Frontier to Postregion: [One] Hundred Years of Western American Literature," in Isaac Sequeira and R. S. Sharma, eds., *Closing of the American Frontier* (Hyderabad, India: American Studies Research Centre, 1994), 40–75.

2. Owen Wister, *Owen Wister Out West: His Journals and Letters,* ed. Fanny Kemble Wister (Chicago: University of Chicago Press, 1958), 30, 31, 29–30, 32.

3. Owen Wister to Sarah Butler Wister, May 15, 1895, Box 9, Owen Wister Papers, Library of Congress, Washington, D.C.; Wister, *Owen Wister Out West*, 112.

4. Wister, *Owen Wister Out West*, 136.

5. Wister, "The Promised Land," *Harper's Monthly* 88 (April 1894): 791–92; "Little Big Horn Medicine," *Red Men and White* (New York: Harper and Brothers, 1896), 11; "The General's Bluff," *Red Men and White*, 88.

6. Wister, *Owen Wister Out West*, 61; Wister to Sarah Butler Wister, August 23, 1900, Box 11, Owen Wister Papers; "La Tinaja Bonita," *Red Men and White*, 180; "A Pilgrim on the Gila," *Red Men and White*, 215.

7. Wister, "The Evolution of the Cow-Puncher," *Harper's Monthly* 91 (September 1895): 603; *Lin McLean* (New York: Harper and Brothers, 1897), 1.

8. Wister, *The Virginian: Horseman of the Plains* (New York: Macmillan, 1902), 114.

9. James H. Maguire, *Mary Hallock Foote* (Boise, Idaho: Boise State College, 1972); Mary Hallock Foote, *A Victorian Gentlewoman in the Far West: The Reminiscences of Mary Hallock Foote*, ed. Rodman W. Paul (San Marino, Calif.: Huntington Library, 1972), 114.

10. Foote, *The Led-Horse Claim: A Romance of a Mining Camp* (Boston: J. R. Osgood, 1883).

11. Foote, *The Last Assembly Ball: A Pseudo Romance of the Far West* (Boston: Houghton, Mifflin and Company, 1889), 7.

12. Quoted in Foote, "Introduction," *Victorian Gentlewoman*, 17.

13. Foote, *Victorian Gentlewoman*, 264, 265.

14. Foote, "Maverick," *The Cup of Trembling and Other Stories* (Boston: Houghton, Mifflin and Company, 1895), 92; "The Maid's Progress," *A Touch of Sun and Other Stories* (Boston: Houghton, Mifflin and Company, 1903), 126.

15. Foote, "A Cloud on the Mountain," *In Exile and Other Stories* (Boston: Houghton Mifflin and Company, 1894), 156, 157; "On a Side-Track," *Cup of Trembling*, 164, 121.

16. Paul, "Introduction," 26, 28.

17. Foote, "The Trumpeter," *Cup of Trembling*, 182, 183, 248, 249, 253.

18. Mary Hallock Foote to Helena [de Kay Gilder], Letter 358, May 23, 1888, Mary Hallock Foote Letters, Henry E. Huntington Library, San Marino, California.

19. Lee Ann Johnson, *Mary Hallock Foote* (Boston: Twayne Publishers, 1980), 146.

20. The most useful introduction to Jack London the writer is Earle Labor and Jeanne Campbell Reesman, *Jack London*, rev. ed. (New York: Twayne, 1994).

21. London, "The White Silence" (1898), reprinted in *The Complete Short Stories of Jack London*, ed. Earle Labor et al. (Stanford, Calif.: Stanford University Press, 1993).

22. London, "In a Far Country" (1899), *Complete Short Stories*, 1: 209, 211.

23. London, *Call of the Wild* (1903), reprinted in *The Portable Jack London*, ed. Earle Labor (New York: Penguin Books, 1994), 357, 358, 417.

24. London, "How I Became a Socialist," *The Comrade* 2 (March 1903): 123; see also Jack London, *Jack London on the Road: The Tramp Diary and Other Hobo Writings*, ed. Richard W. Etulain (Logan: Utah State University Press, 1979).

25. London, "The Class Struggle," *War of the Classes* (New York: Macmillan, 1905), 8–9.

26. London, *The Road* (New York: Macmillan, 1907), 152; *The Tramp* (Chicago: Charles H. Kerr, 1904), reprinted in London, *Jack London on the Road*, 135; see also pp. 21–22.

27. London, *The Valley of the Moon* (New York: Macmillan, 1913), 484, 530.

28. Frank Norris, *The Literary Criticism of Frank Norris*, ed. Donald Pizer (Austin: University of Texas Press, 1964), 29, 30.

29. Frank Norris, *The Letters of Frank Norris*, ed. Franklin Walker (San Francisco: Book Club of California, 1956), 3.

30. Frank Norris, *Blix* (1899), reprinted in Frank Norris, *A Novelist in the Making: A Collection of Student Themes and the Novels* Blix *and* Vandover and the Brute, ed. James D. Hart (Cambridge, Mass.: Harvard University Press, 1970), 226–27.

31. Norris, "The Literature of the West," in Norris, *Literary Criticism*, 105, 107.

32. Norris, "The Frontier Gone at Last," "The National Spirit as It Relates to the 'Great American Novel,' " and "A Neglected Epic," in Norris, *Literary Criticism*, 116, 117, 118, 121–22.

33. For revealing examples of Norris's literary criticism, see the essays collected in his *The Responsibilites of the Novelist and Other Literary Essays* (New York: Doubleday, Page & Company, 1903).

34. Donald Pizer, *The Novels of Frank Norris* (Bloomington: Indiana University Press, 1966), 70.

35. Norris, *McTeague* (New York: Doubleday, Page & Co., 1899), 442.

36. George W. Johnson, "The Frontier Behind Frank Norris' *McTeague*," *Huntington Library Quarterly* 26 (November 1962): 91–104; Don B. Graham, "Frank Norris," in J. Golden Taylor and Thomas J. Lyon et al., eds., *A Literary History of the American West* (Fort Worth: Texas Christian University Press, 1987), 373.

37. Norris, *The Octopus* (Boston: Houghton Mifflin Company, Riverside Edition, 1958), 395, 396, 10, 448.

38. Quoted in Jane Tompkins, *West of Everything: The Inner Life of Westerns* (New York: Oxford University Press, 1992). Tompkins provides a feminist interpretation of Grey and several other western writers.

39. For helpful discussions of Zane Grey and the Mormons, see Ann Ronald, *Zane Grey* (Boise, Idaho: Boise State University, 1975); and Gary Topping, "Zane Grey in Zion: An Examination of His Supposed Anti-Mormonism," *Brigham Young University Studies* 18 (Summer 1979): 483–90.

40. Grey, *Riders of the Purple Sage* (New York: Penguin Books, 1990), 8, 9.

1. This chapter draws heavily on Richard W. Etulain, "Introduction: The Rise of Western Historiography," and "After Turner: The Western Historiography of Frederic Logan Paxson," in Etulain, ed., *Writing Western History: Essays on Major Western Historians* (Albuquerque: University of New Mexico Press, 1991), 7–12, 137–65.

2. Frederick Jackson Turner to William Allen, October 31, 1888, Box 1, Turner Papers, Henry E. Huntington Library (HEH), quoted in Wilbur R. Jacobs, ed., *The Historical World of Frederick Jackson Turner: With Selections From His Correspondence* (New Haven: Yale University Press, 1968), 77; Turner to Carl Becker, December 16, 1925, quoted in Ray Allen Billington, *The Genesis of the Frontier Thesis: A Study in Historical Creativity* (San Marino, Calif.: Huntington Library, 1981), 234.

3. Turner, "Problems in American History," *The Aegis*, November 4, 1892, reprinted in *The Early Writings of Frederick Jackson Turner* (Madison: University of Wisconsin Press, 1938), 72; "The Significance of History," *Early Writings*, 64, 52.

4. Turner to Constance L. Skinner, March 15, 1922, Box 31, Turner Papers, HEH, as quoted in Billington, *Genesis*, 214.

5. Turner reviewed volumes of Rossevelt's *Winning of the West* in *The Dial* 10 (August 1889): 71–73; *The Nation* 60 (March 28, 1895): 240–42; *The Nation* 63 (October 8, 1896): 277; *American Historical Review* 2 (October 1896): 171–76; quotations are from *AHR*, p. 171, and *The Nation*, p. 241. Turner, review of Justin Winsor, *The Westward Movement*, in the *American Historical Review* 3 (April 1898): 556–61; quotations are from p. 557. Turner, review of Reuben Gold Thwaites, *Early Western Travels*, in *The Dial* 37 (November 16, 1904): 298–302; 41 (July 1, 1906): 6–10. Turner, "Francis Parkman and His Work," *The Dial* 25 (December 16, 1898): 451–53; quotations are from 451–53. Turner's reviews are expertly summarized in Martin Ridge, "A More Jealous Mistress: Frederick Jackson Turner as Book Reviewer," *Pacific Historical Review* 55 (February 1986): 49–63.

6. Billington, *Genesis*, 10. Like all students of Turner, I am much indebted to Ray Billington's magisterial biography, *Frederick Jackson Turner: Historian, Scholar, Teacher* (New York: Oxford University Press, 1973).

7. Turner, *The Character and Influence of the Indian Trade in Wisconsin*, eds. David Harry Miller and William W. Savage, Jr. (1891; Norman: University of Oklahoma Press, 1977), 85, 5, 3.

8. Turner, "The Significance of History," 52–53, 58, 44, 64.

9. "Problems in American History," 72, 74, 75–76, 77, 83.

10. Turner, "The Significance of the Frontier in American History," in *History, Frontier and Section: Three Essays by Frederick Jackson Turner*, ed. Martin Ridge (Albuquerque: University of New Mexico Press, 1993), 77, 60, 59, 62.

11. Ibid., 61, 91.

12. Turner, *Rise of the New West, 1819–1829* (New York: Harper & Brothers, 1906), 68, 69.

13. William Cronon, "Revisiting the Vanishing Frontier: The Legacy of Frederick Jackson Turner," *Western Historical Quarterly* 18 (April 1987): 157–76; Cronon, "Turner's First Stand: The Significance of Significance in American History," in Etulain, *Writing Western History*, 73–101.

14. The best general introduction to Paxson is Earl Pomeroy, "Frederic Logan Paxson and His Approach to History," *Mississippi Valley Historical Review* 39 (March 1953): 673–92.

15. Paxson to Claude H. Van Tyne, October 22, 1905, March 17, 1905, Van Tyne Papers, Michigan Historical Collections, Bentley Historical Library, University of Michigan, Ann Arbor; Turner to Paxson, January 12, 1906, Turner Papers, HEH.

16. Paxson, Preface in *The Last American Frontier* (New York: Macmillan, 1910).

17. Paxson, *History of the American Frontier 1763–1893* (Boston: Houghton Mifflin Company, 1924).

18. Paxson, *When the West is Gone* (New York: Henry Holt and Company, 1930).

19. Paxson, "A Generation of the Frontier Hypothesis: 1893–1932," *Pacific Historical Review* 2 (March 1933): 51.

20. Turner, "The Significance of the Frontier," 59, 88.

21. David M. Wrobel, *The End of American Exceptionalism: Frontier Anxiety from the Old West to the New Deal* (Lawrence: University Press of Kansas, 1993), 115, 114.

22. Billington, "Frederick Jackson Turner and the Closing of the Frontier," in Roger Daniels, ed., *Essays in Honor of T. A. Larson* (Laramie: University of Wyoming, 1971).

23. Norman Foerster, ed., *The Reinterpretation of American Literature* (New York: Harcourt, Brace, 1928), 28; Richard W. Etulain, "The American Literary West and Its Interpreters: The Rise of a New Historiography," *Pacific Historical Review* 45 (August 1976): 311–48.

24. Charles A. Beard, *New Republic* 25 (1920): 349–50; Wilbur R. Jacobs, *On Turner's Trail: 100 Years of Writing Western History* (Lawrence: University Press of Kansas, 1994), 107–8, 177–78.

CHAPTER 3. FRONTIER ART

1. For a useful discussion of the West's impact on Remington, Roosevelt, and Wister, see G. Edward White, *The Eastern Establishment and the Western Experience* (New Haven: Yale University Press, 1968). Especially thorough is the narrative life story by Peggy and Harold Samuels, *Frederic Remington: A Biography* (Garden City, N.Y.: Doubleday, 1982). The best cultural study of Remington the artist is Ben Merchant Vorpahl, *Frederic Remington and the West: With the Eye of the Mind* (Austin: University of Texas Press, 1978). The quotation is from p. xii.

2. Frederic Remington, "A Few Words from Mr. Remington," *Collier's Weekly,* March 18, 1905, p. 17, quoted in Vorpahl, *Frederic Remington and the West,* 26.

3. White, *The Eastern Establishment,* 99.

4. Poultney Bigelow, *Seventy Summers,* 1:304, quoted in White, *The Eastern Establishment,* 100.

5. Royal Cortissoz, *American Artists,* 232, as quoted in Peter H. Hassrick, *Frederic Remington . . .* (New York: Abrams, 1973), 26.

6. Hassrick, *Frederic Remington,* 68.

7. Vorpahl, *Frederic Remington and the West,* 192–202. Most of the Remington letters concerning Wister's "Evolution of the Cow-Puncher," including those containing Remington's sketches, are deposited in the Wister Papers in the Library of Congress. Several of these letters are quoted in Vorpahl, *My Dear Wister: The Frederic Remington–Owen Wister Letters* (Palo Alto, Calif.: American West, 1972). Wallace Stegner argues in his foreword to this volume that in their several collaborations Remington and Wister virtually created the cowboy hero of western mythology.

8. White, *The Eastern Establishment,* 104.

9. Quoted in White, *The Eastern Establishement,* 109.

10. Hassrick, *Frederic Remington,* 37.

11. Jane Tompkins, *West of Everything: The Inner Life of Westerns* (New York: Oxford University Press, 1992), 182. For another revisionist treatment of Remington, see Alex Nemerov, " 'Doing the "Old America" ': The Image of the American West, 1880–1920," in William H. Truettner, ed., *The West as America: Reinterpreting Images of the Frontier, 1820–1920* (Washington, D.C.: Smithsonian Institution Press, 1991), 285–343.

12. Quoted in Samuels and Samuels, *Frederic Remington,* 306–7.

13. Brian Dippie, *Remington and Russell* (Austin: University of Texas Press, 1982), 10.

14. Ibid., 52.

15. Vorpahl, *Frederic Remington and the West,* 268.

16. Two pioneering studies of Charles Russell are Harold McCracken, *The Charles M. Russell Book: The Life and Work of the Cowboy Artist* (Garden City, N.Y.: Doubleday, 1957), and Frederic G. Renner, *Charles M. Russell . . .* (New York: Harry N. Abrams, 1974).

17. Quoted in Charles M. Russell, *"Paper Talk": Charlie Russell's American West,* ed. Brian W. Dippie (New York: Alfred A. Knopf, 1979), 7.

18. Ibid., 5.

19. McCracken, *Russell Book,* 103–8.

20. John C. Ewers, "Charlie Russell's Indians," *Montana: The Magazine of Western History* 37 (Summer 1987): 36–53; Raphael Cristy, "Charlie's Hidden Agenda: Realism and Nostalgia in C. M. Russell's Stories about Indians," *Montana: The Magazine of Western History* 43 (Summer 1993): 2–15.

21. Ewers, "Charlie Russell's Indians," 53. One should note, however, that Russell's little-known *Joy of Life* (n.d.) presents a discordant note. Depicting an Indian man and two Indian children waiting outside a tepee, the painting hints at a cowboy and Indian woman's tryst inside. With the aid of an inserted coin, the curious could raise the flap of the tepee to view those inside. Nancy Russell tried to destroy the painting, but it remained out of her grasp in the Mint Saloon in Great Falls.

22. Brian W. Dippie makes this point in his provocative study, *Looking at Russell* (Fort Worth, Tex.: Amon Carter Museum, 1987).

23. See Dippie, "Charlie Russell's Lost West," *American Heritage* 24 (April 1973): 4–21, 89; and Robert Archibald, "C. M. Russell and Montana: The End of the Frontier," in *Charles M. Russell: American Artist* (St. Louis: Jefferson National Expansion Historical Association, 1982), 36–43.

24. Dippie argues that Dame Progress may also reflect Charlie's ambivalent attitude toward his wife, Nancy, who tried to divorce him from what she considered the detrimental influences of his cowboy days. See Dippie, "Charlie Russell's Lost West," 9–13.

25. Russell, *"Paper Talk"*, 86, 103, 81 (quote).

26. Quoted in Dippie, *Looking at Russell,* 125.

27. Russell to Friend Ted, May 13, 1919, in Russell, *"Paper Talk,"* 153.

28. Quoted in Archibald, "Russell and Montana," 39.

29. Dippie, *Looking at Russell,* 125.

30. The two best collections of paintings by the Taos artists are Mary Carroll Nelson, *The Legendary Artists of Taos* (New York: Watson-Guptill Publications, 1980), and Patricia Janis Broder, *Taos: A Painter's Dream* (Boston: New York Graphic Society, 1980). Much more analytical are the essays collected in Charles C. Eldredge, Julie Schimmel, and William H. Truettner, *Art in New Mexico, 1900–1945: Paths to Taos and Santa Fe* (Washington, D.C.: National Museum of American Art, 1986). I have relied heavily on this source for my discussions of southwestern artists.

31. Arrell Morgan Gibson, *The Santa Fe and Taos Colonies: Age of the Muses, 1900–1942* (Norman: University of Oklahoma Press, 1983).

32. Quoted in Laura M. Bickerstaff, *Pioneer Artists of Taos,* rev. ed. (Denver: Old West Publishing, 1983), 31.

33. Quoted in Charles C. Eldredge, "The Faraway Nearby: New Mexico and the Modern Landscape," *Art in New Mexico,* 152–53.

34. Eldredge, "The Faraway Nearby," 172.

35. Ibid., 156.

36. For an alternative view of Higgins's *Winter Funeral,* which reads the painting as a depiction of the mourners "surrounded and overwhelmed by the magnitude and power of nature," see Broder, *Taos,* 192.

37. A very useful overview of modern western art, with major emphasis on ethnic topics, appears in H. Wayne Morgan, "Main Currents in Twentieth-Century Western

Art," in Gerald D. Nash and Richard W. Etulain, eds., *The Twentieth-Century West: Historical Interpretations* (Albuquerque: University of New Mexico Press, 1989), 383–406.

38. William Truettner, "The Art of Pueblo Life," *Art in New Mexico*, 85.

39. Gibson, "Hispanic Muses," *Santa Fe and Taos Colonies*, 163–75; Kay Aiken Reeve, *Santa Fe and Taos 1898–1942: An American Cultural Center*. Southwestern Studies, Monograph No. 67. (El Paso: Texas Western Press, 1982), 25–35; Julie Schimmel, "The Hispanic Southwest," *Art in New Mexico*, 101–45.

40. Keith L. Bryant, Jr., "The Atchison, Topeka and Santa Fe Railway and the Development of the Taos and Santa Fe Art Colonies," *Western Historical Quarterly* 9 (October 1978): 437–53.

41. Melody Graulich, "Profile of Mary Hallock Foote," *Legacy* 3 (No. 2) (1986): 43–52; Shelley Armitage, "The Illustrator as Writer: Mary Hallock Foote and the Myth of the West," in Barbara Howard Meldrum, ed., *Under the Sun: Myth and Realism in Western American Literature* (Troy, N.Y.: Whitston, 1985), 150–74.

42. This series, accompanied by Foote's one- to two-page comments on each illustration, is conveniently reprinted in Mary Hallock Foote, *The Idaho Stories and Far West Illustrations of Mary Hallock Foote*, ed. Barbara Cragg et al. (Pocatello: Idaho State University Press, 1988), 265–303. Foote furnishes illuminating comments about her illustrations in Mary Hallock Foote to Mr. Fraser (*Century* magazine, June 10, [1887?]), #196, Mary Hallock Foote Collection, Henry E. Huntington Library, San Marino, California.

43. W. J. Linton, "The History of Wood-Engraving in America: Part IV," *American Art and American Art Collections* 1 (Boston, 1889), 459; Regina Armstrong, "Representative American Women Illustrators: The Character Workers," *Critic* 37 (August 1900): 131; Robert Taft, *Artists and Illustrators of the Old West, 1850–1900* (New York: Charles Scribner's Sons, 1953), 173.

44. Graulich provides a brief but provocative reading of Foote's understanding and use of female voice in her fiction and art in "Profile of Mary Hallock Foote." Armitage, meanwhile, suggests that Foote's perspective provides a countermyth to the usual Old West myth of cowboys and Indians, "The Illustrator as Writer."

45. In 1903, Foote wrote to Austin, saluting her efforts to bring a woman's point of view to writing about the West; Mary Hallock Foote to Mary Austin, October 12, 1903, Austin Collection, Box 9, Huntington Library.

PART II. THE WEST AS REGION

CHAPTER 4. REGIONAL NOVELS

1. H. L. Davis and James Stevens, *Status Rerum: A Manifesto, Upon the Present Condition of Northwestern Literature, Containing Several Near-Libelous Utterances, Upon Persons in the Public Eye* (The Dalles, Oregon: N.p., 1927), n.p.

2. H. G. Merriam, "Endlessly the Covered Wagon," *The Frontier* 8 (November 1927): 1.

3. Ibid.

4. The fullest account of American regionalism between the wars is Robert L. Dorman, *Revolt of the Provinces: The Regionalist Movement in America, 1920–1945* (Chapel Hill: University of North Carolina Press, 1993). Also, see Richard Maxwell Brown's brief but superb overview "The New Regionalism in America, 1970–1981," in William G. Robbins et al., eds., *Regionalism and the Pacific Northwest* (Corvallis: Oregon State University Press, 1983), 37–96.

5. Josiah Royce, "Provincialism," *Race Questions, Provincialism, and Other American Problems* (New York: Macmillan, 1908), 62; Richard W. Etulain, "Frontier, Region and Myth: Changing Interpretations of Western American Culture," *Journal of American Culture* 3 (Summer 1980):84.

6. Edwin R. Bingham, *Charles F. Lummis: Editor of the Southwest* (San Marino, Calif.: Huntington Library, 1955), 190–91.

7. Mary Austin, "Regional Culture in the Southwest," *Southwest Review* 14 (July 1929): 476.

8. Stark Young, "On Reeking of the Soil," *Texas Review* 1 (June 1915): 80–81; Jay B. Hubbell, "The New Southwest," *Southwest Review* 10 (October 1924): 91, 98; Hubbell, "*Southwest Review*, 1924–1927," *Southwest Review* 50 (Winter 1965): 1–18.

9. Henry Nash Smith, "McGinnis and the *Southwest Review*: A Reminiscence," *Southwest Review* 40 (Autumn 1955): 305.

10. Milton M. Reigelman, *The Midland: A Venture in Literary Regionalism* (Iowa City: University of Iowa Press, 1975), 42.

11. Reigelman, *The Midland*, 20.

12. H. G. Merriam, "Expression of Northwest Life," *New Mexico Quarterly* 4 (May 1934): 127–32.

13. B. A. Botkin, "Regionalism: Cult or Culture?" *English Journal* 25 (March 1936): 184.

14. Ibid.

15. Carey McWilliams, *The New Regionalism in American Literature* (Seattle: University of Washington Book Store, 1930).

16. Willa Cather, *O Pioneers!* (Boston: Houghton Mifflin Company, 1913), 15, 3, 75, 76, 83.

17. H. L. Davis, *Collected Essays and Short Stories* (Moscow: University of Idaho Press, 1986), 301, 302, 31.

18. Richard W. Etulain, "Frontier, Region, and Border: Cultural Currents in the Recent Southwest," *Montana: The Magazine of Western History* 44 (Winter 1994): 64–70.

19. John Steinbeck, "The Leader of the People," *The Red Pony* (1937; New York: Bantam, 1948), 91–92

20. Ibid., 90–91.

21. James N. Gregory, *American Exodus: The Dust Bowl Migration and Okie Culture in California* (New York: Oxford University Press, 1989).

CHAPTER 5. REGIONAL HISTORIES

1. Most of the papers presented at the Boulder conference appear in James F. Willard and Colin B. Goodykoontz, eds., *The Trans-Mississippi West* (Boulder: University of Colorado, 1930).

2. Turner, "Problems in American History," *The Early Writings of Frederick Jackson Turner* (Madison: University of Wisconsin Press, 1938), 79; Fulmer Mood, "The Origin, Evolution, and Application of the Sectional Concept, 1750–1900," in Merrill Jensen, ed., *Regionalism in America* (Madison: University of Wisconsin Press, 1965), 87.

3. Mood, "Sectional Concept," 91, 96.

4. Turner to Mr. MacVeagh, April 5, 1921, Henry Holt Correspondence, Firestone Library, Princeton University, Princeton, N.J.; Turner, "Is Sectionalism in America Dying Away?" *American Journal of Sociology* 13 (March 1908): 661–75; Turner, "Sections and Nations," *Yale Review* 12 (October 1922): 1–21; Turner, "Geographical Sectionalism in American History," *Annals of the Association of American Geographers* 16 (June 1926): 85–93; Turner, "The West—1876 and 1926: Its Progress in a Half-Century," *World's Work* 52 (July 1926): 319–27; Turner, "Draft on Sectionalism," in Wilbur R. Jacobs, ed., *Frederick Jackson Turner's Legacy* (San Marino, Calif.: Huntington Library, 1965), 50–51.

5. Turner, "The Significance of the Section in American History," *Wisconsin Magazine of History* 8 (March 1925): 255, 274, 280.

6. For a superb overview of Turner as regionalist, see Michael C. Steiner, "The Significance of Turner's Sectional Thesis," *Western Historical Quarterly* 10 (October 1979): 437–66.

7. Quoted in Elliott West, "Walter Prescott Webb and the Search for the West," in Richard W. Etulain, ed., *Writing Western History: Essays on Major Western Historians* (Albuquerque: University of New Mexico Press, 1991), 168.

8. A letter from Walter Prescott Webb to John P. Howe of the University of Chicago, dated May 22, 1938, reveals much about Webb's painful memories and reactions to his experiences at Chicago; Webb Papers (2M260), Eugene C. Barker History Center, University of Texas, Austin.

9. Webb to Professor Lee Benson, January 10, 1951, Webb Papers (2M284), Barker Center. Webb's notes on Keasbey's lectures are in the W. P. Webb Papers, Texas State Library, Austin.

10. Undated, untitled twenty-two-page autobiographical typescript in the Webb Papers, Texas State Archives, Texas State Library; Frederic Logan Paxson, review of Webb, *The Great Plains*, *American Historical Review* 37 (January 1932): 359–60.

11. Webb, *The Great Plains* (Boston: Ginn and Company, 1931), vi.

12. Webb, *Divided We Stand: The Crisis of Frontierless Democracy* (New York: Farrar & Rinehart, 1937), 12, 9.

13. Wallace Stegner, *The Uneasy Chair: A Biography of Bernard DeVoto* (Garden City, N.Y.: Doubleday, 1975), ix–x.

14. Bernard DeVoto, "The West: A Plundered Province," *Harper's Magazine* 169 (August 1934): 355–64; DeVoto, "The West Against Itself," *Harper's Magazine* 194 (January 1947): 1–13.

15. Malin's major writings are conveniently sampled in James C. Malin, *History and Ecology: Studies of the Grassland,* ed. Robert P. Swierenga (Lincoln: University of Nebraska Press, 1984).

16. On Bolton and the Borderlands school, see David J. Weber, "Turner, the Boltonians, and the Borderlands," *American Historical Review* 91 (February 1986): 66–81; and Albert L. Hurtado, "Herbert E. Bolton, Racism, and American History," *Pacific Historical Review* 62 (May 1993): 127–42.

17. Frederick J. Hoffman et al., *The Little Magazine: A History and a Bibliography* (Princeton, N.J.: Princeton University Press, 1947), 139.

18. John R. Milton, *Three Wests: Conversations with Vardis Fisher, Max Evans, and Michael Straight* (Vermillion, S. Dak.: Dakota Press, 1970), 11, 9.

19. Jerre Mangione, *The Dream and the Deal: The Federal Writers' Project, 1935–1943* (Boston: Little, Brown, 1972), 201–8.

CHAPTER 6. REGIONAL ART

1. Matthew Baigell, *Thomas Hart Benton* (New York: Henry N. Abrams, 1975), 43.

2. Thomas Hart Benton, *An Artist in America* (1937), reprinted as *Tom Benton's America: An Artist in America* (New York: Robert M. McBride and Company, n.d.), 76–77.

3. Thomas Hart Benton, *An American in Art: A Professional and Technical Autobiography* (Lawrence: University Press of Kansas, 1969), 58–59.

4. Benton, *Tom Benton's America,* 202–3. For the fullest comment on *Boomtown,* see Karal Ann Marling, "Thomas Hart Benton's *Boomtown*: Regionalism Redefined," in Jack Salzman, ed., *Prospects* 6 (1981): 73–137.

5. Quoted in Henry Adams, *Thomas Hart Benton: An American Original* (New York: Alfred A. Knopf, 1989), 261.

6. Grant Wood, *Revolt against the City,* pamphlet, Iowa City, Iowa, 1935, reprinted in James M. Dennis, *Grant Wood: A Study in American Art and Culture* (Columbia: University of Missouri Press, 1986), 231.

7. Wanda M. Corn, *Grant Wood: The Regionalist Vision* (New Haven, Conn.: Yale University Press, 1983), 74.

8. Ibid., 132.

9. Matthew Baigell, *The American Scene: American Painting of the 1930's* (New York: Praeger Publishers, 1974), 110.

10. John Steuart Curry to *Life* magazine, February 28, 1942, roll 166, Curry Papers, Archives of American Art, Smithsonian Institution, Washington, D.C.

11. Mrs. Henry J. Allen to William Allen White, December 16, 1931, roll 166; William Allen White to John Steuart Curry, December 18, 1931, roll 168, AAA, Smithsonian; *Kansas City Star,* June 27, 1947, quoted in Calder M. Pickett, "John Steuart Curry and the Topeka Murals Controversy," *Kansas Quarterly* 2 (Fall 1970): 30–41.

12. Pickett, "Murals Controversy," 32; M. Sue Kendall, *Rethinking Regionalism: John Steuart Curry and the Kansas Mural Controversy* (Washington, D.C.: Smithsonian Institution Press, 1986), 132.

13. Baigell, *The American Scene,* 129.

14. Lee Rosson DeLong, *Nature's Forms / Nature's Forces: The Art of Alexandre Hogue* (Norman: University of Oklahoma Press, 1984), 19, 120, 104.

15. Rick Stewart, *Lone Star Regionalism: The Dallas Nine and Their Circle* (Austin: Texas Monthly Press, 1985).

16. Peter Hurd, *My Land Is the Southwest: Peter Hurd Letters and Journals,* ed. Robert Metzger (College Station: Texas A&M University Press, 1983), 126, 166; Tonia L. Horton, " 'I Did What I Knew I Could Do': Peter Hurd and American Regionalism," in *Peter Hurd: Insight to a Painter* (Phoenix: Phoenix Art Museum, 1983), 21.

17. *Regionalism: The California View: Watercolors 1929–1945* (Santa Barbara: Santa Barbara Museum of Art, 1988).

18. Nancy Boas, *The Society of Six California Colorists* (San Francisco: Bedford Arts, 1988), 187.

19. Martha Kingsbury, "Four Artists in the Northwest Tradition," in *Northwest Traditions* (Seattle: Seattle Art Museum, 1978); interviews with Mark Tobey by William Sietz, 1962, Tobey Papers, Box 10, Folder 23, University of Washington Library, Seattle; Kingsbury, *Celebrating Washington's Art: An Essay in 100 Years of Art in Washington* (Olympia: Washington Centennial Commission, 1989).

PART III. THE WEST AS POSTREGION

INTRODUCTION

1. Gerald D. Nash, *The American West Transformed: The Impact of the Second World War* (Bloomington: Indiana University Press, 1985); Earl Pomeroy, *The Pacific Slope: A History of California, Oregon, Washington, Idaho, Utah, and Nevada* (New York: Alfred A. Knopf, 1965).

1. For an excellent brief overview of western fiction, see James Maguire, "Fiction of the West," in Emory Elliott et al., eds., *The Columbia History of the American Novel* (New York: Columbia University Press, 1991), 437–64. For a comprehensive listing of the major books and essays on more than 300 western writers, consult Richard W. Etulain and N. Jill Howard, eds., *A Bibliographical Guide to the Study of Western American Literature*, 2d ed. (Albuquerque: University of New Mexico Press, 1995).

2. Joan Didion, *Run River* (1963; New York: Pocket Books, 1978), 5.

3. Walter Van Tilburg Clark to Walter Prescott Webb, September 1, 1959, quoted in Webb, Afterword to *The Ox-Bow Incident* (New York: Signet Classic Edition, 1960), 224, 222; John R. Milton, "Conversation with Walter Van Tilburg Clark," *South Dakota Review* 9 (Spring 1971): 27–38.

4. A. B. Guthrie, *Big Sky, Fair Land: The Environmental Essays of A. B. Guthrie, Jr.*, ed. David Peterson (Flagstaff, Ariz.: Northland Press, 1988).

5. Wallace Stegner and Richard W. Etulain, *Conversations with Wallace Stegner on Western History and Literature*, rev. ed. (Salt Lake City: University of Utah Press, 1990), 47, 43.

6. Stegner, *Angle of Repose* (Garden City, N.Y.: Doubleday, 1971), 22; Etulain, "Western Fiction and History: A Reconsideration," in Jerome O. Steffen, ed., *The American West: New Perspectives, New Dimensions* (Norman: University of Oklahoma Press, 1979), 152–74.

7. Quoted in *Rocky Mountain News*, May 10, 1992, p. 127.

8. Antonya Nelson, "Turf Wars in New Mexico," *New York Times Book Review,* November 29, 1992, p. 22.

9. Kittredge, *Hole in the Sky: A Memoir* (New York: Alfred A. Knopf, 1992), 234–35.

10. James N. Gregory, *American Exodus: The Dust Bowl Migration and Okie Culture in California* (New York: Oxford University Press, 1989); William W. Bevis, *Ten Tough Trips: Montana Writers and the West* (Seattle: University of Washington Press, 1990).

CHAPTER 8. POSTREGIONAL HISTORIES

1. In addition to the books and essays cited in these notes, thousands of other sources are listed in Richard W. Etulain, et al., eds., *The American West in the Twentieth Century: A Bibliography* (Norman: University of Oklahoma Press, 1994).

2. Overviews of western historiography include Gerald D. Nash, *Creating the West: Historical Interpretations, 1890–1990* (Albuquerque: University of New Mexico Press, 1991); and Etulain, ed., *Writing Western History: Essays on Major Western Historians* (Albuquerque: University of New Mexico Press, 1991). John W. Caughey, "Historians' Choice: Results of a Poll on Recently Published American History and Biography," *Mis-*

sissippi Valley Historical Review 39 (September 1952): 289–302; W. N. Davis, Jr., "Will the West Survive as a Field in American History? A Survey Report," *Mississippi Valley Historical Review* 50 (March 1964): 672–85.

3. For a particularly probing evaluation of Smith's *Virgin Land*, see Lee Clark Mitchell, "Henry Nash Smith's Myth of the West," in Etulain, *Writing Western History*, 247–75.

4. Henry Nash Smith to Richard W. Etulain, May 22, 1976.

5. Smith, *Virgin Land: The American West as Symbol and Myth* (Cambridge, Mass.: Harvard University Press, 1950), v.

6. Earl Pomeroy, "Toward a Reorientation of Western History: Continuity and Environment," *Mississippi Valley Historical Review* 41 (March 1955): 579–600.

7. Julie Roy Jeffrey, *Frontier Women: The Trans-Mississippi West, 1840–1880* (New York: Hill and Wang, 1979); John Phillip Reid, "Some Lessons of Western Legal History," *Western Legal History* 1 (Winter-Spring 1988): 3–21; Terry G. Jordan, *North American Cattle-Ranching Frontiers: Origins, Diffusion, and Differentiation* (Albuquerque: University of New Mexico Press, 1993); John D. W. Guice, "Cattle Raisers of the Old Southwest: A Reinterpretation," *Western Historical Quarterly* 8 (April 1977): 167–87. Urban historians that emphasize eastern continuities in western towns and cities include Lawrence H. Larsen, *The Urban West at the End of the Frontier* (Lawrence: Regents Press of Kansas, 1978); William Issel and Robert W. Cherny, *San Francisco, 1865–1932: Politics, Power, and Urban Development* (Berkeley: University of California Press, 1986); and Carl Abbott, *The Metropolitan Frontier: Cities in the Modern American West* (Tucson: University of Arizona Press, 1993).

8. Pomeroy's large influence on western historiography is traced and evaluated in Howard R. Lamar, "Earl Pomeroy, Historian's Historian," *Pacific Historical Review* 56 (November 1987): 546–60; and Michael P. Malone, "Earl Pomeroy and the Reorientation of Western American History," in Etulain, *Writing Western History*, 311–34.

9. Wallace Stegner, *Beyond the Hundredth Meridian: John Wesley Powell and the Second Opening of the West* (Boston: Houghton Mifflin, 1954).

10. The remainder of this chapter draws heavily on Etulain, "Visions and Revisions: Recent Interpretations of the American West," in *Writing Western History*, 335–58; and Richard W. Etulain, "Prologue: A New Historiographical Frontier: The Twentieth-Century West," in Gerald D. Nash and Richard W. Etulain, eds., *The Twentieth-Century West: Historical Interpretations* (Albuquerque: University of New Mexico Press, 1989), 1–31.

11. Earl Pomeroy, *The Pacific Slope: A History of California, Oregon, Washington, Idaho, Utah, and Nevada* (New York: Alfred A. Knopf, 1965), 3.

12. Gerald D. Nash, *The American West in the Twentieth Century: A Short History of an Urban Oasis* (Albuquerque: University of New Mexico Press, 1977); Nash, *The*

American West Transformed: The Impact of the Second World War (Bloomington: Indiana University Press, 1985); Nash, *World War II and the West: Reshaping the Economy* (Lincoln: University of Nebraska Press, 1990).

13. Rodman W. Paul and Michael P. Malone, "Tradition and Challenge in Western Historiography," *Western Historical Quarterly* 16 (January 1985): 27–53.

14. Robert Berkhofer, "The Political Context of a New Indian History," *Pacific Historical Review* 40 (August 1971): 357–82.

15. Albert Camarillo, *Chicanos in a Changing Society: From Mexican Pueblos to American Barrios in Santa Barbara and Southern California, 1848–1930* (Cambridge, Mass.: Harvard University Press, 1979); Mario T. García, *Desert Immigrants: The Mexicans of El Paso, 1880–1920* (New Haven: Yale University Press, 1981); Ricardo Romo, *East Los Angeles: History of a Barrio* (Austin: University of Texas Press, 1983); Richard Griswold del Castillo, *The Los Angeles Barrio, 1850–1890: A Social History* (Berkeley: University of California Press, 1979).

16. Rodolfo Acuña, *Occupied America: A History of Chicanos*, 3d ed. (New York: Harper and Row, 1988); Juan Gómez-Quiñones, *Mexican American Labor, 1790–1990* (Albuquerque: University of New Mexico Press, 1994); Oscar Martínez, *Troublesome Border* (Tucson: University of Arizona Press, 1988); Robert J. Rosenbaum, *Mexicano Resistance in the Southwest: "The Sacred Right of Self-Preservation"* (Austin: University of Texas Press, 1981).

17. Frederick C. Luebke, *Immigrants and Politics: The Germans of Nebraska, 1880–1900* (Lincoln: University of Nebraska Press, 1969); Luebke, "Ethnic Minority Groups in the American West," in Michael P. Malone, ed., *Historians and the American West* (Lincoln: University of Nebraska Press, 1983), 387–413.

18. Joan Jensen and Darlis Miller, "The Gentle Tamers Revisited: New Approaches to the History of Women in the American West," *Pacific Historical Review* 49 (May 1980): 173–213.

19. Sandra L. Myres, *Westering Women and the Frontier Experience, 1800–1915* (Albuquerque: University of New Mexico Press, 1982); Glenda Riley, *The Female Frontier: A Comparative View of Women on the Prairie and the Plains* (Lawrence: University Press of Kansas, 1988); Jeffrey, *Frontier Women*; Lillian Schlissel, *Women's Diaries of the Westward Journey* (New York: Schocken Books, 1982); John Mack Faragher, *Women and Men on the Overland Trail* (New Haven: Yale University Press, 1979).

20. *Journal of American History* 76 (March 1990).

21. Cronon, *Nature's Metropolis: Chicago and the Great West* (New York: W. W. Norton, 1991), xxi.

22. Franklin Walker, *San Francisco's Literary Frontier* (New York: Alfred A. Knopf, 1939); Carey McWilliams, *Southern California: An Island on the Land* (New York: Duell, Sloan, & Pearce, 1946).

23. John Cawelti, *The Six-Gun Mystique* (Bowling Green, Ohio: Bowling Green University Popular Press, 1984); Christine Bold, *Selling the Wild West: Popular Western Fiction, 1860–1960* (Bloomington: Indiana University Press, 1987); Norman Yates, *Gender and Genre: An Introduction to Women Writers of Formula Westerns, 1900–1950* (Albuquerque: University of New Mexico Press, 1995).

24. D. W. Meinig, "American Wests: Preface to a Geographical Interpretation," *Annals of the Association of American Geographers* 62 (June 1972): 159–84; Raymond D. Gastil, *Cultural Regions of the United States* (Seattle: University of Washington Press, 1975); David Montejano, *Anglos and Mexicans in the Making of Texas, 1836–1986* (Austin: University of Texas Press, 1987); James Gregory, *American Exodus: The Dust Bowl Migration and Okie Culture in California* (New York: Oxford University Press, 1989).

25. White, "Trashing the Trails," in Patricia Nelson Limerick, Clyde A. Milner II, and Charles E. Rankin, eds., *Trails: Toward a New Western History* (Lawrence: University Press of Kansas, 1991), 26–39.

26. Ray Allen Billington and Martin Ridge, *Westward Expansion: A History of the American Frontier*, 5th ed. (New York: Macmillan, 1982); Robert V. Hine, *The American West: An Interpretive History*, 2d ed. (Boston: Little, Brown and Company, 1984); Rodman W. Paul, *The Far West and the Great Plains in Transition, 1859–1900* (New York: Harper and Row, 1988); Nash, *The American West in the Twentieth Century*; Michael P. Malone and Richard W. Etulain, *The American West: A Twentieth-Century History* (Lincoln: University of Nebraska Press, 1989).

27. "Trails: Toward a New Western History," Conference Program, September 27–29, 1989, Santa Fe, New Mexico.

28. Limerick's one-page statement was published in Limerick, "Western History: Why the Past May Be Changing," *Montana: The Magazine of Western History* 40 (Summer 1990): 61–64.

29. Patricia Nelson Limerick, *The Legacy of Conquest: The Unbroken Past of the American West* (New York: W. W. Norton, 1987), 26, 22. Challenges to Limerick's views include Michael P. Malone, "The 'New Western History': An Assessment," *Montana: The Magazine of Western History* 40 (Summer 1990): 65–67; Daniel Tyler, "Barbecuing a 'Paleo-Liberal': Western Historians React to Patricia Nelson Limerick's *The Legacy of Conquest: The Unbroken Past of the American West*," *Gateway Heritage* 9 (Winter 1988/89): 38–42; William W. Savage, Jr., "The New Western History: Youngest Whore on the Block," *AB Bookman's Weekly* 92 (October 4, 1993): 1242–47. Also see note 31 below.

30. Wilbur Jacobs provides a lucid, balanced discussion of Richard White's works and those of other New Western historians in his *On Turner's Trail: 100 Years of Writing Western History* (Lawrence: University Press of Kansas, 1994), esp. 203–37. Although rarely called a New Western historian, Elliott West provides a stunning example of post-

regional scholarship in a synthetic case study that enlarges the meaning of traditional topics through the adroit use of recent innovative scholarship. See his *Way to the West: Essays on the Central Plains* (Albuquerque: University of New Mexico Press, 1995).

31. For challenges to the New Western history, see Gerald D. Nash, "Point of View: One Hundred Years of Western History," *Journal of the West* 32 (January 1993): 3–4; and Gerald Thompson, "The New Western History: A Critical Analysis," *Continuity* 17 (Fall 1993): 6–24. Essays criticizing and advocating the New Western history are conveniently collected in Gene M. Gressley, ed., *Old West/New West: Quo Vadis?* (Worland, Wyo.: High Plains Publishing Company, 1994).

CHAPTER 9. POSTREGIONAL ART

1. Richard White, *"It's Your Misfortune and None of My Own": A New History of the American West* (Norman: University of Oklahoma Press, 1991), 3.

2. Thomas Albright, *Art in the San Francisco Bay Area 1945–1980: An Illustrated History* (Berkeley: University of California Press, 1985). This is an extraordinarily useful book for understanding West Coast art.

3. April Kingsley, *The Turning Point: The Abstract Expressionists and the Transformation of American Art* (New York: Simon and Schuster, 1992), 134, 137.

4. Katharine Kuh, "Clyfford Still," in John P. O'Neill, ed., *Clyfford Still* (New York: Metropolitan Museum of Art, 1979), 12.

5. Peter Plagens, *Sunshine Music: Contemporary Art on the West Coast* (New York: Praeger Publishers, 1974), 40–41.

6. Caroline A. Jones, *Bay Area Figurative Art 1950–1965* (Berkeley: University of California Press, 1990), 6–11. The following discussion draws heavily on this major study.

7. Letter from Clyfford Still to Mark Rothko, quoted in O'Neill, *Clyfford Still*, 57.

8. Albright, *Art in the San Francisco Bay Area*, 57. Caroline Jones doubts the authenticity of the story; see *Figurative Art*, 12.

9. Paul Mills, *The New Figurative Art of David Park* (Santa Barbara, Calif.: Capra Press, 1988); the Diebenkorn quotation is from p. 70.

10. Paul Mills, *Contemporary Bay Area Figurative Painting* . . . (Oakland, Calif.: Oakland Art Museum, 1957), 12, as quoted in Albright, *Art in San Francisco Bay Area*, 66.

11. Gerald Nordland, "The Figurative Works of Richard Diebenkorn," in *Richard Diebenkorn: Paintings and Drawings, 1943–1976* (Buffalo, N.Y.: Albright-Knox Art Gallery, 1976), 25–41. The criticism of figurative art is in Hubert Crehan, "Reviews and Previews," *Art News* 58 (January 1960): 12, quoted in Jones, *Figurative Art*, 61.

12. Gerald D. Nash, *The American West in the Twentieth Century: A Short History of an Urban Oasis* (Englewood Cliffs, N.J.: Prentice-Hall, 1973).

13. Irving Sandler, *American Art of the 1960s* (New York: Harper & Row, 1988), 143–49.

14. Daniel Wheeler, *Art since Mid-Century: 1945 to the Present* (Englewood Cliffs, N.J.: Prentice-Hall, 1991), 154.

15. Nancy Marmer, "Pop Art in California," in Lucy R. Lippard, *Pop Art* (New York: Frederick A. Praeger, 1966), 139–61.

16. Ibid., 154, 155.

17. Ibid., 154.

18. Lawrence Alloway, *American Pop Art* (New York: Collier Books, 1974), 37; Wheeler, *Art since Mid-Century*, 250–51.

19. Sandler, *American Art of the 1960s*, 199, 203; Louis K. Meisel, *Photorealism Since 1980* (New York: Harry N. Abrams, 1993).

20. Meisel, *Photo-Realism* (New York: Harry N. Abrams, 1980); the quotation is from p. 336.

21. Ibid., 25–27.

22. Ibid., 274, 275.

23. Sandler, *American Art of the 1960s*, 331.

24. *The Writings of Robert Smithson*, ed. Nancy Holt (New York: New York University Press, 1979).

25. Quoted in Sandler, *American Art in the 1960s*, 333.

26. Wheeler, *Art since Mid-Century*, 262–65; Corinne Robins, *The Pluralist Era: American Art, 1968–1981* (New York: Harper, 1984), 82–91.

27. Anita Pollitzer, *A Woman on Paper: Georgia O'Keeffe* (New York: Simon and Schuster, 1988), 146. The fullest and most dependable biography of O'Keeffe is Roxana Robinson, *Georgia O'Keeffe: A Life* (New York: Harper & Row, 1989).

28. Charles C. Eldredge, *Georgia O'Keeffe* (New York: Abrams, 1991).

29. Pollitzer, *A Woman on Paper*, 158.

30. Sharyn Rohlfsen Udall, *Modernist Painting in New Mexico* (Albuquerque: University of New Mexico Press, 1984), 145.

31. Eldredge, *Georgia O'Keeffe*, 123, 122.

32. Jacinto Quirarte, *Mexican American Artists* (Austin: University of Texas Press, 1973); Richard Griswold del Castillo et al., eds., *Chicano Art: Resistance and Affirmation, 1965–1985* (Los Angeles: Wright Art Gallery, University of California, Los Angeles, 1991).

33. Victor A. Sorrell, "Articulate Signs of Resistance and Affirmation in Chicano Public Art," in Griswold del Castillo et al., *Chicano Art*, 148; Sylvia Gorodezky M., *Arte Chicano como cultura de protesta* (Mexico City: Universidad Nacional Autónoma de Mexico, 1993).

34. Amalia Mesa-Bains, "El Mundo Femenino: Chicana Artists of the Movement—A Commentary on Development and Production," in Griswold del Castillo et al., *Chicano Art*, 131–40.

35. Tomas Ybarra-Frausto, "Rasquachismo: A Chicano Sensibility," in Griswold del Castillo et al., *Chicano Art*, 155, 161; Gorodezky M., *Arte Chicano*, 88–93.

36. Dorothy Dunn, *American Indian Painting of the Southwest and Plains Areas* (Albuquerque: University of New Mexico Press, 1968); Clara Lee Tanner, *Southwest Indian Painting: A Changing Art,* 2d ed. (Tucson: University of Arizona Press, 1973).

37. Two useful brief introductions to modern Indian art are available in William H. Goetzmann and William N. Goetzmann, *The West of the Imagination* (New York: W. W. Norton, 1986); and Patricia Janis Broder, *The American West: The Modern Vision* (Boston: Little, Brown and Company, 1984).

38. Broder, *The American West,* 261–62.

39. Quoted in John Wilmerding, "The Mystery and History of Fritz Scholder's Art," in *Fritz Scholder: Paintings and Monotypes* (Altadena, Calif.: Twin Palms, 1988), n.p.

40. Joshua Taylor et al., *Fritz Scholder* (New York: Rizzoli, 1982). I draw here on an overview chapter on Indian art by James J. Rawls in *Chief Red Fox Is Dead: A History of Native Americans since 1945* (Ft. Worth, Tex.: Harcourt Brace 1996), 177–99.

41. Quoted in Broder, *The American West,* 270.

INDEX

Note: Boldface numerals indicate an extended treatment of the subject.

murals, 120, 123–24

My Ántonia (Cather), 93, 94–96

myth and symbol school, 161, 176–77

Nash, Gerald D., 139, 167–69, 178–79, 190

naturalism, 23

Nature's Metropolis (Cronon), 176

Nebraska, 93, 94, 95

Neihardt, John G., 89, 92, 98

New, Lloyd Kiva, 205

New Deal, 116–18, 203

New History, 33

New Indian history, 170–71

New Mexico, 68–72, 130–32, 197–98, 199

New Mexico Quarterly, 87, 91, 99

New Regionalism, 90

New Social History, 172, 173

New Western historiography, **170–79**, 181

New Western history, 40–41, 170, 176, 179–81, 207

New York City, 21, 53, 57, 88; as art center, 68, 183–84, 190, 191

New York School, 183–85, 187

Nichols, John, 156

1960s, 102, 141, 149, 190, 209

Norris, Frank, **20–26**, 29

Northwest School of Art, 133–34

Northwest tradition, 134

novels. *See* fiction

Nudes by a River (Park), 188

Octopus, The (Norris), 24–26

Odum, Howard, 111, 116

Okada, John, 157

O'Keeffe, Georgia, 134, 182–83, **196–200**, 207

Okies, 102, 144

One Flew Over the Cuckoo's Nest (Kesey), 158–59

O Pioneers! (Cather), 93–94, 95

Orchard Windbreak, The (Foote), 74

Oregon, 44, 81, 96–97

Overland Monthly, xxiii, 16, 144

Ox-Bow Incident, The (Clark), 146

Pacific Coast, 41, 132

Pacific Northwest, 90, 96–97, 98; and literary regionalism, 79, 82–83; and regional art, 133–35

Pacific Slope, The (Pomeroy), 165, 168–69

Paris, 68, 120, 124, 183

Park, David, 187–89

Parkman, Francis, xxii–xxiii, 8, 33, 34, 35

Paxson, Frederic Logan, 4, **42–48**, 109

Pearce, T. M., 91

Pearl Harbor, 141, 143, 183

Pecos Bill, xx

Phillips, Bert Geer, 68, 71, 72

photographs, 191, 193

Photo Realism, 183, 193–95

Pickers, The (Baca), 202

Pictures of the Far West (Foote), 74–76

place. *See* in-the-West idea

Play It as It Lays (Didion), 145–46

Pollock, Jackson, 182–83

Pomeroy, Earl, 47, 48, 139, 163–66, 167–69

Pop Art, 183, 191–93

Populists, 14, 46, 47, 120

Portage, Wisconsin, 75

possibilism, 113

postmodernism, 141, 192

postregionalism, xiv, 102, 135, 141, 212; in art, **182–207**; in fiction, **143–59**; in historiography, **160–81**

Powell, John Wesley, 105, 166–67

Prairie Schooner, 87, 98, 116

Price, C. S., 133

"Problems in American History" (Turner), 37–38, 105

process. *See* to-the-West idea

Progressives, 19, 20

provincialism, 84

Pulitzer Prize, 45, 46, 50, 96, 100, 109, 148, 165

racism, 57

82, 122; as hegemonic myth, 74, 141, 158; in art, 56, 60; in frontier writings, 8, 39

Wild West show, xix–xx, xxviii, 22

Wilson, Woodrow, 36, 49, 92

Wimar, Charles, 62

Wimberly, Lowry C., 117

Winsor, Justin, 33, 34, 35

Winter in the Blood (Welch), 151–52

Wister, Owen, 4, **5–10**, 29, 53, 55–56

Woman on Porch (Diebenkorn), 189–90

Woman Warrior, The (Kingston), 157

women's experiences, 9, 40, 63; and World War II, 140–41; as depicted in fiction, 73–76, 93–96, 149–50; as treated in historiography, 173–74

Wood, Grant, 80, 109, 124–26

World War I, 51, 76, 79, 87, 92, 121

World War II, 98, 102, 133, 139–42, 161, 169, 183, 190, 203

Worster, Donald, 165, 167, 174–76

Wright, Louis B., 164

Wrobel, David M., 49

Wyeth, N. C., 130

Wyoming, 6, 8, 154